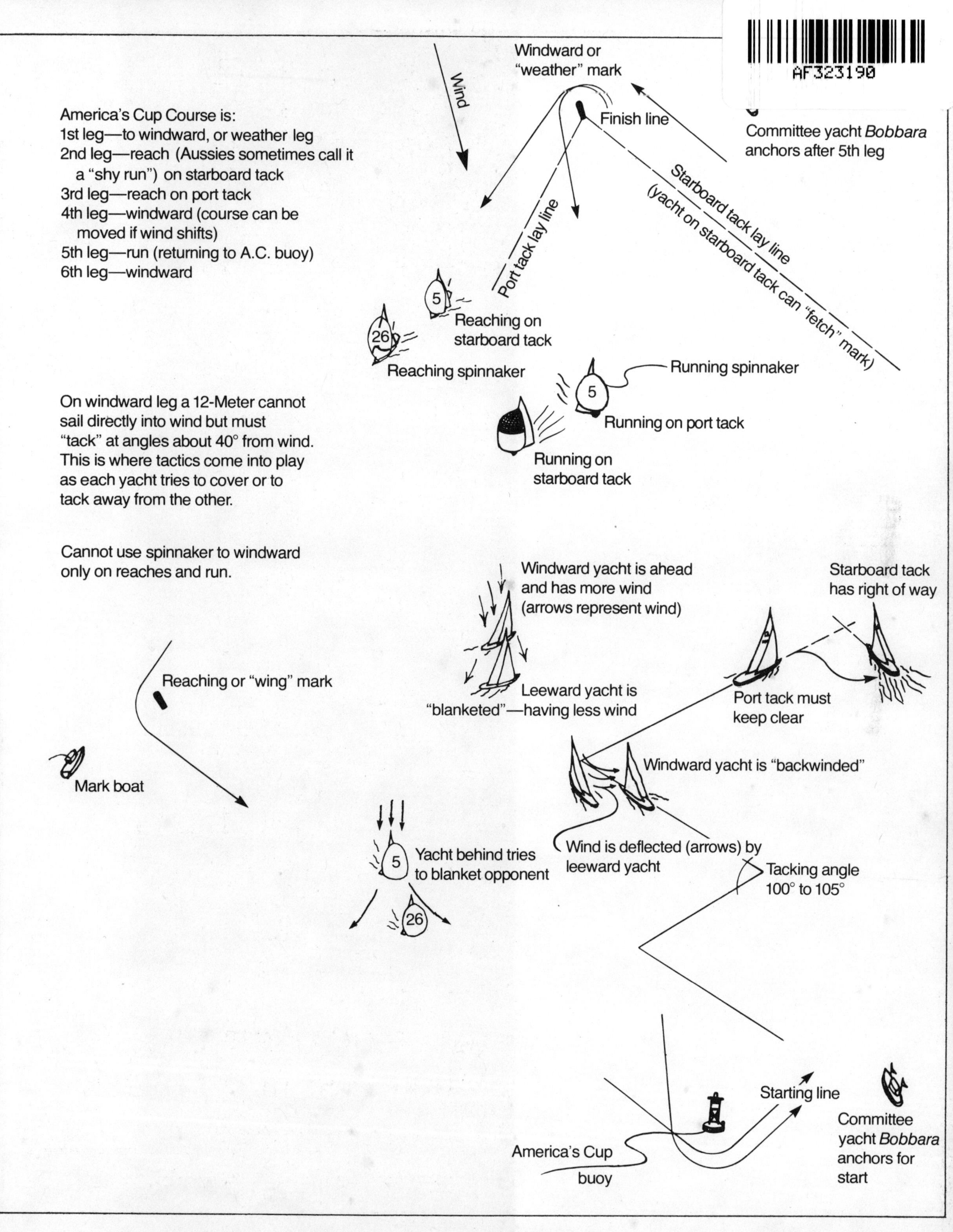

America's Cup Course is:
1st leg—to windward, or weather leg
2nd leg—reach (Aussies sometimes call it a "shy run") on starboard tack
3rd leg—reach on port tack
4th leg—windward (course can be moved if wind shifts)
5th leg—run (returning to A.C. buoy)
6th leg—windward

On windward leg a 12-Meter cannot sail directly into wind but must "tack" at angles about 40° from wind. This is where tactics come into play as each yacht tries to cover or to tack away from the other.

Cannot use spinnaker to windward only on reaches and run.

Wind
Windward or "weather" mark
Finish line
Committee yacht Bobbara anchors after 5th leg
Port tack lay line
Starboard tack lay line (yacht on starboard tack can "fetch" mark)
5
26
Reaching on starboard tack
Reaching spinnaker
Running spinnaker
5
Running on port tack
Running on starboard tack
Reaching or "wing" mark
Mark boat
Windward yacht is ahead and has more wind (arrows represent wind)
Leeward yacht is "blanketed"—having less wind
Starboard tack has right of way
Port tack must keep clear
Windward yacht is "backwinded"
5
26
Yacht behind tries to blanket opponent
Wind is deflected (arrows) by leeward yacht
Tacking angle 100° to 105°
Starting line
America's Cup buoy
Committee yacht Bobbara anchors for start

Challenge '77
Newport and the America's Cup

S1
12
S-A
-3
S1
12
S3
12
S3

CHALLENGE '77

NEWPORT AND THE AMERICA'S CUP

by Ted Jones

W · W · NORTON & COMPANY · INC · *NEW YORK*

Copyright © 1978 by W. W. Norton & Company, Inc.
Published simultaneously in Canada by George J. McLeod Limited,
Toronto. Printed in the United States of America.

All Rights Reserved

First Edition

Library of Congress Cataloging in Publication Data

Jones, Theodore A.
Challenge '77.

1. America's Cup Races.   I Title.
GV830 1977.J66 1978   797.1'4   77–19254
ISBN 0–393–08811–1

1 2 3 4 5 6 7 8 9 0

To Tara

CONTENTS

Contents

APPENDICES

ACKNOWLEDGMENTS

The author believes that almost any one of the many reporters and photographers who spent the summer chasing daily stories could have written a book about the 1977 America's Cup. In many ways they each helped to write this one. The daily reporters with the continuing pressure of a story and early deadlines must drag out the salient facts and quotes of a day's sailing, often between two sets of races held on widely separated parts of the ocean, with little time to think about what they are writing. It is only after they have gone on to other assignments that the book writer gets down to cases and renews his acquaintance with his typewriter, and then he has the benefit of the responses to the all cogent questions asked by others. With the luxury of time it has been possible to put the summer's events in perspective, but much of the raw data was largely pried loose by the daily reporters. One in particular did an excellent job. Barbara Lloyd, writing for the *Newport Daily News*, came out of the summer with a much greater knowledge of the America's Cup and sailing in general than that which she possessed when she began her Cup coverage. She made only a few errors, and those were never repeated. Other yachting reporters, who shall remain nameless, who have been on the beat for years could take lessons. I am grateful to Barbara not only for the daily reporting, which I referenced frequently, but also for contributing Chapter VI, "Gatsby in Topsiders," an account of the America's Cup Ball.

Leonard Panaggio, of the Rhode Island Department of Economic Development, did a masterful job of organizing the press office. His staff, headed by Lois Muessel, was always helpful. Almost all of the back-up material compiled in the Appendix came from the press office.

There were many in each of the syndicates who went out of their way to be helpful even when there were more pressing matters to attend to. Press contacts for the various syndicates were: Bob Hemery, *Australia*; Hanne Marie Bense, *Gretel II*; Lars Ahren, *Sverige*; Bruno Bich, *France*; Richie Sayer, *Courageous* and *Independence*; and Ed du Moulin, who was syndicate manager for *Enterprise*. Their continuing assistance is gratefully acknowledged.

Ted Turner frequently went out of his way to invite me inside the latticed gates at Bannister's Wharf. For all the gaff that was heaped upon Lee Loomis, I always found him cooperative and friendly.

Bill Manning, syndicate manager for *Gretel II*, earned my gratitude many times over for among other things inviting me aboard *Ursa Major* and *La Costa Brava* to watch crucial races. Peter Campbell and Bruce Stannard provided much valuable information and friendly counsel—as did many other broadcasters and magazine reporters.

Suzanne Landrieu provided an inside view of many facets of the summer that only a woman would be in a position to know. Her candid comments form a valuable part of Chapter X, "Hanging Out in Newport."

Among the many crew members who were helpful, Jeff Neuberth, Pete Lawson, and Steve Lirakas—from *Independence*; Gary Jobson—from *Courageous*; and Jack Gale—from *Gretel II* deserve special thanks.

Among the skippers, Gordon Ingate stood out as a marvelous sportsman and a true gentleman who many times bared to the press what must have been his innermost thoughts. Gordon was always open and honest, and he never begged a question from anyone. He made many friends in Newport and contributed immeasurably to the thoughts and information that went into this book.

Thanks to Cynthia Rex of Homs Services for help in transcribing audio tapes into readable copy, and special thanks (for a second time) to Lucia Carpenter who provided a tremendous amount of information, background, and helpful suggestions. In addition, Lucia contributed Chapter IX, "Upstairs, Downstairs on the Tub Derrière," and she performed admirably as copy editor of the manuscript.

Lucia Carpenter receives thanks also for contributing photographs along with Dan Nerney, Stan Rosenfeld, Barbara Lloyd, and Jim Quigley, and Bob Foley deserves credit for his careful and speedy processing of my films and proof sheets.

INTRODUCTION

This is a narrative about people—those who race for the America's Cup. It is also about the people who form the syndicates which support and finance the contenders as well as the people who follow the fleet with worshipful devotion to the skippers and crews. It is a narrative about the general craziness, the *ambiance*, and the mystique that surrounds an America's Cup summer in Newport, Rhode Island. This is also an account of an event—really a series of events—which determines whether or not the United States, as exemplified by the New York Yacht Club, is still the undisputed ruler of the sailing seas.

The America's Cup is a summer-long happening. The intensity is that of an Olympiad. It attracts competitors and spectators alike from all over the world. Fortunes are spent to win it. Millions are spent to defend it. It has a major impact on the economy of the area —three million visitors spent 35 million dollars, according to a Newport Chamber of Commerce estimate, during the 1977 season. (The year-round population is 34,000.) The world's two leading sailmakers with businesses worth tens of millions put their reputations on the line for the prestige of being the defender, and both lost.

The America's Cup has not always enjoyed such fame. In fact, the New York Yacht Club, which has held the America's Cup since 1851, has always considered the defense of the Cup its private domain. The Club is a private organization, it holds the America's Cup, it decides whether or not to accept a challenge, it determines the racing conditions under which a challenger must operate, it runs the races, its members finance the defenders. If the New York Yacht Club had a preference it would be perfectly happy to conduct the races in a vacuum, in some remote part of the ocean reserved for the competitors, race committee, flag officers (commodores and fleet captains who are entitled to fly flags from their yachts designating rank), and a *few* special members and invited guests.

The Club's motives are pure enough. The competition is for sport—to determine which yacht club conducting races in the open ocean can produce the best yacht and crew in the world. The Club maintains that since 1851, when the schooner yacht *America* defeated the entire Royal Yacht Squadron fleet in England, the New York Yacht Club is the best in the world. Anyone who disputes that fact is welcome to come to its home waters and prove otherwise. Anything which distracts from this basic premise and the central objective of the racing is a nuisance to be avoided if possible.

Not surprisingly this attitude has gotten the Club in difficulty over the years with challengers, the media, and even potential defenders. Lord Dunraven, a challenger in 1893 and 1895, accused the New York Yacht Club defender of several misdeeds including shifting ballast during the series. He was summoned to a hearing which exonerated the accused, and when his apology was not forthcoming he was expelled from his honorary membership in the Club. In 1901 a Boston yachtsman, Thomas J. Lawson, wanted to defend the Cup but the New York Yacht Club insisted that Lawson become a member. Lawson argued—which did no good of course—and became so embittered that he tried to rewrite the history of the Cup. *The Lawson History of The America's Cup* is a beautiful, extravagant, and biased limited edition volume, a very battered remnant of which resides in the library of the New York Yacht Club. In 1962, when the Australians' first challenge very nearly won the Cup using American-made Hood sails, the press generally lambasted the New York Yacht Club for backtracking and insisting that future challengers follow the letter of the Deed of Gift that *all* of the defender must be built in the country from which the challenge originates.

Whether in spite of or because of the New York Yacht Club's attitude that the America's Cup is a private affair, the spectacle of the America's Cup has intrigued spectators and would-be spectators throughout its history. Unfortunately, spectator craft threaten the safety of the competitors as they move in close for a better view, and even a well-disciplined and controlled fleet of spectators creates a confused sea condition from the combined wakes that disrupts the normal sailing of the competitors. Thus, there is some justification for the Club's attitude.

In 1974 the appeal for public funds for the Intrepid Syndicate sparked a massive support for this West Coast yacht as "the people's boat." They financed much of their costs through public contributions, and the idea that an old boat, which had twice before defended the Cup, could make a comeback for an unprecedented third defense on a shoestring budget supported by public contributions, caught the imagination of people all over the country. For the first time the America's Cup was a national event, not limited to that part of the country east of the Hudson River—as one boating magazine editor once chided me. Now, with sailmakers vying for honors and the obvious commercial spin-off if they win, commercial considerations once abhorred by the New York Yacht Club are blatantly present and reluctantly condoned.

As someone with a lifelong interest in sailing who has made an occupation out of writing about the sport, it is not difficult to understand what has drawn me to Newport, Rhode Island, the site of each recent America's Cup series. The America's Cup is in many important respects the pinnacle of yacht racing. Some will argue this point and say the Olympics or an event such as the Star Class World Championships are more meaningful. I do not take issue with this except to say that it all depends on your point of view. The America's Cup has been held by the New York Yacht Club for 126 years—the longest unbroken string of victories in any sport. Incredible sums have been spent trying to win it and even more incredible sums have been spent defending it. For sheer effort and determination among the sailors who vie for the Cup and among the millionaires who pay the bills, the America's Cup competition is unsurpassed by any other sailing event. Since it is a match between two competitors, there is something almost animal in the intensity with which the protagonists do battle. Yet, it is undersood that this is a gentlemanly sport on the highest level of personal integrity and honesty.

There is an innate grace to the vessels which gives their maneuvers a dream-like quality. They never touch (or if they do the rule offender must retire or be disqualified) but their coming together close aboard each other conjures up visions and sounds of knights clanging lance to armor as in an Elizabethan-age joust. The slow, deliberate movements of the large yachts is like a precision ballet where the patterns are random but the movements are precisely programmed. To the aficionado, the America's Cup races and the events that precede them present an endless fascination. I am hooked. I am back in Newport once again, as I have been back in 1962, 1964, 1967, 1970, and 1974 each time there has been a challenge and a successful defense of the America's Cup.

Once again I swelter in the stuffiness of the old National Guard Armory which has been temporarily converted to serve as a press headquarters. Once again I roam the docks in search of the latest secrets from the contenders. Once again I bob in the waves of Rhode Island Sound in hopes of a close-up of one of the Twelves. Once again I jump at the chance to sail one of the yachts or to ride on one of the tenders. Once again I tread the cobbled streets of Newport that have become an integral part of the modern era of America's Cup racing. And as I look from the skylight of my house, which surveys the reaches of Newport Harbor, I wonder if this will be the last. Will the challenger finally win this time? Come along with me, and we shall see!

Ted Jones
Newport, Rhode Island

September, 1977

CHALLENGE '77
NEWPORT AND THE AMERICA'S CUP

1977 was the year of the seventh challenge in the modern history of America's Cup competition which began with the introduction of 12-Meter Class yachts in 1958. While this 19-year period is relatively brief in the 126-year history of the America's Cup, it was packed with events which had a great influence on future challenges—particularly the 1977 challenge. Nowhere has this history been set down in a single volume, and much of the significance of the 1977 challenge and defense is lost if viewed out of context of this recent history of the event.

The purpose of this prologue is to provide a brief chronicle to establish a background for the events of 1977. It is by no means a complete history. Rather it focuses on the salient events that provoked changes, established trends, or encouraged people to continue trying to win and defend the Cup.

If you are new to the America's Cup and are anxious to get into the events of 1977, to come to grips with characters like Ted Turner and Alan Bond, it is permissible—if not desirable—to skip this prologue and get right into things beginning with Chapter I on page 47. Perhaps, after getting your feet wet, you will want to return to this *history. If you prefer to skip back and forth, the subheads identifying the sections dealing with each challenge will guide you to the right section.*

If you are an America's Cup fanatic, this prologue will serve as a reminder of how and when things happen. I found, in doing the research for this history, that some events which I thought I had remembered well didn't happen exactly as I had remembered them or didn't happen when I thought they had. This attempts to set the record straight for you as well as reminding you of events which signalled the future.

HOW IT ALL BEGAN

Soon after they returned to New York from England where their yacht had won a "100 Guinea Cup" from the best of Great Britain, the owners of the yacht *America* offered their prize to the New York Yacht Club for perpetual international competition between yacht clubs from different countries.

The New York Yacht Club, which was only six years old in 1850, had been invited by England to send a representative to the sailing events of the World's Fair that was being organized for the summer of 1851. Intrigued by the possibility of showing the former mother country a thing or two about yacht design, to say nothing about the prospect of winning a substantial quantity of the Queen's gold, Commodore John Cox Stevens and five other members commissioned the building of a yacht for that purpose.

The *America*, as the new yacht was christened, was something of a marvel in her time as were the conditions under which she was built. Her builder agreed to deliver her fully found for $30,000 and to take her back if she wasn't the fastest yacht in New York. She was actually beaten by one yacht in her trials, and as Herbert L. Stone and William H. Taylor wrote:

"Of course the schooner wasn't ready on contract time (April 1st). Boats never are. It was May 3rd before she was launched, and on May 24th, when she was still not ready, the syndicate offered to purchase her outright for $20,000. She was finally delivered on June 8th."[1]

[1] Herbert L. Stone and William H. Taylor, *The America's Cup Races* (Princeton, New Jersey: D. Van Nostrand Company, Inc. 1958), p. 6.

A replica of the *America* built in Maine in the 1960s is probably worth, today, 100 times the contract price of the original.

America thoroughly frightened English yachtsmen with her speed when she easily beat the yacht sent to escort her into the Solent. Consequently, she was unable to find any matches until she was finally invited to race with the Royal Yacht Squadron fleet in August of 1851. It was this race, which she won handily, that provided her owners with the cup which now bears her name.

Since the *America* had crossed the ocean on her own bottom and had defeated the entire RYS fleet, the conditions laid down for the America's Cup competition made similar demands of the challenger. After the first challenge, which the challenger lost, conditions were changed to have the challenger face a single defender. In the second challenge the New York Yacht Club had the right to name the defender on the day of each race. This challenge failed also as the defender was a light weather boat on light weather days and a heavy weather boat on heavy weather days. Thereafter, the matches were fairer with the defender remaining the same throughout the series. Still, no challenger has ever won a match in 24 attempts over a period of 126 years, and only two have come close.

Modern America's Cup history began in 1958. The previous match in 1937 had been held in J-boats which were a class of yacht about 130 feet in overall length with towering marconi-rigged masts (with a single triangular-shaped mainsail similar to today's conventional rigs) nearly as high as 30-story buildings. In the postwar economy such behemoths would have been prohibitively expensive to build, and it would have been nearly impossible to find the 22 professional seamen required to sail them. However, it was not possible to race in yachts under 65 feet waterline length under the Deed of Gift until the New York Yacht Club was able to obtain a court order altering this provision to allow competition for the Cup to resume in yachts not less than 44 feet waterline length. The Court Order also permitted the challenger to be shipped to the defending country instead of sailing there on her own bottom—a time-consuming and unrealistic requirement today.

Holding that the America's Cup should be sailed in the largest and most prestigious yachts in vogue, the New York Yacht Club let it be known that it would consider challenges in International 12-Meter Class yachts.

"Twelves," as they are called, had raced actively in England and in the New York Yacht Club fleet before the war. Harold S. Vanderbilt had taken his Sparkman & Stephens designed Twelve *Vim* to England in 1939 and had demonstrated her outstanding superiority during that summer. With this background in both countries the 12-Meter seemed a logical choice rather than an ocean racer, which was also considered. "In informal discussions among British and American yachtsmen, the Twelves seemed to appeal more to those who had the most to say about it," wrote Stone and Taylor.[2]

England had been the only country to challenge, except for two early challenges from Canada, and ocean racers were designed to divergent rating rules in Britain and the U.S. in 1958, which seemed to mitigate against ocean racers as America's Cup yachts. (There continues to be some sentiment to race in ocean racers as the Twelves are now used only for America's Cup racing, but it is unlikely that there will be a change as those who have "the most to say about it" still prefer the 12-Meters in spite of certain anacronistic characteristics.)

THE 1958 CHALLENGE

1958, the first summer of America's Cup racing in 21 years, racing in 12-Meters, set patterns for all the summers which have followed.

The 1958 season began for the Matthews family in 1952. Captain John Matthews purchased Harold S. Vanderbilt's 12-Meter *Vim* (it is said that this was the first sailing yacht that Vanderbilt had ever sold—the others, like the previous Cup defender *Ranger*, were all scrapped). Matthews converted *Vim*, installed an engine, and gave her to his two sons, Don and Dick—not yet 20—to race in the cruiser races out of Long Island Sound and in the New York Yacht Club Cruise.

When it was announced that competition for the America's Cup would resume in 12-Meters in 1958, it was natural for the Matthews family—with the fastest Twelve then in existence and several seasons of racing experience—to decide to become a candidate for the defender's role.

Commodore Henry Sears of the New York Yacht Club went to the elder Matthews when the challenge for the 1958 series was ac-

[2] *The America's Cup Races*, p. 235.

cepted and asked him if *Vim* would participate in a defense effort. Sears headed the syndicate building a new Olin Stephens design, the Henry Mercer syndicate was commissioning Philip L. Rhodes to design a Twelve, and Chandler Hovey of Boston was going ahead with a C. Raymond Hunt design. The inclusion of *Vim* would make an even fourth so that two pairs could be matched each day of the trials, and since *Vim* was a known quantity she would, in all likelihood, prove to be a valuable yardstick. Matthews agreed and set about returning *Vim* to competitive racing condition.

Always thereafter, until 1977, the New York Yacht Club was able to muster four 12-Meters—albeit some of them hardly worthy as contenders—to vie for the right to defend.

The Matthews family started working up for the 1958 season in the fall of 1957. Practice sails, crew workouts, and planning went on until late November. This early experience gave them an important edge over their rivals, all of which would be new boats with inevitable problems to sort out. Going into the winter, the Matthews and their budding crew knew how to get nearly maximum potential from their yacht. The changes they would make over the winter were based upon experience—they were not merely unproven ideas.

Even so, Captain Matthews felt that *Vim* would be fighting an uphill battle against the newer boats. Olin Stephens was thoroughly committed to the new Sears syndicate yacht, but he agreed to design a new keel for *Vim* with the proviso that he could use *Vim* as a benchmark for testing his new design in the Davidson Laboratory towing tank at Stevens Institute.

For *Vim*'s new sails, Matthews selected a young man from Marblehead who was virtually unheard of west of Boston—Frederick E. (Ted) Hood. Hood had been working with his father, an engineer, making sails for small one-designs and weaving his own sailcloth on secondhand looms. In Hood, who was also destined to sail on *Vim*, Matthews saw an eager and capable new hand who could provide *Vim* with something extra over her rivals. Not only were Hood's sails to provide *Vim* with a competitive edge, but the search for "something extra" was to be the continuing philosophy of the *Vim* effort throughout the summer.

With *Vim* laid up for the winter, the Matthews turned their efforts toward final crew selection. Don was to be the skipper and Dick the navigator—roles they had practiced aboard *Vim* for several years. During January and February of 1958 they had several meetings with Bus Mosbacher and gradually convinced him to join the crew. Don Matthews says that he had been impressed by Mosbacher, having raced against him in International One-Designs. Bus had also raced in Six-Meters, having skippered the Gold Medal-winning Six in the 1948 Olympics, and he had done quite a bit of match racing in Sixes as well. His experience in the afterguard of *Vim* would, it was hoped, add considerable depth of talent.

Vim and her crew were out sailing early in the spring of 1958. Captain Matthews had chartered the prewar Twelve *Gleam* as a trial horse, and with two boats to sail and plenty of time to practice, the *Vim* crew developed a considerable edge over their competitors in general teamwork, sail handling, and match race starts. Hood had never made a sail as large as those used by 12-Meters and this early season experience allowed him time to develop his ideas to their fullest extent.

The first time all the Twelves raced together was the New York Yacht Club Annual Cruise in July. *Vim* won five out of the seven races to establish herself as a serious contender. Contemporary press reports gave the edge to *Vim* and the Mercer syndicate's *Weatherly*, which seemed to be the first of the new boats to sort herself out. *Columbia*, Commodore Sears's Twelve, had been beset by various problems, having changed skippers and several other crew positions, and *Easterner*—the Hovey family's Twelve—was inconsistent.

Columbia gradually began to get herself together during the final trials. As her crew work improved and as the light summer winds gave way to more blustery autumn weather, *Columbia*'s superiority to windward began to show.

"There was no question that *Columbia*'s was the better hull," Don Matthews said, and the Selection Committee kept the series going until *Columbia* proved it.

At the end of the summer, *Vim* and *Columbia* had even scores, but *Columbia* had won more races toward the end. While there was some bitterness expressed at the time (not necessarily from the *Vim* camp) that the New York Yacht Club had kept the trials going until their commodore's boat could finally be selected, Don Matthews harbored no hard feelings years later.

"We knew Burr Bartram, Mike Vanderbilt, George Hinman, Commodore Morgan—people who were on the Committee—and there's no question that any committee would always lean toward the newer boat," said Matthews. "There's no question that you would bend over backwards for the newer boat to give them that option. We never were critical of that—that we expected—we knew we were fighting an uphill battle all the way—that we were an underdog.

"Even though there were moments of pique and the competition was carried to the point of anger, maybe, there was never any hostility. It was really a clean, hard-fought game."

As has been the case in subsequent Cup history when the new boat has been pushed hard by a worthy crew in an inherently slower design, *Columbia* owed much of her success to *Vim*. The Matthews team effort, always looking for something extra, added many new wrinkles not only to the America's Cup contenders but to other aspects of sailing.

In 1958, the America's Cup courses were either a 24-mile triangle or a 24-mile windward-leeward. This was the first time, according to Matthews, that anyone had seen 30 or 40 tacks initiated in a 12-mile beat. It was exhausting work for both the crew and the helmsman. Consider the fact that all the boats had coffee grinder winches with only two speeds, that they were inefficient—with considerable friction—by today's standards. Yet *Vim*, because of their precision teamwork, found that they always gained while tacking. When behind, they would throw tack after tack at their rival, and they often wore down the other crew. Also, Matthews and Mosbacher had learned early how to steer *Vim* through a tack by gradually accelerating the turn, holding just off head to wind and gaining a precious boat length on the new tack before falling away to accelerate. This is a standard feature of the helmsman's repertory today, but it was considered a *Vim* innovation in 1958.

Perhaps the most significant contribution *Vim* made was the dip-pole jibe. Previously all jibes were made "end-for-end." That is, the spinnaker pole was unhooked from the mast, swung athwartships (across the boat), and that end was hooked to the spinnaker so that both ends of the pole were attached to both clews of the spinnaker. As the boat jibed, the new inboard pole end was tripped from the spinnaker and attached to the mast—a difficult and dangerous maneuver!

Don Matthews can't recall any specific flash of inspiration that led them to develop the dip-pole technique. He thinks that they first did it in a light air race when they wanted to cover *Columbia*, which had surprised them with a quick jibe. *Vim's* afterguard wanted to jibe, someone suggested that they just trip the pole and go ahead and jibe with the spinnaker left to fend for itself. It worked!

Vim's crew used to talk over the events of the day after their evening meal, and after this particular day it was suggested that they try to perfect this maneuver. Matthews says the whole crew contributed ideas. Ted Hood made up some special sheets and guys, and the system was perfected by the "cut and try" method in the next few days.

Vim's crew was the first in the history of America's Cup competition to be housed together. Previously, most of the crew had been professionals who stayed wherever they could while the afterguard might have stayed together at a mansion ashore or individually on large yachts afloat. Don Matthews feels that this was an important innovation for *Vim* as it allowed the crew to develop as a homogeneous team.

Unlike many later crew houses, Lily Pond House—where they quartered—had few rules. When the racing for the day was over each crew member was on his own. He could come to dinner or not, and no one checked him in at night. Woe be unto the crew member who showed up with a hangover the next day, but nobody prevented him from acquiring it. Wives lived at the house, and girlfriends were welcome visitors. "The house was a place where we could have fun together in an informal setting," Matthews recalled. "We had a tight ship but a happy ship. We came away from that summer closer friends —all of us."

Don Matthews feels that this lesson has not been carried forward in other crews. "I think this was some of the trouble they've had in later years," he said, "where they've tried to organize everything— dictate to everybody what the schedule shall be—you know, dinner at six, seven o'clock you may have coffee, nine o'clock we will all show in the hall because we're going to somebody's house and we'll arrive en masse . . . kind of like prep school.

"It's very tough to take people out of their personal lives and put them in a situation where they (syndicate managers) dictate everything. You've got to have the discipline when you're racing but it's like professional sports today where they've found if they get too restrictive it's counterproductive."

The 1958 America's Cup campaign brought innovation to our sailing lives. It launched Ted Hood on an international career. Similarly, Bus Mosbacher earned legendary status among America's Cup skippers as he went on from 1958 to defend the Cup successfully in 1962 and again in 1967.

More than anything else, however, the Matthews and *Vim*'s crew set a standard that others have emulated in the years that followed. Their contribution cannot be measured in real terms, of course, but their dedication and ability have surely helped continue the dominant winning streak that the New York Yacht Club has enjoyed.

The British challenger *Sceptre* was soundly trounced by *Columbia* in the America's Cup match of 1958. The defeat was so decisive that most observers felt that any of the American Twelves could have beaten her easily. There was some bitterness expressed within the New York Yacht Club that so much effort and money was expended for so unworthy a challenger. There was also the fear that faced with so impressive an array of potential defenders, future challenges might not be forthcoming.

When one came, it came from a most unlikely quarter—halfway around the world—from Australia.

THE 1962 CHALLENGE

The Royal Sydney Yacht Squadron challenge for the America's Cup was issued in behalf of Sir Frank Packer, a Sydney newspaper tycoon. *Gretel* (pronounced *Gryt'l* in Australian) was designed by Alan Payne, a promising young yacht designer whose work was virtually unknown outside the Antipodes.

Following the 1958 series, Sir Frank Packer had chartered *Vim* from the Catholic charity to which she had been donated by Captain Matthews. There was speculation at the time that Captain Matthews had allowed *Vim* to go to Australia out of bitterness for the treatment he received at the hands of the New York Yacht Club Selection Committee. This may have been a counter expression of bitterness by some Yacht Club members that Matthews had let the country's second-fastest 12-Meter go to a potential challenger.

Whatever the motivations, *Vim* was in Australia. Taking her lines as a point of departure, testing them in the Stevens Institute towing tank where all the American Twelves were tested, and developing several new models with the help of the Stevens tank, Payne was able to design a very competitive Twelve on his first try.

On the American side Henry Mercer, who owned a major share of the 1958 contender *Weatherly*, was anxious to see *Weatherly* defend the America's Cup against the Australians. Mercer was impressed by Bus Mosbacher's performance as the primary helmsman aboard *Vim*, and he invited him to skipper *Weatherly* in 1962. Mosbacher, for his part, was interested in captaining his own crew and wanted to prove that with a competitive design he could successfully defend the Cup.

Weatherly had been designed by Philip L. Rhodes and built at Luders' Shipyard in 1958. A. E. (Bill) Luders, a designer himself, had several ideas for improving *Weatherly*, and modifications were made under his supervision. Mosbacher also had definite ideas about deck layout and weight saving. Every questionable piece of gear or structure was removed. The transom and 18 inches of hull and deck planking were cut off. Toe rails came off the bow, and superfluous winches and other hardware were removed. The weight thus saved was added to a new keel for additional stiffness.

Easterner was again sailed by the Hovey family but with Boston yachtsman George O'Day at the helm. *Columbia*, the 1958 defender, was purchased by Paul Shields and skippered by his nephew, Cornelius ("Glit") Shields, Jr., who was coached by his father "Corny." *Nefertiti*, the only new Twelve in 1962, was designed by Ted Hood. She proved to be a strong performer in heavy weather, but she was definitely slower than the others in light air.

Weatherly, always a good light weather boat, was considerably improved by Luders and Mosbacher and now was a good all-around performer. Skillfully handled by Mosbacher and an experienced crew which included many of those who had sailed on *Vim* and *Columbia* in 1958, *Weatherly* proved to be the outstanding Twelve of 1962 and won decisively over *Columbia* after *Nefertiti* and *Easterner* had been eliminated by the Selection Committee.

Unlike the hard-fought battles of 1958, *Weatherly* selected herself in 1962. There were some lost races and some close wins, but mostly *Weatherly* won selection because she was well organized and almost flawlessly sailed. She shone ever more brightly in contrast to the deficiencies of the others which seemed disorganized and unable to put together a winning combination. Hood replaced Don McNamara as skipper aboard *Nefertiti*, but she still could win only in heavier weather. C. Raymond Hunt, *Easterner's* designer, replaced O'Day, but in spite of flashes of speed, *Easterner* was never a contender. Glit Shields probably should have been replaced (his father might have stepped in had it not been for his doctor's warnings that skippering a Twelve could be too much for the elder Shields's sailing heart).

In the 1962 America's Cup series it was nearly a foregone conclusion that *Weatherly* would win, and shortly after the start of the first race it appeared that it would be another walkover for the defender. Mosbacher took the start—he is the master by which we still measure match-race tactics—and *Weatherly* lengthened her lead in the 24-mile windward-leeward race on each leg. She finished nearly four minutes ahead of *Gretel*, skippered by Jock Sturrock.

In the second race, *Weatherly* was ahead at the end of the eight-mile beat which was the first leg, and it appeared that she would win in four straight. However, in the fresh 20-knot winds, *Gretel* caught up considerably on the second leg, a reach.

Shortly after rounding the second mark for the eight-mile reach to the finish, *Gretel* caught a wave, and with a great aboriginal whoop from her crew she sped past the defender while the American crew was still settling down with sail trim. Suddenly, the score was even at 1-1, and there was nervous speculation that the defender was in trouble.

If it had been generally known how much trouble Mosbacher and *Weatherly* were in, the eventual outcome might have been different, but Mosbacher, who admitted later to spending some of the most nerve-wracking days of his life staying ahead of the Aussies, kept his concerns to himself and toughed it out.

Mosbacher won every windward leg from Sturrock, but he soon found that *Weatherly* could not tack with *Gretel*. One of the factors was *Gretel's* linked "coffee grinder" winches which allowed four crew members to crank in the genoa sheet drum instead of only two, which was the limit aboard *Weatherly*. This allowed *Gretel's* genoa to be trimmed much faster. To compensate, Mosbacher refused to cover *Gretel* tack for tack, preferring a loose cover staying generally between *Gretel* and the windward mark to protect against wind shifts. In earlier races that summer Mosbacher had ignored the unwritten rule, which calls for close cover of your opponent. This tactic was heretofore unheard of in America's Cup Competition, and fortunately for Mosbacher, it worked.

The third race was another windward-leeward course in light

winds, and *Weatherly* won this easily with a margin of 8:40. Everyone but Mosbacher breathed more easily.

The fourth race was another triangular course. It started in light winds, but they increased as the afternoon progressed. *Gretel* had another surprise in store for the *Weatherly* crew when she changed from a light genoa to a heavier one without first having to remove the light one. Their light sail had no hanks attaching it to the headstay, and the replacement sail had a zippered sleeve along the luff which allowed it to be zipped around the headstay as it went up. To change sails, *Weatherly*'s crew had to first remove the old headsail before the new one could be hoisted. This time-consuming maneuver made Mosbacher reluctant to change headsails while on the weather leg.

Still, *Weatherly* remained ahead at the weather mark and at the first reaching mark. On the final reach to the finish, however, *Gretel* threatened. Noting that *Gretel* was catching up under spinnaker, Mosbacher took a bold gamble. *Weatherly*, slightly ahead and to windward, dropped her spinnaker and headed up (closer to the wind)

Weatherly (right) stays ahead of *Gretel* in the critical fourth race of the 1962 America's Cup series. By daring strategy Bus Mosbacher, *Weatherly*'s skipper, was about to squeak out a 24-second victory over the Aussies to seal the Americans' win. Note that *Gretel* is using Hood sails that appear identical in shape to *Weatherly*'s. (*Stanley Rosenfeld photo*)

under genoa. Sturrock, sensing a wind shift that would be to his disadvantage if he stayed low, under spinnaker, followed Mosbacher's lead. Under genoa the yachts were even, and *Weatherly* maintained her slim margin. But sooner or later *Weatherly* would have to come down to the mark. Mosbacher timed it perfectly, and when his crew reset *Weatherly*'s spinnaker, they were close enough to the finish that *Gretel* could not get by. The difference was only 24 seconds, the closest finish in America's Cup history.[3]

With a windward-leeward course for the fifth race, Mosbacher began to breathe a little easier. *Weatherly* seemed capable of holding *Gretel* on this course, and she did on this final race to win the series 4-1. However, as we have seen, the contest was much closer than the score indicated.

Pierre DeSaix, who is in charge of the Davidson Laboratory, wrote in the September 1962 issue of *Yachting* Magazine from the vantage of having tank tested both challenger and defender. In his article, which was written before the series, DeSaix said he could predict which yacht would be the winner on the basis of their tank test results. We know now, although DeSaix had not acknowledged it, that he would have picked *Gretel* to win the America's Cup.[4]

There was one other subtle but important change to come to the America's Cup scene as a result of the Australian challenge. Heretofore, between the stuffiness of the New York Yacht Club and the reserve of the British challengers, the general public had little reason to know much about the America's Cup and had even less reason to be interested in it. The Aussies changed all that. Here was a bunch of guys who were much more like the average American than New York Yacht Club and Royal Yacht Squadron members. The Australian crew took to hanging out at a bar on Pelham Street, just a few steps from Port 'O Call where *Gretel* and *Vim* were moored, called the Cameo. Renamed the "Royal Cameo Yacht Squadron," the Cameo, which was just another of the many bars in the area before the Aussies adopted it, attracted a following of Americans who came to rub elbows with 12-Meter sailors.

The Aussies, who love to celebrate—getting drunk and uproariously jocular—even when they lose, staged a wind-up party after they had lost their challenge that almost wrecked the Cameo. It was the party of the decade.

[3] In 1920 *Resolute* and *Shamrock IV* finished in a dead heat, but the time allowance difference gave *Resolute* the victory by 7:01.

[4] Pierre DeSaix, "Tank Testing the Twelves," *Yachting*, September 1962, p. 124.

Alas, the Cameo has gone the way of most if its contemporaries —plowed under in the general clean-up of Newport's waterfront to make way for the genteel tourist shops that now line Pelham Street West in the popular Bannister's/Bowen's Wharf area. But the friendliness and fun-loving enthusiasm that the Aussies brought to Newport and the America's Cup scene helped interest the general public in both Newport and the Cup races. For the first time in its history, the America's Cup was being contested by "real people" instead of the unapproachable wealthy.

For his first 12-Meter design, Alan Payne had produced a truly innovative boat with great potential.

Part of *Gretel's* success was due to her Hood sails. The Aussies had asked for permission to use sails made in the U.S. because they had no sailmaking industry in Australia at that time that could produce competitive 12-Meter sails. Permission had been granted, and it was a source of continuing frustration for Mosbacher to work out, with Hood, a design for a fast spinnaker, for example, only to have an identical copy appear on *Gretel* a few days later. Photos show *Gretel* and *Weatherly* side by side in the fourth race flying spinnakers and mainsails of identical cut—even to the flaws!

It was this close call that prompted the New York Yacht Club to interpret the Deed of Gift more strictly, and in December 1962 it issued a resolution adopted by the Board of Trustees:

"WHEREAS, certain citizens or subjects of foreign countries, members of yacht clubs which qualify under the Deed of Gift of the America's Cup, and which yacht clubs are considering challenging for the America's Cup, have raised the question as to whether the obtaining of components (other than raw materials), fittings and sails, or the use of design facilities such as a towing tank, outside the country of the challenging club would be construed as falling outside the Board's Resolution of March 27, 1958, construing the word 'constructed' in the Deed of Gift as 'designed and built'; and

"WHEREAS, by Resolution dated March 27, 1958, the Board construed the word 'constructed' wherever it appears in the Deed of Gift of the America's Cup as meaning 'designed and built'; it is

"RESOLVED that the word 'designed' includes the use of a design facility such as a towing tank, and that the word 'built' includes components, fittings and sails; and

"WHEREAS, the Board recognizes that components, fittings

and sails and the availability of design facilities such as towing tanks may not be obtainable in the country of the challenging club; it is

"RESOLVED, that recognizing that such design facilities may not be available and components, fittings and sails may not be obtainable in the country of the challenging club, the New York Yacht Club, at the instance of a challenging club, will consider a request for permission to obtain certain of the aforesaid components, fittings and sails to use the aforesaid design facilities in any country other than that of the defending club;

"RESOLVED, that whenever the Deed of Gift of the America's Cup is printed, this Resolution with preamble adopted December 7, 1962 and the Resolution with preamble adopted by the Board of Trustees on March 27, 1958, intrepreting the word 'constructed' to mean 'designed and built,' be printed with the Deed of Gift."

W. Mahlon Dickerson,
Secretary.

THE 1964 CHALLENGE

The English were sadly disappointed when the New York Yacht Club turned down their challenge for 1963. It was too soon, New York said, and after some heated debate the Royal Thames Yacht Club issued a challenge for 1964 which was accepted. Ultimately, the challenger, *Sovereign*, was defeated in four straight races by the defender *Constellation* by lopsided margins. The largest was 20 minutes, 34 seconds—the greatest margin of victory in America's Cup history.

There were several significant developments from the 1964 series, in spite of the lopsided outcome, that set patterns for the future.

For the first time a challenging club sent two yachts eligibile to be challenger. In this case, two identical hulls were built to designs by David Boyd, who had also designed the ill-fated *Sceptre* in 1958. These yachts *Kurrewa V*, owned by the Livingston Brothers of Australia challenging through the English club, and *Sovereign*, built by a syndicate headed by Tony Boyden, raced each other with completely separate crews in a series to determine which would be the challenger. It had been observed that part of the Americans' success lay in their strenuous eliminations. If the challenger could have as good a work-up it was believed that it would have a better chance. The idea had merit, but the execution was flawed. Boyd, not the best regarded designer in Britain, had improved on *Sceptre*, but not much. *Sovereign* pitched horribly in the seas of Rhode Island Sound, and to say she was no match for *Constellation* is being overly kind. By choosing one hull design, the British thought that they would have closer competition, but they banked too much on Boyd's design. It would, in hindsight, have been better to have two different designs.

For the New York Yacht Club's defense, two new Twelves were built. *Constellation* was a Sparkman & Stephens design, and *American Eagle* was designed and built by Bill Luders from ideas he developed after working with *Weatherly*. Eric Ridder, who organized the syndicate which financed *Constellation*, was named her skipper, but he was replaced in midseason by Robert N. Bavier, Jr., after *Constellation* had been beaten consistently by William S. Cox, skipper of *American Eagle*. Bavier was to know the sting of rejection ten years later when he was replaced by Ted Hood in much the same circumstances that found Bavier replacing Ridder. But Bavier was unstoppable at the helm of *Constellation* in 1964.

THE 1967 CHALLENGE

The Aussies were back with a challenge for 1967. The New York Yacht Club had issued another policy statement to the effect that it would prefer to entertain challenges no sooner than three years following a successful defense. It also stated that it would consider all challenges received within 30 days after the last race of a successful defense as having been received simultaneously, thus obviating the need for potential challengers to be first (and risk being run over on 44th Street in Manhattan—where the New York Yacht Club is located—trying to be first to the door).

This challenge came, not from Sir Frank Packer but another group of Sydney yachtsmen. They commissioned Warwick Hood (not related to Ted Hood), who had designed some popular small cruising yachts in Australia, to design a new Twelve named *Dame Pattie* after the prime minister's wife.

Warwick Hood was a diligent and conscientous worker, but we will never know how close he came to improving on the likes of *Gretel*, *Constellation*, or *American Eagle* because Olin Stephens designed a super 12-Meter later named *Intrepid*.

A group of very serious-minded New York Yacht Club members

headed by William Strawbridge commissioned Sparkman & Stephens to do the design. They left no stone unturned and convinced Bus Mosbacher to come out of retirement to be the new yacht's skipper. They also purchased *Constellation* which would be campaigned by Robert W. McCullough as a full-fledged defender—not just a trial horse.

Intrepid was built in great secrecy at Minneford's Yacht Yard in City Island, New York. She was in many ways a radical departure from *Constellation.* Her bow had an ugly (by contemporary standards) knuckle which extended her effective waterline. She had a very short keel with small rudder attached. Protruding aft of the keel was a long full skeg with another small rudder attached to it at the aft ending of the waterline. The two rudders were to be used very effectively in combination. The forward one as a trim tab to improve the lifting action of the keel—much like flaps on an airplane wing, while the aft one was primarily used for steering. However, they could also be coupled to allow *Intrepid* to turn very quickly inside any competitor as in the expected circling maneuvers before a start. Mosbacher even anticipated a rule infraction by asking for a ruling as to whether using the rudders opposite each other to act as a brake would be in violation of the racing rules. The New York Yacht Club, the final authority in rule matters at that time, said that such use would not be considered a violation.

There were no other Twelves built in 1967. (The Club always seems able to come up with at least one new boat to meet a challenge, and usually there are two or more.) Besides *Constellation,* there was *Columbia,* considerably rebuilt by her West Coast owner Pat Dougan. A "dusted off" *Weatherly* came out for some of the trials before *Columbia* was able to get East. The Aurora syndicate was organized out of the old *American Eagle* backers, but there was not too much enthusiasm in this group for fighting Strawbridge's syndicate.

It wouldn't have mattered if there were no other Twelves besides *Intrepid.* She was so superior to any of the others that she lost only one race all summer (to *American Eagle*). Again the defender selected herself.

Dame Pattie arrived in Newport early enough for sailing trials, but she had no trial horse. When, in mid-August, Jock Sturrock (again named as skipper) and his crew were observed sitting dock-bound reading magazines, it was apparent that they would not be a serious threat to the defender. What was not known to the outside world at that time was that the Australians had exhausted their funds, and no additional money was raised to allow them to train as extensively as they might wish or buy new equipment or sails.

Sturrock and his mates seemed beaten before the series had begun. There wasn't much of the old fight that the *Gretel* bunch had shown even though there were many old *Gretel* hands aboard. Warwick Hood worked extremely hard, but there isn't much you can do without the funds. Soon *Dame Pattie* was being referred to as "Damn Pity," which was probably unfair. While she was no match for *Intrepid*, she was by no means the disgrace that *Sceptre* and *Sovereign* had been. Nevertheless, Hood went back to Australia never to be heard from again. He had devoted over two years to *Dame Pattie's* design, construction, and campaign. His design business had dried up or gone to others in the meantime, and he was blamed for *Dame Pattie's* failure. Hood has drifted into obscurity as a result.

THE 1970 CHALLENGE

Following the defeat of *Dame Pattie*, three challenges were received: a new one from Australia, one from England, and one from France. The latter was the first challenge from a country whose native language was not English. To accommodate more than one challenge, the New York Yacht Club agreed to allow the challengers to hold a run-off series to name the challenger. The Royal Sydney Yacht Club was named the "challenger of record" and it was left to this club and the two other clubs to work out their method of deciding how it would be done. Eventually, the Royal Thames challenge evaporated, leaving a series to be sailed between the French and Australian contenders.

Sir Frank Packer was back with *Gretel II*, a new boat designed by Alan Payne and skippered by Jim Hardy.

The French effort was a substantial one financed personally by ballpoint pen manufacturer Baron Marcel Bich. Bich had purchased *Constellation* from the Intrepid Syndicate following the 1967 series. He also purchased both *Sovereign* and *Kurrewa V*. In addition, he commissioned U.S. designer Britton Chance, Jr., to design a new Twelve to be built in Switzerland. This boat, named *Chancegger* after her designer and builder Hermann Egger, was not eligible to challenge as she was not designed and built in France. However, Bich intended to use her as a trial horse and as a trial run for Egger, who had never built anything as large as a 12-Meter before. For his challenger, Bich commissioned André Mauric to do the design—using Chance's design as a point of departure—and he built a new facility just over the Swiss border in France for Egger to use to build the hull. The new boat was named *France*.

The Baron put on a splendid show. His fleet of two Twelves, *Chancegger* and *France*, arrived in Newport complete with a large *entourage* and much fanfare. Bich tried out many helmsmen, and never did settle on any. In the final race against *Gretel II* (*France* lost four straight) in a dashing move the baron took command himself resplendent in white yachting attire—complete with white gloves. This race ended in disaster as *France* was unable to find the finish line in thick fog.

What the baron's challenge lacked on the race course was more than made up for by flamboyance. That, coupled with the emotional nature of the French, attracted much attention among the American public.

Another attention-getter was Charlie Morgan, a Florida designer, sailmaker, and boat builder, who entered the America's Cup fray (he had crewed aboard *Columbia* in 1964) as a one-man band. Morgan not only designed and built his own Twelve, his firm also made the sails, he was the skipper, *and* he personally financed the whole effort. Morgan's yacht was not a threat to the other contenders primarily, it was felt, because he tried to do too much himself. However, Morgan caught the imagination of the American public, and interest in the America's Cup was heightened by a nationally televised film showing all the U.S. contenders and concentrating on Morgan's anguish as his hopes crumbled.

Robert McCullough, who had skippered *Constellation* in the shadow of Mosbacher and *Intrepid* in 1967, formed a syndicate to build a new Sparkman & Stephens Twelve, *Valiant*, for the 1970 challenge.

The Intrepid syndicate turned to Britton Chance to design modifications to *Intrepid* and California architect Bill Ficker was signed on as skipper.

Former Commodore George Hinman chartered the aged *Weatherly* to provide four yachts for the selection trials. Hinman and *Weatherly* were impressive against the new Twelves, beating *Valiant* once and Morgan's yacht, *Heritage*, twice. Hinman's success with the old boat was to lead him to a key role as a contender in 1974.

Weatherly and *Heritage* were eliminated early in the final trials. *Heritage* was much improved, but her improvements came too late. Besides, the others had improved also. *Intrepid* and *Valiant* fought it out, but a cool Bill Ficker and *Intrepid* were consistently better than McCullough's disappointing *Valiant*. The new Olin Stephens design was decidedly not an improvement on *Intrepid*, even though most keen observers thought that Chance's modifications to *Intrepid* had slowed her down. Nevertheless, *Intrepid* was chosen to defend the Cup.

Meanwhile, *Gretel II* had won the right to challenge.

The two yachts came together for the first time seven minutes before the start of the first race and almost collided. *Gretel*, on starboard tack with the right of way, matched *Intrepid*'s movements first bearing off (away from the wind) and then heading up. As they approached, *Gretel* luffed (headed up) and had to tack to avoid colliding with *Intrepid*. *Gretel II* immediately flew a protest flag. They started, and *Intrepid* went on to win the race by a large (5:52) margin.

The basis of *Gretel II*'s protest was that *Intrepid*, on port tack, was obliged to keep clear under the fundamental port/starboard rule. However, the Committee found that *Gretel* had ignored another rule which requires the right-of-way yacht to give ample opportunity to the burdened yacht to keep clear. It found no violation of the rules since no collision occurred, and the results of the race were allowed to stand.

The fact that the New York Yacht Club Committee also was the arbiter of protests did not sit well with the Australians. They felt that they had an open and shut case against the defender and that the first race rightfully belonged to them. There was some public outrage as well, and the formal and unbending demeanor of Chairman B. Devereux Barker III did nothing for the Club's image in the minds of the public or the Australian challengers.

The incident so shook *Gretel*'s skipper, Jim Hardy, that he lost his confidence in starting situations and turned over the helm to Martin Visser, his tactician, for the second race. This had a definite bearing on the events that followed.

Just before the starting gun, *Intrepid* was approaching near the

Committee Boat end of the line, and *Gretel* was in position to force *Intrepid* to either steer behind *Gretel* or sail on the wrong side of the Committee Boat. It was an excellent position. However, as the seconds ticked away and *Intrepid* shot for the gap between *Gretel* and the Committee Boat, *Gretel's* mainsail continued to luff long after it should have been sheeted in to go for the line. Having switched unfamiliar roles with Visser, who normally trimmed the mainsail at the start, Hardy may have clutched. Perhaps, watching the situation develop he was seeing it through the eyes of helmsman rather than tactician, and when it was time to trim the main he temporarily forgot that the job was his responsibility. Whatever the reason, *Gretel* was too late to close the gap. Ficker was quicker and *Intrepid* sped through. *Gretel* continued to head up, however, and the two yachts collided shortly after the starting gun had fired.

This was one of the most controversial episodes in America's Cup history. Both yachts flew protest flags and continued racing— *Gretel* with part of her stem missing. *Intrepid* assumed an early lead, but *Gretel* passed the American yacht on the run (next to last leg) and won the race by 1:07. There was joy in the Australian camp. However, there was a protest to be heard.

The Australians were woefully unprepared for legalistic situations. Martin Visser had to borrow a rule book from Bruce Kirby, a sailing magazine editor, to take to the protest hearing. The Australians lost again, and there was even more outrage than before. Instead of a 2-0 score for *Gretel II* as most believed should be the case, it was 2-0 for the defender. Both wins had been provided by the New York Yacht Club's own Race Committee as announced by the unsmiling and irreversible B. Devereux Barker III, Chairman.

John Hopf, a Newport photographer, was in the Goodyear blimp directly above the starting line and recorded the sequence in still photographs. Movies were also taken from the same vantage point, and a UPI photographer got aerial shots from another angle. These were all considered by the Committee which concluded that the photographs supported *Intrepid's* contention that *Gretel's* action, which would have been appropriate prior to the starting gun, was in violation of the rules afterward.

Sir Frank Packer, in a letter to Barker six days later, when one race remained to be sailed, contended that the photographs showed *Intrepid* in violation of a different rule. Barker replied that this had been considered, as had the photographs, and as no additional evidence was presented by Sir Frank, the hearing would not be reopened.

The day after the last race, Sir Frank wrote again asking for redress and a meeting among interested parties. This letter cited a cable from England's international rule authority G. Sambrooke Sturgess.

This request was also denied by Barker citing consultation on the part of the New York Yacht Club Race Committee with U.S. international rule authority F. Gregg Bemis—not a member of the New York Yacht Club, Barker said.

The Race Committee could not deny *Gretel* her victory in the fourth race, however. *Intrepid* led at the start and managed to sneak away to a 1:02 lead at the fifth mark. It appeared to be over—another four straight for the defender—but under the eyes of an incredulous Race Committee and amid a deafening roar of approval from the spectator fleet—*Gretel* sneaked past *Intrepid* in dying wind as they both approached the finish line.

Gretel supporters now wanted blood. The score should stand 3-1 in her favor, they reasoned, instead of 3-1 for *Intrepid*. It was a moot point as *Intrepid* won the next race to conclude a successful—though controversial—defense.

The Aussies took their defeat with good grace. Hardy was particularly gracious in defeat, earning for himself the nickname "Gentleman Jim."

The controversy raged for some time following the event. Sailing magazines rehashed it and second guessed the Race Committee's decision. In the heat of the arguments on the second race protest, the controversy of the first protest was forgotten. In the end, most experts studying the photographs and the findings of the Race Committee came to believe that the decision was correct. However, it remains one of those thorny problems that will never be clearly resolved in the minds of many.

Never since the Lord Dunraven affair had the New York Yacht Club been in so much trouble with a challenger. Realizing the difficulty of their position having the Club's own Race Committee decide protests, it subsequently agreed to establish an impartial International Jury under the terms of the International Yacht Racing Rules. To the credit of both sides, the controversy had been neutralized. Both the New York Yacht Club and the Australian challengers have gone ahead with subsequent series with feelings of goodwill and mutual respect.

Socially, the America's Cup took another step toward becoming the superbowl of sailing. People came from all over the U.S. as well as Australia, Canada, England, France, and other countries to be a part of the excitement. With attractions like Charlie Morgan, Baron Bich, and the Aussies, they were not disappointed even if most of them couldn't get to see the races and many of those that did didn't understand much of what transpired.

The 1970 season saw two new watering holes develop in Newport. The French discovered a small, inexpensive restaurant that had been ignored for years because it was upstairs from a run-of-the-mill Thames Street bar. The Salases had been in business for many years, but until the public learned that the French had discovered Salas's Dining Room it was relatively unknown. Now, one waits hours for a table even in the winter season, and during an America's Cup season —forget it!

The drinking crowd migrated from the Black Pearl to an undistinguished bar on Thames Street which had been known as Dorians. Renamed "The Candy Store" it became *the* in place for 1970 with sailors and spectators from all over the world laughing and jostling on the open porch bar just to be able to say they'd been there.

THE 1974 CHALLENGE

Following the 1970 series, San Diego yachtsman and boat builder Gerry Driscoll acquired *Intrepid*. He believed that *Intrepid* had been slowed down by the Chance modifications. The original was faster, he thought, so he arranged for *Intrepid* to be purchased and shipped to his yard in San Diego.

I happened to be in Driscoll's boat yard the day she arrived, and I have never seen a sorrier mess that wasn't headed for a fire. Her keel was off, her deck hardware had been removed, her planking was dried out from the sun, and her seams were opened from the drying and jarring of a transcontinental truck ride. She looked like a large, dead whale waiting to be cut up for blubber. *Intrepid* was restored nearly to her 1967 shape. The stern was rebuilt, a new keel was made and attached, and a new deck layout was installed. Before long, *Intrepid* looked like a brand-new 12-Meter.

At the end of the 1970 series, the International Yacht Racing Union (IYRU) agreed to a request from the New York Yacht Club (in consultation with several past and potential future challengers) to set up scantling rules for aluminum construction for 12-Meters.

The IYRU controls the 12-Meter Class rules, and the strict construction specifications (scantlings) allowed only wood construction. These new scantlings, which took over a year, were developed in conjunction with Lloyds and other shipping bureaus. Therefore, the challenges from England, France, and Australia were postponed from 1973, the customary three-year period, to 1974. The Royal Thames Yacht Club's challenge was accepted as the "challenge of record" and it was left to the Royal Thames and the other clubs to work out suitable arrangements—similar to 1970 when there were only two clubs—for selecting the challenger. Once again the Royal Thames challenge evaporated by 1973, but they were left with the responsibility, and the considerable expense, of running the challenger's series.

The baron was behind the French challenge once again. However, he did not build a new yacht. Instead he planned slight modifications to *France I*. Compared to 1970, this was a very low-key effort—so low, in fact, that few people gave the French much of a chance against the Australians.

The Australian challenge came from Western Australia—near Perth—instead of Sydney in the East. The sole backer was Alan Bond, a brash real estate developer of Yanchep Sun City. Bond was in it strictly for the publicity value and admitted as much. He was not a stranger to sailing, however, having campaigned a number of ocean racers. His latest was a Bob Miller design, and he chose Miller to design the new Twelve, *Southern Cross*. Miller's boat was radical for a modern Twelve in that it was long (over 70 feet overall) and had an unusual break in the profile forward just below the waterline. Bond's PR corps cranked out the propaganda like confetti. One would have to believe *Southern Cross* was the fastest 12-Meter in the world if quantity of rhetoric was any measure of speed.

Bond also bought *Gretel II* to use as a trial horse. She was eligible to be the challenger, and many people believed that she was still the fastest 12-Meter ever designed. But if Alan Payne had succeeded in producing the two "fastest" Twelves of their times—as both *Gretel*'s very likely were—it was yet to be proven on the race course. Bond maintained, to his ultimate defeat, that *Southern Cross* was faster, and in practice matches in Newport *Southern Cross* usually beat *Gretel II*. However, Bond was accused of allowing *Gretel* to grow a foul bottom and she was not provided with any new gear. Either of these factors would have slowed her down considerably below her potential. Jim Hardy later admitted that he would rather have sailed *Gretel II* if she had been brought up to full potential.

Southern Cross beat *France* with reasonable dispatch in four straight.

Two New York Yacht Club syndicates built new 12-Meters for the 1974 defense. George Hinman was first to announce a syndicate through the U.S. Maritime College at Kings Point, Long Island. He commissioned Britton Chance to design a new boat. Chance was convinced that he could produce a winning design if allowed to start from scratch instead of being confined by the constraints of an existing form (designed by somebody else) as he had been with his *Intrepid* modifications. Key to this syndicate was the signing of Ted Turner as the new boat's skipper. Turner, an Atlanta, Georgia, advertising and broadcasting tycoon, had been talking with Chance for several years about an America's Cup defender, but he was never able to raise enough money on his own. Thus Hinman, who wanted to head a syndicate; Chance, who wanted to design his own Twelve; and Turner, who wanted to skipper an America's Cup defender were thrown together into a common pot. As has been well chronicled by Roger Vaughn in *The Grand Gesture*, it was an indigestive stew.[5]

Chance took a chance with a very radical design. He assured Hinman and Turner that his data from the Davidson Laboratory towing tank proved that he had a breakthrough design. Through a long summer, agonizing for all those involved, the boat, named *Mariner*, proved to be a dud. She was modified to make her more conventional in July and early August, but as is usual in these cases, the modifications—while definite improvements—were too late. *Mariner* was eliminated along with her stablemate the old *Valiant*.

Robert McCullough, now vice commodore of the New York Yacht Club, did not share Hinman's confidence in Chance, and was dismayed that there was no one to commission Olin Stephens to design a new Twelve. *Valiant* went to the *Mariner* syndicate, and using the clout that went with his office McCullough was able, with

[5] Roger Vaughn, *The Grand Gesture* (Boston: Little, Brown and Co., 1975).

some difficulty, to form a syndicate to build a new Sparkman & Stephens design. The new boat was named *Courageous*.

It was believed that the aluminum Twelves would be noticeably superior to the old wooden hulls, and that *Intrepid*, *France*, and *Valiant* would be hopelessly outclassed by the three new aluminum Twelves, *Courageous*, *Mariner*, and *Southern Cross*. Doubtless this belief lent credence to Alan Bond's insistence that *Gretel II* would not be a suitable contender.

Gerry Driscoll was not convinced. Working diligently to remove extraneous weight from the hull, deck, rig, and hardware on *Intrepid* (in much the same way that Mosbacher and Luders did with *Weatherly* in 1962), Driscoll was able to achieve a ballast to displacement ratio equal to the aluminum hulls. (Since weight is one of the factors in the formula used in the measurement of a 12-Meter, it is constant as long as other measurements are constant. Therefore, weight saved in other areas can be put into the ballast to provide more stability.)

Not only was *Intrepid* competitive, she very nearly won the selection trials. It was not until the last race on the last possible day that *Courageous* won to finally tip the score and the Selection Committee in her favor. It was a series reminiscent of the 1958 battle between the old *Vim* and the new *Columbia*—the establishment's pride and joy.

Excitement was added through the public support of *Intrepid*. West Coast yachtsman Peter Davis had paved the way for tax write-off's for America's Cup defenders several years before when he established a foundation for sail training. This organization was used as the basis of the syndicate of West Coast yachtsmen who joined Driscoll in the defense effort. The group actively solicited public contributions to the fund, which were tax deductible. This was a first for America's Cup competition, and the public responded with enthusiasm—the combination of old boat and the anti-establishment image (rightly or not) of a West Coast effort was irresistible.

The *Intrepid* people created buttons, bumper stickers, and posters to promote their cause. A favorite bumper sticker simply said, "Knock on Wood," a reference to *Intrepid*'s hull material. This prompted supporters of *Courageous*, whose sail number is 26, to counter with, "26— Pick Up Sticks."

Robert N. Bavier, Jr., skipper of *Courageous*, had obtained permission from the America's Cup Selection Committee to sail with twelve in crew during the observation trials. The twelfth man was sailmaker Ted Hood, whose products had been on every defender since 1958. Hood was taken on as adviser and sail-trimmer. Bob Bavier, who skippered *Constellation* to a successful Cup defense in 1964, had gotten that berth as a replacement for Eric Ridder. After being defeated by *Intrepid* for the third straight race on August 30th Bavier was replaced as *Courageous's* skipper by Ted Hood.

The battle that had raged between *Intrepid* and *Courageous* all summer had been, in some ways, a battle of sailmakers. Hood's sails were being used almost exclusively aboard *Courageous* and North sails were being used almost exclusively aboard *Intrepid*. North sails had been used on contenders before, but never successfully. Therefore, as the rivalry developed between the two 12-Meter camps, so did the rivalry between the world's most prestigious sailmaking firms. This was the forerunner of the big confrontation in 1977 between Hood and North.

As had so often been the case, the America's Cup Races themselves were anticlimactic compared to the excitment of the trial races between *Intrepid* and *Courageous*. *Courageous* swept the series in four straight.

Once again there were protests from both competitors resulting from an incident in prestarting maneuvers of the second race. The protest was heard by the International Jury which disallowed both. However, there was considerable feeling among knowledgeable observers that *Southern Cross* had fouled *Courageous* which probably avoided a collision by tacking. Perhaps the Jury's decision was a *politically* correct one, as *Courageous* won the race anyway.

Bond had made much of the signing on by *Courageous* of Dennis Connor, who had been the first tactician and then skipper of *Mariner*. Connor's aggressive starting tactics had been noteworthy, and after *Mariner* was eliminated he was signed aboard *Courageous* as starting helmsman for the defense. Bond, hollering before he could be hurt, maintained that Connor's tactics were dangerous, unsportsmanlike, and marginally legal. However, all the table thumping and name calling were for nothing. *Southern Cross's* prestart confrontation with *Courageous* in the second race may have been a deliberate move to call Connor out, but after the series was over, Bond put on a "gracious loser" smile and all was forgiven—if anyone had ever taken his bravado seriously in the first place.

One of the "gifts and antiques" offered by the Army/Navy Surplus Store was an old oxen yoke. It was suggested as the perfect gift for your mother-in-law.

Chapter I NEWPORT

It was late in the evening of September 10, 1967. I was bounding across southern Rhode Island skipping from bump-top to bump-top as fast as I dared push my six-year-old Corvair (having just found out before turning off route I-95 that its top speed is 90 mph downhill). The reason for my haste was that I had to make the last ferry from Jamestown to Newport or I would not only miss the party but I would have to spend the night in the car. The alternative, to drive up to Providence and down to Newport over the Mount Hope Bridge, was an extra hour-and-a-half unattractive. Finally, the ferry slip was in sight. She was still there, but it looked like they were getting ready to pull out. With horn blaring and lights flashing, I zoomed through the village of Jamestown, through the many lanes of the empty parking queue and got waved impatiently aboard the waiting ferry. The gates slammed down behind me, chains rattled, a bell sounded, and we were off to Newport before I could stagger, shaken and relieved, out of my smoking car. This was my last of many such frantic trips to Newport on an America's Cup Eve. By the time the 1970 series was sailed, the new Newport suspension bridge across Narragansett Bay was completed, and an institution of great charm and influence on Newport was gone.

The Jamestown Ferry was unquestionably a hindrance to Newport's development. In busy times it was a bad bottleneck. Friday afternoons one would wait for hours in Jamestown with traffic backed way up Route 138. One such afternoon I was stopped next to a maroon Rolls Royce whose passengers were Schweppes' Commander Whitehead and two luscious-looking blondes—a welcome distraction. Late on Sundays the whole of Newport's waterfront would be crammed with cars funneling down Spring Street to Mill Street and the ferry lanes. Everything in town stopped until the jam could be broken late in the afternoon or early evening.

The ferry slips are gone now. The large dusty area that once held rows of cars queued for the next boat is now the Treadway Inn—one of two recent waterfront hotels which cannot keep up with the demand for rooms. But gone, also, is the charm of remoteness that the ferry brought to the city, and the sense of adventure and anticipation that accompanied boarding the ferry in Jamestown is hard to describe and irretrievably lost.

In its heyday as a navy port, Newport's waterfront was a conglomeration of sleazy bars, ptomaine palace luncheonettes, odd shops, and tattoo parlors. But in the early 1970s the U.S. Navy pulled almost all of its operations out of Newport. The city, which had only to hold out its hand for the windfall of jobs and commerce the navy and its personnel brought, was faced with a major problem of existence. An obvious solution would be to foster a growing tourist trade and develop the natural assets that make it an attractive yachting center. However, before this could be done the sleaze of central Thames Street had to go. The bridge made all these things possible.

Except for the navy, Newport had been by-passed since early Colonial days. While the industrial revolution raged in nearby Fall River, Massachusetts, and north toward Providence, it left Newport— once the largest city along the New England Coast—to stay a sleepy fishing town. Wealthy society found Newport and built mansions (called "summer cottages") for their idle amusement. Society was, perhaps, attracted to Newport because of its remoteness which kept it from participating in New England's busy commerce of the 19th century, but the wealthy built their summer cottages south and east of the town on the stately rock promontories overlooking the ocean. There was no development pressure in Newport all the way back to Colonial days, and as a result there are more original Colonial buildings

The Bowen's/Bannister's Wharf area provided a variety of entertainment both by day and by night.

Contributions gratefully received.

And then there was the other kind of entertainment on the other side of Thames Street.

surviving in Newport than in any other city in the U.S. It is this combination of stately mansions of the very rich—most now turned into museums—and the fine old homes of the Colonial middle class—scores now restored to their original spartan utility and antique charm—that makes Newport a unique attraction for vacationing families. The same things attract visiting yachtsmen plus an excellent harbor with good shipyards and chandleries surrounded by unsurpassed sailing waters and pleasant anchorages. And of course, every three or four years an America's Cup, which has been sailed off Newport since 1930, attracts yachtsmen and landlubbers alike.

Following the 1970 America's Cup, plans were initiated to redevelop the Thames Street area between Broadway (Washington Square) and Memorial Boulevard. This section of town had a checkered past. It was mostly old buildings of little or no historical significance. At one time or another—especially when the navy was in town—most of these buildings had been saloons, the kind you would not take a "lady" to.

In later years Thames Street was not nearly as rowdy as it had been during and just following World War II, but there were still more reasons for tearing it down than for keeping it up. There was little to restore. What there was was saved or moved. Traffic was a continuing problem getting continually worse, and the city fathers felt that renewal would present a better image.

With the ferry gone, America's Cup Avenue could be started. The new Treadway Inn was built on old navy land, more recently the ferry's queue area, between the ferry slips and Long Wharf at the north end of the harbor. What had once been a wasteland of gravel and dust was transformed into an attractive hotel site with a spec-

The Brickmarket Place is a recently developed combination of shops, offices, and condominiums located adjacent to the old Brick Market between Washington Square and the Treadway Inn. The many shops included such specialties as candles, tobacco, stained glass, and many varieties of curios.

tacular view of the harbor. This was the cornerstone around which the renewal project grew.

Much of Bowen's Wharf and the properties at the foot of Mill Street adjacent to the Treadway and the Seaman's Institute building were acquired by a young visionary, Bart Dunbar. Dunbar transformed a run-down, smelly fishing boat wharf into an attractive collection of shops. He restored most of the old buildings, laid cobblestones on the wharf, repaired bulkheads, and rented out new shop spaces, apartments, and studios. The Aquidneck Lobster Company, one of the largest wholesalers in the country, with its iced trucks and quaint fishing boats remains at the end of Bowen's Wharf as a reminder of Newport's oldest surviving form of commerce. Bowen's Wharf and the Treadway Inn compliment each other very well, both attracting and serving the tourists and boat owners who visit the city.

America's Cup Avenue was scheduled to be completed from the Treadway to Memorial Drive in time for the America's Cup Races of 1974. However, several old and new Newport institutions were in the road, and they had to be moved or torn down before construction could begin. Among these were the Candy Store, Mario's Delicatessen, the Army-Navy Surplus Store, the Cameo, the Roman Gardens, and the Tides-Inn.

David Ray had done so well in 1970 and '71 with the Candy Store that he was very reluctant to move. One can always relocate a business, but a restaurant/bar has a fragile relationship with its clientele. Subtle changes in décor or menu can turn off the faithful. A drastic change in location or another type of building could be devastating. Besides, the Candy Store was housed in an 18th-century home called the Clarke Cooke House so it had considerable historical significance.

Ray managed to find space for the Clark Cooke House nearby on West Pelham Street on the site of Gilbert Stuart's residence while he was learning to paint. The building was jacked up, turned 90 degrees, and deposited on new foundations next to the Black Pearl, and across the street from Bowen's Wharf. This was accomplished over the winter of 1973–74, and with a completely restored structure, the same atmosphere (back porch overlooking the harbor), a new gourmet restaurant named after the original home, and a new downstairs disco called the Daisy, the Candy Store was more successful than ever.

One of the literally hundreds of shops on or near the waterfront. This one, located in an old firehouse, offers a mixture of antiques, modern china, glassware, and bric-a-brac. One of their oddities is an old fire alarm system.

Mario's Delicatessen had been a favorite stop for cruising yachtsment, Bermuda-bound racers, and anyone else needing deli supplies or a good sandwich and a cold beer. Mario's was fortunate to find a spot for a new building between The Moorings—which, along with Christie's, is the oldest marina on the waterfront—and the General Electric plant. Now one must order sandwiches the night before if one is going sailing before 11 A.M., Mario is that busy.

The Army-Navy Surplus Store, a junk shop complete with wooden Indian, found a suitable place to relocate across Thames Street from where it had been. There are those who say they would have preferred to see this venerable institution turned under by the bulldozer blades, but it adds a charm of its own and serves as a reminder of Thames Street's past.

The Cameo, alias the "Royal Cameo Yacht Squadron," alas did not survive. All that remains are some photographs somewhere showing Sir Frank Packer hoisted up onto the bar and Alan Payne swinging from the overhead light fixture that famous night in 1962 when they had almost won the America's Cup.

Washburn's Bookstore on Spring Street offered bargains even at the height of the tourist season.

The Roman Gardens is mourned by the few who tired of the Pier and Christie's seafood and high prices and found delicious and reasonable alternatives in the Gardens' lasagna and pizza. The traffic light which stands where the Roman Gardens' bar once was is no substitute for the dime beer and the dollar pizza.

Few will remember the Tide's-Inn and virtually no one will be sorry that it's gone. However, it was the most convenient place for outward bound sailors to have a final breakfast. The floors were white tile, the ceilings embossed tin, and the vinyl covers on the booth seats were patched with tape. The scrambled eggs were brown with grease, and the coffee—made with Newport water and served in white pottery mugs—was terrible. However, it was convenient, and if one was unlucky enough to be seasick later it could always be blamed on breakfast.

With the Black Pearl and the Candy Store in close proximity on West Pelham Street and Bowen's Wharf adjacent, this area has become a focus of daytime and nighttime activity. The Bowen's Wharf shops which once were tentative attempts to establish boutiques and craft exhibits are now in full flower with more buildings and small businesses being added every year. Following the 1974 series, David Ray bought Port-O'-Call Marina and transformed its cement-block arcade into a cedar-shingled chic shopping area which he restored to its original name, Bannister's Wharf. There is now no reason to venture forth to other parts of the Thames Street area. Where people once roamed the street from the Pier to the Treadway, they now cram into the Bannister's Wharf/Bowen's Wharf area where their every need can be satisfied. Elsewhere, Thames Street is often almost deserted in the evening which seems ridiculous when there are more people jostling for dinner tables at the Chart House, the Clark Cooke House, and the Pearl than can possibly be accommodated, yet there are tables going begging at some equally fine restaurants 200 yards north and east. Lemmings!

Me too!

About the time the Newport city fathers were seriously considering redeveloping the Thames Street area, the Newport Restoration Foundation began buying up old houses and restoring them. The Foundation retains the houses once they are completed and rents them as residences, offices, and stores. The Foundation's policies require tenants to maintain the interiors in the period appropriate

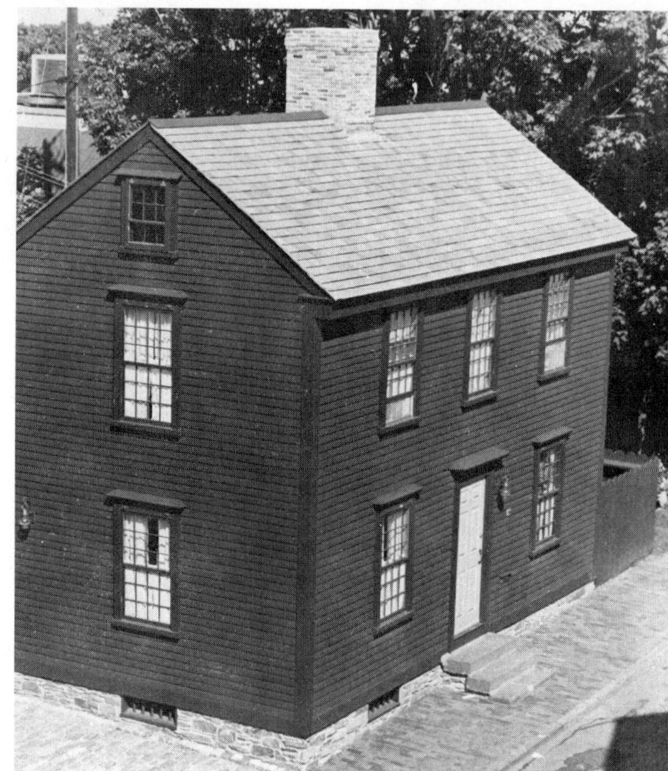

Newport Restoration Foundation houses are painstakingly restored with authentic details such as forged nails in the siding, stone foundaions, 12-pane sash, paneled doors, and proper trim. The only clues that this is not an 18th-century setting are the doorbell button and the front door lock. Also, if one looks closely, the bricks in the walk are larger than Colonial brick.

A small Restoration Foundation house on William Street.

New York Yacht Club Vice-Commodore Harry Anderson owns this restored colonial house on Spring Street.

to the houses. For instance, only curtains—no venetian blinds or shades —may be used in windows.

Fearing that the Foundation, which is funded largely by tobacco heiress Doris Duke, would eventually buy up all the old houses, an organization, which calls itself "Operation Clapboard," was formed to encourage private individuals to buy and restore Colonial homes. Most restored homes have a plaque stating the date and naming the home after one of its early owners. The two types "NRF" and "OC" differentiate between the buildings owned by the Newport Restoration Foundation and private homes whose owners were assisted by Operation Clapboard.

The restorations, which in 1977 had accounted for probably half of the restorable houses in Newport, have added greatly to the values of real estate in Newport. The house in which I live, for instance, is an unrestored 1801 single-family home which recently changed hands for a price in the low 30s. At the closing, one of the bank officers quipped that a few years ago the whole neighborhood could have been bought for that. In fact, an old house across the street was reportedly bought for one dollar and was restored by a 16-year-old boy! It is probably worth over $60,000 in today's market. Sadly, the inflationary spiral of these houses is so steep that few native New-porters can afford to take advantage of it. Friends who bought a restored Colonial for a price in the upper 40s in 1975 were told at that time that they paid too much for the house. In early 1977 a similar house in the same neighborhood sold for $95,000!

Restoration is expensive, however. Jim Gibbons, who specializes in chimney and fireplace reconstruction, told me that the price of Colonial bricks, which he claims are necessary to assure proper authenticity, is between 25 and 35 cents each. When I asked Jim to look at my house to see what would be required to replace the original chimney and fireplaces he said that it would be a year before I could expect to have any work done but that I should buy $1,500 or $2,000 worth of bricks now because they were available for 25 cents and next spring they would undoubtedly be priced higher. Perhaps Newporters will one day be investing in "brick futures" on the local commodity market.

Newport still has its isolated bits of sleaze. There are a couple of old-time bars left on Thames Street, but they are dying out rapidly. The Skipper's Dock on the corner of Thames and Pelham

Streets is a classic. The one-story building is painted a sort of barn red all over—including some of the windows. One window not painted over has contained a sign proclaiming "Exotic Dancer" and underneath in the same Magic Marker style are the words "Friday and Saturday." In felt tip above this is the word "Thursday," and in ballpoint pen around the periphery of the sign the word "Nightly" is printed several times. The real estate boom has hit commercial establishments as well as Colonial homes. This particular building with a small empty lot in back was for sale, asking $125,000. In addition, the asking price for the Skipper's Dock business—with no lease—was $25,000.

Newport had been a resort town even in Colonial times. Wealthy plantation owners and merchants from southern cities, such as Charleston, South Carolina, found Newport's moderate summer climate more comfortable than the sweltering heat of their southern homes. Newport never quite recovered its importance as a seaport and center of commerce following the Revolutionary War, the War of 1812, and the "hurricane of 1815."[1] However, it was able to advance its importance as a summer colony because of its unique climate and location by the sea.

The first summer hotels were built in the 1840s, and the mansion-like summer cottages began to appear at the same time. These homes differed drastically from the early Colonial homes of the merchants and seafarers. The latter are simple, practical structures suited to the needs of everyday living. While some of the more wealthy decorated the interiors of these houses with fancy stairways, mantels, and paneling, their structures were simple boxes—many of them using barn-type construction. Many of these homes, both fancy and plain, can be seen in the "historic hill" area of Newport and on the "Point," both adjacent to the harbor. By contrast, the summer cottages are ornate, many-faceted structures. These developed along Bellevue Avenue to the south of the commercial center of Newport. Today this area begins at the Bellevue Casino, built in 1879–81 as a recreational center for the summer colony.[2] This building now houses the Tennis Hall of Fame, a fine restaurant, and many shops. The summer cottages—

[1] Antionette F. Downing and Vincent J. Scully, Jr., *The Architectural Heritage of Newport, Rhode Island,* second edition, revised (New York: Bramhall House, 1967), p. 129.

[2] Downing and Scully, *Architectural Heritage,* p. 162.

Trinity Church was completed in 1726 . . .

Although it was lengthened at a later date.

The original organ which came from London in 1733 has been replaced, but the case remains unchanged. The pews at the back of the church under the organ were reserved for prisoners, who were required to spend Sunday in church along with everyone else.

The poop of the Revolutionary War frigate *Rose* was one of the only places from which to look down on the goings-on at the dock where *Independence* and *Courageous* were moored . . .

mansions—to the south along Bellevue and the ocean, which were built by the Lorillards, the Vanderbilts, and their ilk, stand in majestic testimony to a bygone era when the very rich lived in incredible splendor and luxury. These ornate, rambling dinosaurs are open to the public who come in droves to gawk and drool over things they can scarcely dream about no less aspire to.

Many of the old mansions have been turned into schools most of which have been absorbed by Salve Regina College. It was at this school's Conley Hall that the *Courageous* and *Independence* crews lived during the 1977 America's Cup. The *Enterprise* syndicate lived at Sea View Terrace, overlooking the Cliff Walk, and other syndicates in 1977 and over the years have lived in a variety of these former summer cottages.

One of the last privately owned mansions, Bois Doré, owned by the late Elinor Dorrance Ingersoll of the Campbell Soup fortune, was put up for sale and its contents auctioned off just after the America's Cup series. It was the first "house" auction ever conducted in this country by the famed Christie's. The auction grossed over $400,000 after the "good stuff"—paintings and the best furniture—had been removed to their galleries in New York.

The Cliff Walk is a public way which extends from Memorial Boulevard between the sea and the mansions above, down to the small beaches south and around the point called "Land's End" to Bailey's Beach. The Cliff Walk is about two-and-a-half miles long, and well worth the time and effort to walk it, with the pounding surf rolling in from Rhode Island Sound to break on the rocks below and the stately mansions with their manicured lawns and flourishing gardens above.

Kathleen Bond, the mother of *Australia* syndicate head Alan Bond, tried to chase some tourists away from the portion of the Cliff Walk in front of their rented "summer cottage," Plaisance. The "tourist" turned out to be the next-door neighbor Nuala Pell, wife of U.S. Senator Claiborne Pell. It was tactfully pointed out to Mr. Bond that the Cliff Walk is a public way and that many past attempts to close it to the public have been met with stormy rejection.

The only other way to find out what was happening on Bannister's Wharf was to try to peer through this lattice-work.

Tom Hardy, brother of *Southern Cross*'s skipper Jim Hardy, was aboard the press boat *Hel-Cat* every day of the 1974 America's Cup series. Not only did the *Hel-Cat* provide him a better view than he might have had aboard any other craft in the spectator fleet, it also provided Hardy with relative anonymity. He was scouting the series, in a very low-key way, in preparation for a possible challenge for 1977.

The Hardy brothers are in the wine business in Australia. Jim had been skipper of two America's Cup challengers—for Sir Frank Packer aboard *Gretel II* in 1970 and for Alan Bond aboard *Southern Cross* in 1974. Jim Hardy has been an America's Cup fan since his youth when he first read *The Lawson History of the America's Cup*. Now, having skippered two challengers he was thoroughly bitten. However, he wanted to put the whole thing together himself with maximum control over the things he felt had gone wrong in 1970 and '74. Thus, while Jim labored fruitlessly on the race course, Tom was observing as much as he could so that the Hardy brothers could come back with their own boat next time. During a dull moment aboard *Hel-Cat* (and there were many) Tom Hardy was noticed figuring up how many barrels of wine they'd have to sell to finance the campaign.

The Hardys were not in Newport in 1977. Their challenge through the Royal Sydney Yacht Squadron was accepted by the New York Yacht Club following the 1974 series. The Hardys did not put any of their own money up front and early in 1976 it was admitted that they had not been able to raise the money to design, build, and campaign a challenger. The Hardys announced that they were abandoning their plans.

Following the defeat of *Southern Cross* in 1974, Alan Bond announced that he would be back. His challenge was entered by the Sun City Yacht Club of Perth, Australia. Bond was reported to be in financial difficulties even while the 1974 series was in progress. However, those who counted him down were premature.

Compared to 1974, Bond's 1977 effort was very low key. He insisted that his was a proper syndicate—that is, that there were lots of financial backers of which he was only one, but there was difficulty from another quarter. The Sun City challenge was an on and off thing, and it appeared for a while that it, too, would falter. Bond and designer Bob Miller were unable to agree on details of the challenger, and for a while the deal was off.

Gordon Ingate had been concerned that the Hardys would not be able to mount their challenge. He had also been casting about for a new boat to replace his aging ocean racer *Caprice of Huon*. Furthermore, he made a study of the 1974 series, comparing finish times of *Intrepid* and *Courageous*, *Courageous* and *Southern Cross*, and practice sessions between *Gretel II* and *Southern Cross*. He came to the conclusion that *Gretel II* must have been as good as if not better than *Courageous* in some conditions.

Ingate confirmed these conclusions with Alan Payne. ". . . And I was just muttering around," said Ingate, "and said well if Jim (Hardy) doesn't get his act together, I'll buy *Gretel II* and we'll convert her into an ocean racer. Then if anything should come up we would have a boat we could go to the America's Cup with.

"Now I didn't see Alan Bond (then *Gretel's* owner) until Christmas of '75. I'd never met the guy, but I went up to him at a garden party and said, 'Excuse me, Mr. Bond, would you be interested in selling *Gretel II*?' "

"Oh, yes, I'll sell it," Bond told Ingate. "What are you going to do with it?"

"Well, I would like to convert it into an ocean racer, what Jock's

Gretel II, with a new deck and other modifications, was the challenger for the Royal Sydney Yacht Squadron challenge.

done with *Gretel I*," Ingate replied referring to Jock Sturrock.

"Well, she's a pretty good boat," Bond replied, "but I don't think she's as good as *Gretel I* for ocean racing."

Ingate continued working on Bond, all the time thinking of the facts and figures indicating that the boat was still pretty competitive as an America's Cup contender.

"Anyway," Ingate said, recalling the conversation with Bond, "he put much too high a price on the boat, and I said, 'Sorry, Mr. Bond, I couldn't afford that.'"

Shortly after this conversation, the Hardy syndicate folded for lack of funds, and the word was out that Alan Bond was having difficulty with his effort. Bond called Ingate to ask if he was still interested in buying *Gretel II*, but the price was still too high.

Meanwhile, Ingate had another talk with Alan Payne. "Look, Alan," Ingate told him, "if we can get *Gretel II*, what sort of changes will we make to it?"

Payne replied, "Gordon, you're wasting your time, the boat should be burned."

Bond called Gordon again, and in June of 1976 an undaunted

Ingate made an offer acceptable to Bond. Several weeks later, Bond announced his withdrawal from the America's Cup competition, citing disagreement with the designers, and Ingate found himself with the only viable Australian challenger.

Gretel's designer Alan Payne, having been released by the abandonment of the Hardy's challenge, was consulted and subsequently commissioned by Ingate, who was putting a syndicate together, to redesign *Gretel II*. Since the 12-Meter rules had been changed following the 1974 series to make the yachts more seaworthy and move the crew from below deck, *Gretel II*, as well as all the existing Twelves, had to have her deck rebuilt. Payne took the opportunity to make other modifications to *Gretel*'s hull as well. While much of her hull forward was removed, not too much of her underwater shape was altered. However, she was narrowed considerably, given more tumble-home (inboard sloping of the upper topsides above the point of maximum beam) to narrow her deck line a foot, and a new aluminum deck was installed to comply with the new rules. Payne told the *G II* syndicate that there were limits to which they could go to improve *Gretel*. He felt that the most logical approach was to concentrate on light weather performance. Studies of past series indicated that the August weather conditions, when the challengers would meet to determine the ultimate challenger for the September match, were predominately light. *Gretel* was redesigned to excel in winds from five to eight knots. Payne told the syndicate that she would be competitive up to 12 knots but that in winds higher than 12 they would have a serious deficiency. It was, admittedly, a gamble to give a yacht such a narrow optimum speed range, but Payne felt that it was the only way, limited as he was to certain basic hull characteristics. If *Gretel* did prove to be superior in light weather and did win the elimination series, could she have a chance to win the America's Cup in September when conditions tend to more wind?

Gordon Ingate was chosen to be *Gretel II*'s skipper. There was insufficient time to develop and train a crew of young sailors for *Gretel* so Ingate gathered around him as many experienced 12-Meter hands as he could find plus people he had sailed with aboard his offshore racer. Graham Newland, with whom Ingate had sailed many offshore races, was selected as tactician and alternate helmsman.

Wrestling with heavy wire genoa sheets (the lines which control the clew, or loose end, of the sail) can be extremely dangerous. The forces are measured in tons rather than pounds, as on small sailboats. A missed step or a finger caught on a winch drum can mean a severed member. The techniques of handling a yacht as large and heavy as a 12-Meter are special and require extensive experience. Therefore, *Gretel* had to go with the older and more experienced men. The average age of the crew was 40. And with great good humor, the *Gretel* crew arrived in the U.S. with *G II* T-shirts which read on the front, "Daughters of America, lock up your mothers." They called themselves "Dad's Navy."

———

Following the commitment of Ingate and the *Gretel II* syndicate to carry the Royal Sydney Yacht Squadron's challenge to Newport, Alan Bond, who had never formally withdrawn his challenge, patched up his differences with Bob Miller. Miller (who later changed his name to Ben Lexan) and his partner Johan Valentijn set about designing a new Twelve to an entirely different concept from Miller's 1974 challenger *Southern Cross*.

Miller had been noted for his speedy light displacement designs when Bond engaged him prior to the 1974 challenge. The 12-Meter rule specifically excludes a light displacement hull so Miller leaned on his experience with long waterline, small sailplan boats and produced a large, heavy Twelve in *Southern Cross*. The result was a boat that was well suited to Australian conditions—particularly those found off Western Australia—but one that was unable to sail as well as the defenders in the conditions found off Newport. *Australia* was the antithesis of *Southern Cross*. The new boat was designed to excel in light to medium conditions, and as a result she is smaller, lighter, and has a larger sailplan. It is easy to see the basic difference in the two yachts. Whereas *Southern Cross*'s photographs show a sailplan which ends well short of the ends of the hull, *Australia*'s headstay terminates just inboard of the stem and her boom almost overhangs her deck aft. This is an oversimplification of a very complicated process—designing a yacht to a rigid set of conditions—but it graphically demonstrates the differences which may be achieved within those conditions.

For *Australia*'s skipper, Alan Bond chose Noel Robins. Robins is a former national and world champion in the YW Diamond keelboat class, and Australian Soling champion. Robins was once a paraplegic, the result of a accident. He still walks with the strained gait characteristic of one who does not have full use of his legs, but there can be no doubt about his determination or of his ability as a sailor. The Soling is a demanding and athletic boat to sail, and the Twelve requires physical strength and uncommon endurance. Win or lose, Noel Robins would be much admired for his courage and skill before the summer was over.

For crew, Bond selected many experienced hands from *Southern Cross* and *Gretel II*'s 1970 and '74 summers.

———

Baron Marcel Bich turned, once again, to André Mauric to design his new Twelve for the 1977 challenge. Mauric produced a boat developed more or less by instinct, without tank testing his ideas or the final model. The yacht, christened *France II*, appeared to be designed for predominantly light weather, but when she was launched she was unable to beat *France I*. From the start, it did not seem that the French were a serious threat in 1977 which was most unfortunate considering the amount of personal effort and money the baron had spent on the America's Cup effort since before the 1970 challenge. And he was yet to get into the finals!

The baron also commissioned Alan Payne to design a spar for *France II*. The mast was almost identical to *Gretel II*'s, and both are extremely sophisticated. They stand very straight athwartships (across the boat) but bend easily and controllably fore and aft to control the shape of the mainsail in varying wind strengths. Rather than being made of extruded aluminum tubes, as is normally the case, these spars are fabricated from formed sections.

Payne spent as much time consulting with the French at Newport as with the *Gretel II* syndicate, and it was just as well for his ease of communication that both groups were headquartered at the same pier at Newport Shipyard off Thames Street.

France I, a smiling Baron Bich at her helm, proved to be faster than the new *France II*. The older boat, which was modified, was the baron's contender.

Australia was designed by Lexan and Valentijn for Alan Bond's challenge from Western Australia.

When it became apparent to the French that their new boat might not be competitive, they asked for—and received—permission from the New York Yacht Club to rebuild *France I* in the U.S. Thus *France* spent the entire month of July at the main yard of Newport Shipyard, at Long Wharf, having her deck rebuilt to conform to the new 12-Meter rules. Valuable time was lost when the two yachts could have been working out with one another.

Key crew members for the baron's effort, whichever boat he eventually would decide to go with, were Pierre ("Poppie") Delfour, who was one of the baron's skippers in 1970, and Robin Fuger, an Englishman who has been with Baron Bich since he acquired *Sovereign* from England in 1968. Fuger has been with the baron for each of his challenges.

A new country to challenge in 1977 was Sweden. The challenge from the Royal Göteburg Yacht Club (GKSS) had come as a surprise following the 1974 series. Few people knew of the Swedes' interest in advance, and few could guess at the seriousness of their challenge. Pelle Petterson (pronounced Pel-la Pet-a-son, but so many people called him "Pellee" that it seemed presumptuous for a non-Swede to try to pronounce it correctly) was little known outside Sweden except for those who knew him as the designer of the Maxi line of sailboats and the cognizanti who recognized him as the Star Class World Champion.

Petterson is not only a top designer of sailboats—it is said that he led the team which designed the Volvo P-1800—he also heads the firm which builds Maxis as well as a sailmaking division. He had no previous experience with 12-Meters, but with characteristic Scandinavian logic set about to learn as much as possible and to make up with effort what was lacking in experience.

The Swedes were determined to do things as "right" as possible. Nothing was overlooked. They attempted to purchase *Intrepid*, which would have been a very good starting point for a new design, but the New York Yacht Club made it known to *Intrepid*'s owners that they would consider it imprudent to let the Swedes have that much of a head start. *Intrepid*'s owners refused to sell. Instead, the Swedes bought the 1958 defender *Columbia* to use as a trial horse. *Columbia* was not as infirm as her vintage might suggest. She was campaigned in 1962, '64, and '67. Her hull form had been rebuilt in '67 to make her nearly equal to *Constellation*, so the Swedes were starting about equal with the French on hull shape.

"Our country's first challenge boat is the result of massive support from a large number of leading Swedish industrial concerns," wrote Peter Adler in *The Swedish Challenge, America's Cup 1977*. "In the whole line of challengers, Pelle Petterson's *Sverige* (pronounced Svair'ee-ya and meaning "Sweden") is the first that can be said to represent a nation's industry."[1]

Petterson, like Hood, was anxious to have his Twelve sailing as early as possible, opting for a thorough full-scale test program rather than relying solely on tank test data derived at the last minute—as had been previous practice with all new Twelves. *Sverige* was launched in September 1976 and christened by Queen Sylvia. Like the other challengers *Sverige*'s design parameters suggested a light weather performer, and her most unusual feature was her tiller steering. All other Twelves, with the exception of *Constellation* which was modified for tiller steering by Denmark's Paul Elvström when he was working for

[1] Peter Adler, *The Swedish Challenge, America's Cup 1977* (Wezäta Idé, Göteborg, Sweden), p. 11.

Sweden's challenger, *Sverige*, was designed and skippered by Pelle Petterson.

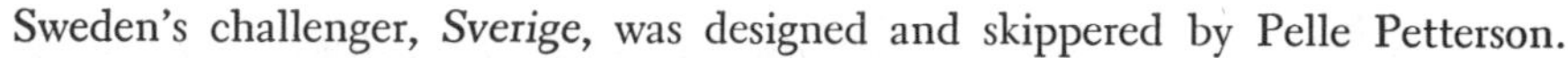

Sverige's tender: the Swedes can make puns in English.

Baron Bich in 1974, are steered with wheels. Most now have two so the helmsman can sit well to windward where he can see best to control the boat, but Petterson—inspired by Elvström—preferred tiller steering and devised a system that would work for *Sverige*. This feature was to play an important part in the tactics of some of the races during the summer.

All the new Twelves—defenders and challengers—were built of aluminum except *France II* and, of course, the old *Gretel II* which had her original wood hull topped with a new aluminum deck. *France*'s hull was built of beautifully laminated mahogany using a system similar to that developed by the Gougeon Brothers in the U.S. in which a relatively light wood (the Gougeons use cedar) is impregnated with epoxy resin laminated diagonally in thin strips of three or more layers over a rigid backbone. While *France II* may have been a failure on the race course, she is beautifully built, and her construction method may be a pioneer of lighter, stiffer composite 12-Meter hulls in the future.

It is interesting to note that all the challengers—not only *Gretel*—were designed to be good in light weather. Others had done their homework too and found light winds predominated off Newport in August when the challenger's series would be sailed. *Gretel II* was, perhaps, extreme in this regard, and while she was given an excellent chance to win the eliminations, it was generally conceded that she would almost surely lose the America's Cup match in the predominantly heavier winds of September if she got that far. In order to get to that point, all challengers obviously felt that light air performance was necessary. The trick would be to produce a good light air boat that would also excel in a breeze.

Courageous, the 1974 defender, was modified by Ted Hood for 1977 and skippered by Ted Turner.

$\mathcal{C}hapter\ III$ THE DEFENDERS

Ted Turner was at or near a lifetime low following his replacement as *Mariner*'s skipper early in the August 1974 trials. When one puts as much effort into something as is required of the skipper of an America's Cup contender, the downer of failure lasts a long time. But Turner is modeled on the prototype of the original positive thinker. He does not stew in his own juice. Rather, he looks ahead to a brighter future and ways to erase the stain of a tarnished image. Even before the 1974 America's Cup series was over, Turner was talking about how he was going to come back and win the America's Cup.

Turner was never a tinkerer, an experimenter, or a blazer of new trails. Therefore, the disastrously disappointing performance of the radical *Mariner* in 1974 was a double disappointment for him. He was caught out of character trying to be a pioneer. His formula for success in sailing was simple: look around for the best proven design, buy one, and campaign hell out of it. Turner relies on his ability to obtain the maximum potential from a proven winner. The result is usually an outstanding success. He did this in 1966 when he made his debut into ocean racing with the Cal-40 *Vamp X* with which he won the Southern Ocean Racing Conference and Transatlantic Race. The next year he joined Bob Derecktor in a partnership to improve on the Cal-40 with a boat Derecktor designed and built. It was only a qualified success. Then Turner bought the converted Luders 12-Meter *American Eagle*—surely not a pioneering ocean racing design, but *Eagle* was a long-term investment with which he won many of the world's most prestigious ocean races including the World Ocean Racing Championship. When *Eagle* was replaced, Turner ordered a German Frers design based on a boat that had done well in the Admiral's Cup two years previously, and his latest ocean racer is a well-travelled Sparkman & Stephens design he purchased (after trying her out on a charter for the 1977 SORC) from a well-known Chicago yachtsman.

With this background and a score to settle in the yachting world following the 1974 disaster with *Mariner*, it was natural for Turner to seek a proven winner. Before *Courageous* had put the final defeat to *Southern Cross*, Ted Turner was already saying that he was going to buy *Courageous* and defend the Cup in 1977.

But before Turner could act, A. Lee Loomis, a prominent member of the New York Yacht Club, approached Ted Hood, *Courageous's* skipper in her successful 1974 defense of the Cup. Loomis, who has owned several Hood-designed offshore racers, believed that the 1977 defense was going to be the toughest yet. He thought that preparations should begin immediately following the 1974 series, and he wanted the man he considered the master, Ted Hood, to put together a spare-no-expense effort. So he could be assured of having an optimum point of departure for a new design, Loomis bought *Courageous* and sent her to Hood's headquarters in Marblehead, Massachusetts.

The plan was for Hood to design a new Twelve that would, hopefully, be an improvement on *Courageous*. So much of the recent history of the America's Cup had demonstrated the folly of last-minute projects. Remembering the success of *Vim* in 1958, *Weatherly* in 1962, and *Intrepid* in 1974, Hood felt that a new design, launched a year early, would have a significant advantage in the trials of the summer of 1977. With *Courageous* as both a point of departure for the new design and a trial horse against which to test the new boat in the fall of 1976, the new boat should be able to reach her maximum potential earlier than any newer rivals. If, when tried against *Courageous* in the fall, the boat was found not to be an improvement, there would be time for modifications. The plan was nearly foolproof.

Independence (US 28) and *Courageous* (US 26), sailing in early practice
sessions off Marblehead, Massachusetts.

When Ted Turner learned that *Courageous* was bought by the Hood group, he offered to join the syndicate if he could be *Courageous*'s skipper and put together a crew to race her as a full-fledged contender. There was some precedent for this—*Constellation*, under Robert W. McCullough, was an "in house" competitor in the *Intrepid* syndicate in 1967—and most people were pretty sure that Hood would be able to design a faster boat than *Courageous*. Her role would probably be much like the one *Constellation* played to super-boat *Intrepid* —glorified trial horse. Besides, Loomis was not about to turn down the substantial contribution Turner was willing to make to the syndicate to assure he would have a free hand with *Courageous*.

The new boat, named *Independence*, was built by Minneford's at City Island, New York—builders of *Constellation*, *Intrepid*, and *Courageous*—and launched in August of 1976. Hood had her sailing in Marblehead from September through December against *Courageous* which was usually skippered by Robbie Doyle, Hood's second in com-

mand at Hood Sailmakers, when Turner was not available. The new *Independence* failed to beat *Courageous* consistently. In fact, insiders reported that they thought *Courageous* was a faster boat.

Care had been taken not to modify *Courageous* in any way from her 1974 configuration. This assured that she would be a true benchmark for *Independence*. However, it was discovered by Hood that *Courageous* had been 1,800 pounds too light when she raced *Southern Cross*. In addition, the 12-Meter Class Rules had been modified subsequent to the 1974 series requiring the rebuilding of the deck and the installation of watertight cockpits. *Courageous* would have to be changed rather extensively from her winning configuration, and since *Independence* was built to the new rules it was felt that she might still be an improvement over *Courageous* in spite of her failure to beat the older boat consistently.

Hood designed modifications to *Courageous* over the winter of 1976–77 to bring her into line with all the 12-Meter rules. Her waterline forward was shortened, her aft sections were changed to relieve some of the tortured curves in her "bustle" (full section just forward of the rudder), and her deck plan was changed to conform to the new rules.

Coming into the June trials it was generally assumed that *Independence* would be faster than her stablemate, that Turner would come out fast and fade in the stretch as the new boat was worked up and improved.

Intrepid had come so close to winning selection as the defender in 1974, and her crew and backers had become so psyched by the whole effort that they vowed to return. Throughout the final America's Cup races between *Courageous* and *Southern Cross* their syndicate spectator yacht *Pearl Necklace* flew a code flag hoist that read "22 in 77" (US-22 being *Intrepid*'s sail number). However, *Intrepid* was sold in 1975.

Andy McGowan, who was a key member of *Intrepid*'s 1974 crew, started developing interest in a new Olin Stephens design for 1977. McGowan was joined by Edward du Moulin, who became syndicate manager, and others—some of whom had been involved with the *Intrepid* group in '74. Since North sails had been the primary motive power for *Intrepid*, it was natural for this group to consider using North sails again, and a natural development from that was the selection of Lowell North to be the new boat's skipper. Among the crew for the new boat, which was also built in Minneford's and was named *Enterprise*, were several of the old *Intrepid* crew members—McGowan, John Marshall—manager of North's East Coast sail loft, Jim Caldwell, and Steve Taft. *Intrepid* was to be used both as a trial horse and as an actual contender—much the same way as *Courageous* would be used by the *Independence* group. However, *Intrepid* was in Hawaii. Her owner had fallen on hard financial times, and it was reported that *Intrepid* was tied up by the courts. The syndicate was able to purchase

Enterprise, US 27 (using multiweight cloth mainsail nicknamed "Jaws"), was designed by Olin Stephens and skippered by Lowell North. US 26 is *Courageous*.

her eventually, and she was shipped to San Diego where Gerry Driscoll commissioned her and became her skipper—as he had in '74.

Unlike the *Independence/Courageous* match, *Enterprise* was consistently able to beat *Intrepid*. Thus, it became a question whether it would be worth the expense to ship *Intrepid* to the East in June. She did not go with *Enterprise*, and there was considerable vacillating in June and even into July whether or not to ship her to Newport for the trials. Including *Intrepid* would ease the burden on the America's Cup Committee by providing four contenders—two pairs could race once each day. In the long run it was decided that there were insufficient funds available to have *Intrepid* sent to Newport. She not only had to be shipped East, her deck had to be modified as those of *Courageous*, *France I*, and *Gretel II* had been, and there would be considerable additional expense to house and feed her crew. Early in July, *Intrepid* was counted definitely out, and the syndicate made it known that she was for sale.

Enterprise was organized under a tax-exempt fund, the Maritime College at Fort Schuyler Foundation, Inc., which supports and raises funds for the Maritime College of the State University of New York. Similarly, *Independence* and *Courageous* were funded by The King's Point Fund, Inc., serving the U.S. Merchant Marine Academy at King's Point, New York. (The two academies are located across the water from each other at the Throgs Neck area which divides the East River from Long Island Sound.) These tax-exempt funds made it possible for contributions to the syndicates to be deducted from the donors' income taxes—providing a definite advantage to the defenders over some of the challengers.

With Lowell North as skipper of *Enterprise* and Ted Hood as skipper of *Independence* the 1977 series shaped up to be a battle between the world's two leading makers of ocean racing sails. The commercial rewards to the winner would be great. The loser? Well, neither talked of the possibility, although one had to lose. As it happened, they both did, but that was to come much later in the summer.

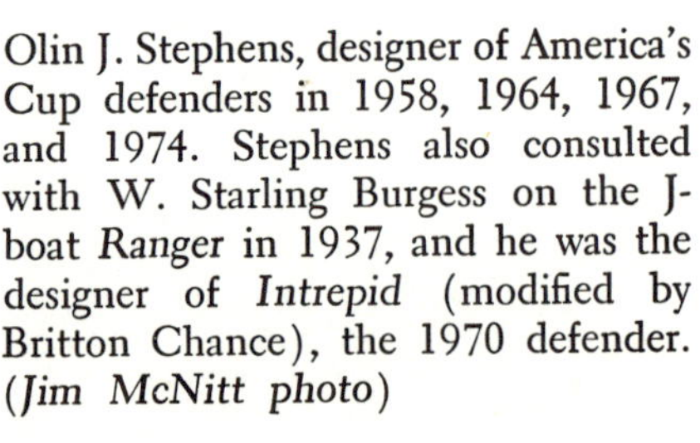

Olin J. Stephens, designer of America's Cup defenders in 1958, 1964, 1967, and 1974. Stephens also consulted with W. Starling Burgess on the J-boat *Ranger* in 1937, and he was the designer of *Intrepid* (modified by Britton Chance), the 1970 defender. (*Jim McNitt photo*)

Chapter IV PRELIMINARY AND OBSERVATION TRIALS

Everyone expected Ted Turner and *Courageous* would be the team to beat in the early trial races for the selection of a defender. The first races were held in June off Newport—the first time that preliminary trials had been held there—and the results were as expected. *Courageous* finished the series with a record of seven wins and one loss.

Since *Intrepid* was not available to make it an even four, with two pairs racing one race every day, the America's Cup Committee raced a pair in two races per day. This provided each yacht with a schedule of four races over two days with the third day off to rest, lick wounds, repair damage, or try new techniques and equipment. The races for the June series were shorter than normal—windward legs of about two miles instead of four—and it was the practice of the America's Cup (or "Selection") Committee to shorten a race when one yacht got so far ahead of the other that the outcome was not in doubt. Practice starts were also run to provide the Selection Committee with a look at the all-important skills of prestart maneuvering.

Independence failed to win a race in this series—losing four races each to *Courageous* and *Enterprise*. *Enterprise* lost three to *Courageous*—winning one race by the narrowest of margins—eight seconds!

Courageous suffered her only loss of the preliminary trials against *Enterprise*. Here *Courageous* threatens on the final leg, but could not quite overtake *Enterprise* on the short, two-mile beat.

Unfortunately, the June trials conflicted with the racing schedule of Block Island Week, and I was occupied most of the week just out of sight, nine or so miles away from the Twelves. However, I convinced my shipmates that a day on the America's Cup course would be fun, and we were lucky enough to see the most exciting race of the series.

In the first race Turner made his commitment to start at the Committee Boat end of the line, and right after the start the boats were headed. This put *Courageous* behind *Enterprise*, which did nothing for Turner's image with his baseball team—the Atlanta Braves—who were watching from aboard an excursion boat Turner had chartered for them. But Turner kept the pressure on upwind, rounded the weather mark about five boat-lengths behind, and gained on both reaches. Turner initiated a furious tacking duel on the second beat and almost crossed *Enterprise* near the weather mark. The Committee had set up a finish line to end the race there, and from our vantage point it appeared that *Courageous* would take the race.

Both yachts were on starboard tack approaching the line with *Enterprise* slightly ahead and to leeward. It appeared to us, off the side of the course, that *Enterprise* would not have been able to cross *Courageous* if the former had to tack for the mark. However, *Enterprise* laid the mark and won the race by a scant eight seconds. Later, my recollection of the finish was that the Twelves were overlapped, but when I saw the photo I had taken there was about half a boat length of water between *Enterprise*'s stern and *Courageous*'s bow. Still, it was the closest 12-Meter race I could remember in 15 years of America's Cup watching. Quite a way to start the America's Cup summer of 1977!

There are many nuances in a 12-Meter match race that are hard for all but the most dedicated race watchers to comprehend. The Atlanta Braves watching their owner split two races with *Enterprise* probably had little idea what was happening. Dave Philips, reporting in the *Providence Journal* on June 24th, quoted the Braves' Hank Aaron as saying, "I didn't understand that circling they were doing before the first race started, but we had somebody explaining things to us and by the time the next race started I was beginning to get the picture."

Besides the circling before the start, which is initiated by one competitor trying to get on the stern of the other, there are other things going on the reasons for which are not readily apparent.

Changes in wind direction can have a drastic affect on the relative positions of the competitors, and unless an observer is very close and has available continual reference to a compass, most of these shifts (except the drastic ones) will go unnoticed by observers. They can be five- to ten-degree oscillations, a series of gradual shifts in one direction, or a drastic, more or less permanent, swing up to 180 degrees.

The windward legs are not sailed directly because a sailboat cannot point directly into the wind. Therefore, it is often difficult from off the Twelves to tell which yacht will cross the other when they converge on opposite tacks.

Before the start the object is to gain control over the other yacht. Normally, a yacht which is directly astern of the other can prevent his opponent from either tacking or jibing, and if the control is maintained the yacht ahead can be forced to one side of the starting line or above it. Therefore, after the starting signal is given the controlling yacht needs only to turn around to be ahead and cross the line. It doesn't matter how long it takes to cross the line after the starting signal, one simply wants to be ahead. Of course, both competitors know these tactics, so the prestart maneuvers are usually "sparring sessions" with each moving warily near the other looking for an opening and hoping not to present one himself. In this league clear-cut control before a start is rare, and both skippers will probably consider themselves lucky to start even and with clear air.

Clear air is crucial. The wind coming off a sail (or from around any obstruction such as a spectator craft) is deflected and disturbed. It should be obvious that to have maximum effectiveness, a sail must use the wind as efficiently as possible. Wind that is turbulent or deflected from its mean direction cannot be used as efficiently as "clear air" that is undisturbed upwind from the sail. Therefore, the ideal position for a yacht ahead is directly upwind of his competitor. Because of the turbulence from the upwind yacht's sail, the yacht behind will find it virtually impossible to pass. Normally the yacht behind will find himself going significantly slower and falling farther and farther behind. This tactic is called "blanketing."

There is another way in which a yacht can affect the efficiency of the sails of his competitor. If a yacht is to leeward of another but close aboard and with his bow slightly ahead of the yacht to windward, the

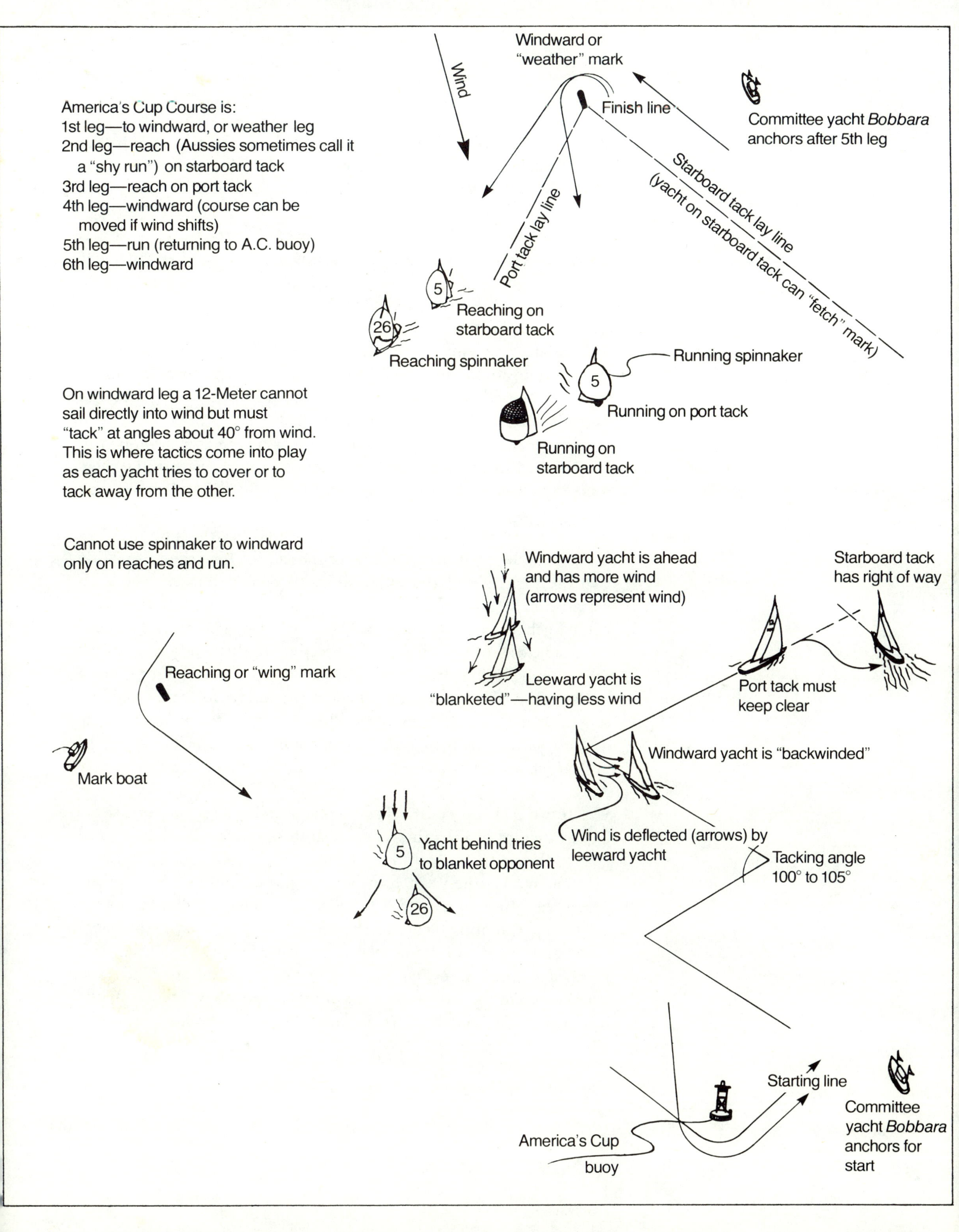

America's Cup Course is:
1st leg—to windward, or weather leg
2nd leg—reach (Aussies sometimes call it a "shy run") on starboard tack
3rd leg—reach on port tack
4th leg—windward (course can be moved if wind shifts)
5th leg—run (returning to A.C. buoy)
6th leg—windward

On windward leg a 12-Meter cannot sail directly into wind but must "tack" at angles about 40° from wind. This is where tactics come into play as each yacht tries to cover or to tack away from the other.

Cannot use spinnaker to windward only on reaches and run.

Wind
Windward or "weather" mark
Finish line
Committee yacht Bobbara anchors after 5th leg
Port tack lay line
Starboard tack lay line (yacht on starboard tack can "fetch" mark)
Reaching on starboard tack
Reaching spinnaker
Running spinnaker
Running on port tack
Running on starboard tack

Reaching or "wing" mark
Mark boat

Windward yacht is ahead and has more wind (arrows represent wind)
Leeward yacht is "blanketed"—having less wind
Starboard tack has right of way
Port tack must keep clear
Windward yacht is "backwinded"
Wind is deflected (arrows) by leeward yacht
Tacking angle 100° to 105°

Yacht behind tries to blanket opponent

America's Cup buoy
Starting line
Committee yacht Bobbara anchors for start

wind deflected from the leeward yacht's sails can be pushed into the leeward side of the windward yacht's sail. The windward yacht slows down, and unless he tacks away into clear air, he will fall behind. This tactic is called "backwinding."

As the two yachts tack up the windward leg, the yacht ahead has the advantage of being able to tack upwind and blanket the yacht behind. Naturally, the yacht behind tries to avoid this and tacks away. Thus, tacking duels are initiated with the yacht behind struggling for clear air and the yacht ahead trying to maintain the covering blanket. If there are wind shifts expected, the yacht ahead tries to force the yacht behind to the unfavorable side of the shifts by covering closely on one tack and loosely on the other. The leader is then in position to take advantage of favorable wind shifts first.

The first rule of match racing is to stay between your competitor and the next mark. If this principle can be applied successfully, there is no way the yacht behind can get past the yacht ahead. It is the crux of the contest.

On the downwind legs, the yacht behind has the advantage because it can be positioned to blanket the sails of the yacht ahead. To give the yacht ahead the opportunity to defend himself, the rules permit him to alter course to keep his wind clear and, if the yacht behind gets so close that the yachts are overlapped, the yacht ahead can head closer to the wind (even directly into the wind) to keep the other from passing. However this maneuver, called "luffing," must be discontinued when the helmsman of the windward yacht—sighting at 90 degrees from his normal position—is opposite the mast of the leeward yacht. He then calls "mast abeam" and the luff must be broken off with the yachts resuming their normal course to the next mark.

If two yachts are relatively even on a windward leg with one ahead and to leeward of the other, a wind shift, no matter how slight, will change their relative positions. If both yachts are headed off (away from the mark), the yacht to windward and behind will fall "down" nearer the other's wake. This is called a "header." If the yachts are headed up (pointing closer to the mark than they were), the yacht ahead and to leeward draws relatively farther behind the other. This is called a "lift." Knowing whether or not there will be shifts and whether or not they will be headers or lifts is extremely important, and it is the tactician's job to keep his skipper positioned to take maximum advantage of shifts while forcing his competitor to be in a position where they can do him the most harm.

Yachts sail at different speeds on different legs of the course—particularly in lighter winds. Sailing to windward, the relative wind speed is greater than the actual wind speed because the forward velocity of the yacht is added as a vector to the actual wind speed. Sailing with the wind, the forward speed of the yacht is subtracted from the actual wind speed. Therefore, a yacht will often sail twice as fast upwind as down. This means that the times at various marks can be misleading if taken as a measure of how much of a lead one yacht has over another. If the yachts are dead even in speed but one reached the windward mark one minute ahead of the other, they will surely be closer at the leeward mark. The lead yacht's speed may have gone from six knots to three as it headed downwind, and for a whole minute the trailing yacht is traveling twice as fast. Conversely, as the yachts round the leeward mark, the lead yacht (whose lead is now considerably less than it was at the windward mark) will increase its speed sooner than the trailing yacht. Also, when winds are light and variable, times around marks will be variable, sometimes wildly so. If two yachts round a mark in very light winds they may be 20 minutes apart in time although relatively close in distance. If the wind increases on the next leg they may be only two minutes apart. This *does not* mean that the trailing yacht has sailed the leg 18 minutes faster than the lead yacht. Only in relatively steady winds and with progressively lengthening mark rounding times can one say with certainty from time alone that one yacht is faster than another.

Going into the observation trials of July, Ted Turner was still the man to beat in *Courageous*, and Turner won the first two races sailed against *Enterprise*. One was taken away from *Courageous*, however, due to a protest over a foul in the second race. Turner had worked into the lead on the first beat, but *Enterprise* caught up on the run and overlapped *Courageous* at the leeward mark. North hailed Turner that he was taking *Courageous* to the wrong side of the mark (which the leeward yacht is permitted to do provided he hails to that effect and goes the wrong side himself), but Turner called "mast abeam" and did not respond with sufficient room. The yachts bumped topsides twice, and when Turner tacked to go back for the mark *Courageous*'s stern hit *Enterprise* in the topsides again.

Enterprise protested, and the America's Cup Committee disqualified *Courageous* for failure to keep clear of a leeward yacht. Turner's "mast abeam" hail did not apply because *Enterprise* had established her overlap from astern and did not have the right to luff *Courageous*. She did, however, have the right to carry *Courageous* to the wrong side of the mark—a normal match race tactic which gives the leeward yacht control once the yachts have passed the mark in much the same way that the trailing yacht has control at the start. He can tack or jibe to go back for the mark first.

Enterprise split with *Independence* the next day. It was the first win for Hood, and it presaged a better contest for the July trials. Betting was that either Hood or North, and perhaps both, would begin getting their acts together and that Turner, with the old boat, would begin to fade.

Courageous and *Enterprise* met once again the third day of the observation trials, and it appeared that the tide was indeed turning. *Enterprise* won twice from *Courageous*. Then, to further mix the pot, *Independence* took two from *Enterprise*. *Enterprise* was beginning to get the better of *Courageous*. *Courageous* was still beating *Independence*, but *Independence* was beating *Enterprise*. Who can pick a winner out of results like that?

The next day *Enterprise* won twice over *Independence* only to have one win taken away over a protest of a foul at the start. *Enterprise* was to windward when the yachts touched slightly, and the America's Cup Committee said that it was her obligation, as windward yacht, to keep clear.

Turner was definitely in a slump, and he was beginning to walk with his head down—talking to his feet in interviews as he often does when things aren't going well. But *Courageous* swept to a final and decisive win over *Enterprise* in the last day of the observation trials. Turner bounced back to life. He was in his winning form again, "Strong, man, strong" (the word drawn out with the emphasis on the "ong" sound), said Turner.

Two reasons were attributable to Turner's mid-series slump. Turner and his afterguard were shaken by their loss of the protest on the first day of the trials. This put them on the defensive and forced a reevaluation of their tactics. In addition, they had not had any new sails until this last race. Then they had used a new genoa made for

Courageous by Robbie Doyle, the Hood Sailmakers' manager and mainsail trimmer aboard *Courageous*.

While Hood's *Independence* was still not living up to expectations on the scoreboard—he finished the series with a 5-7 won/lost record—the racing was extremely close. Two losses to *Courageous* were by margins of six seconds and 18 seconds. As one *Independence* crew member pointed out—that was just 24 seconds away from two wins. The three Twelves appeared extremely close in speed, the wins going to the yacht which was better sailed and/or got the breaks with the wind shifts. It was 12-Meter racing at its finest.

Dyer dhows, closely bunched, dash for the leeward mark in the Demitasse
regatta, which included two representatives from each of the 12-Meters.

The day after the New York Yacht Club's observation trials ended, there was a fun regatta for representatives from all the 12-Meters— U.S. and foreign challengers—called the "Demitasse."

The Demitasse was an afternoon series of races for two representatives from each of the Twelves plus "America's Cup Skipper Emeritus" Arthur Knapp, Jr. "Knappy" was in the afterguard of *Ranger* in 1937, and he was the skipper of *Weatherly*, an unsuccessful defense candidate in 1958. He is a perennial winner in dinghies during the winter "Frostbiting" at the Larchmont Yacht Club in Long Island Sound, and at the age of 70 he may be considered the dean of eastern establishment yachting.

The regatta was the brainchild of Dyer Jones, a prominent member of the Ida Lewis Yacht Club and builder of the Dyer dhows. Jones provided 15 new nine-foot dhows, each with sails especially made to show the colors of the 12-Meters their sailors represented. The Regatta was sponsored by the Rhode Island International Sailing Association and run by Leeds Mitchell in Brenton Cove within the Ida Lewis Yacht Club anchorage.

It couldn't have been a better day. It started out with a light

Turner (third boat from right) got a good start . . .

And moved into the lead (#15) in the first race.

Turner holds the mainsheet in his teeth as he rounds the leeward mark . . .

And staves off all threats to win. He won the regatta as well.

wind from the south with just a few high, whispy clouds to temper the sun. The day was brisk, without being chilly, the sort of day you don't notice whether it's hot or cold. Perfect! Later, the breeze picked up to a not too demanding five to eight knots, which was just about right for the light weather dhows.

Courageous sent her "heavies," skipper Ted Turner and Tactician Gary Jobson, while most of the others sent lesser personages. Besides Knapp, Turner was the only 12-Meter skipper there. While none of the other skippers showed, that did not indicate a lack of talent among the other competitors. There were many top national and international dinghy stars in the fleet.

Once again riding high on *Courageous's* win the previous day, Ted Turner won the first race. Gary Jobson, who figured to walk away with the series, was visibly agitated—bouncing around in the boat on the downwind legs—and just managed to salvage a third. Steve Lirakas was second and Pete Lawson was fourth—both of them are from the *Independence* crew—giving the King's Point syndicate a clean sweep of the first four places.

Turner won the second race with a lead that was virtually unassailable. He was halfway to the finish line before the second boat turned the last mark. The second boat, with an equally impressive lead over those behind, was Arthur Knapp, old enough to be everyone else's grandfather!

Turner slipped to third in the third race and fifth in the fourth race. Jobson finally settled down to finish first in the third race, and the fourth race was taken by *Sverige's* Magnus Olsson.

In the final race, Jobson took the lead at the first mark with Turner a close third. However, Turner's sail clipped the mark, and he had to reround. This was a costly error as the rest of the fleet was close behind him. He finally rounded properly well down in the pack and continued to slip farther and farther back to almost last place. Is this going to be Turner's fate? I wondered aloud to my fellow passengers aboard Chris Cox's 27-foot *Elco*? Is he starting strong and fading in the stretch with *Courageous* just as he started strong only to fade in the end in the Demitasse? Perhaps, but Ted's late slump this day did not prevent him from winning the regatta. The Olympic scoring system allows one race to be thrown out, so Turner's 1,1,3,5

Courageous/Independence supporters came to cheer their representatives who finished 1, 2, 3, and 4 in the first race and 1, 2, 3, and 5 in the regatta!

Geoff Gale thanks the Ida Lewis Yacht Club and Leeds Mitchell for a day of good sportsmanship before the serious business of America's Cup racing was to begin.

was unbeatable. Jobson was second, Lirakas was third, and Joe Cooper from *Gretel II* finished fourth.

When Turner stepped up to accept his first prize, which was an engraved glass wine carafe, he said it looked like a bedpan. Ringing from the crowd over the laughter came a clear voice: "If it is, it's too big." First there was a collective sharp intake of breaths, then uproarious laughter. It was a fitting climax to a day of sparkling weather and equally sparkling good fun and sportsmanship.

When Turner was finally able to regain the stage he made a short speech. "I wanted Robbie Doyle and Gary Jobson, who are our small boat guys, to represent us," said Turner, "but Robbie had to go over to Europe to be in the Admiral's Cup this week, so I filled in for him. And I just came out thinking I was going to get crushed by all the kids, and it's a pleasant surprise, and. . . ." The rest was drowned out by applause and laughter.

Jibing a dhow is a bit simpler than jibing a 12-Meter. Reach out and flip the boom over your head.

Chapter *VI* GATSBY IN TOPSIDERS

by BARBARA LLOYD

Rain began falling the night of August 13 with a few sprinkles grazing the foreheads of 12-Meter crewmen, and within a few hours the sky had opened. The droplets fell like ripened grapes instead of pinheads of water. And, to make matters worse, there wasn't a set of foul weather gear in sight.

Only something quite extraordinary could lead this set of young men, so competent and at home in their usual boating garb, to don blazers, white shirts, and ties (yet retaining their Topsider moccasin deck shoes), but there was nothing usual about the summer of '77, least of all, the America's Cup Ball. Where else could a group of hardened yachtsmen, pampered society matrons, jet setters, and small-town politicians meld so well into an evening that would leave the Shah of Iran dripping with envy?

It was, without a doubt, the highlight of Newport's social season, even for those summer colonists who consider a day at exclusive Bailey's Beach and an evening tête-à-tête with the Princess of Liechtenstein just another dot on the summer calendar. It was a gathering of America's Cup syndicate heads, crewmen, summer colonists (carpet-baggers to winter Newporters), and Preservation Society patrons. It was termed an America's Cup Ball, but the likes of Jacqueline Kennedy Onassis and Lee Radziwill, TV star yachtsman Buddy Ebsen and Gen. William Westmoreland, columnist William Buckley and TV personality Gene Rayburn made it seem more like an Inauguration Ball.

More than one guest equated the evening to a *Great Gatsby* bash, but without the cardboard set. The scene was the same—the expansive front lawn of Rosecliff centered by a circular reflecting pool, and the massive, open-air terrace that framed the ocean side of the white marble mansion, where *Gatsby* was filmed two summers before. Baskets of fresh summer flowers from the Preservation Society's greenhouse and garlands of pink, silken roses on the walls gave an ephemeral quality to the "summer cottage." It was built in 1902 as a copy of The Grand Trianon at Versailles, and was a gift to the Society by its most recent owners, Louise and J. Edgar Monroe of New Orleans. On this evening, the Preservation Society was putting the house to work by creating a party that Newport hadn't seen since the heyday of the robber barons.

The party was by invitation—a summer get-together to raise money for the American 12-Meter syndicates and the Preservation Society. The $50-a-person tickets and the extra $10-a-person table fee was like charging a nickel for a popsicle on a hot summer's day. Preservation headquarters was battered with requests for more invitations, and the guest list stretched like Pinocchio's nose. By 10 P.M. that Saturday, when the first cars started rolling down the long, gravel drive off Bellevue Avenue, officials knew they had to count on at least 1,700 people.

The proceeds from the evening put $10,000 each into the bottomless 12-Meter coffers, and the Preservation Society of Newport ended up $30,000 richer. It was a benefit dance with an America's Cup twist, but the party had a way of making the world of filled spinnakers and sleek, 12-Meter hulls a thousand wharves away.

Jackie O and entourage arrived at midnight as pipers in full Scottish regalia marched up the lawn from the sea to the edge of the reflecting pool. As the national anthems were played the French, Swedish, Australian, and American flags fluttered to the top of stately staffs. Jackie, who was one of the few who knew the words, sang along to "La Marseillaise" in a glare of flashbulbs.

Shortly after the soft rainfall began, leaving the yacht club com-

Jackie Onassis is welcomed to the America's Cup Ball by Rhode Island Governor J. Joseph Barrahy. Making the introduction is Hugh Auchincloss. (*Ed Quigley photo*)

modores and syndicate heads huddled in small groups under five large, pink canopy tents, drinks in hand, listening to faint music from Palm Beach's Cliff Hall Orchestra playing on the Rosecliff terrace. Besides New York Yacht Club Commodore Robert C. McCullough, the ball attracted five other past commodores, including John Nicholas Brown, Henry S. Morgan, George R. Hinman, Clayton Ewing, and Donald B. Kipp.

The crewmen could have cared less about the rain. "I get a lot wetter than this every day on the boat," said one, his navy blue blazer hanging wet and limp on his shoulders as he swung his date around the outdoor dance floor. She, equally carefree, kicked off her shoes, and seemed oblivious to the rain that was turning her white dress into a soggy handkerchief. Inside Rosecliff, the Kennedy mystique was working its usual magic. Jacqueline Onassis and her sister, Lee Radziwill, daughter Caroline, cousin Stephen Smith, and mother Janet Auchincloss, sat together at a table in the main ballroom. Photographers spun around the gathering like hawks at prey, and celebrity gawkers milled by with the aplomb of Groucho Marx, leaving the little cluster about as much anonymity as the Statue of Liberty. A guest edging his way to a table nearby was heard grumbling, "This is worse than the Rangers and the Bruins."

But the family was gracious, and now and then, the curiosity seekers would move out enough to give Jackie time to chat with escort Jack Fallon, a Boston real estate financier, and sister Lee's friend, Peter Tufo, chairman of New York City's Board of Corrections. Caroline, looking very "debutante," in a green chiffon gown, took the dance floor with her cousin Stephen and family escorts. "Mummy" Auchincloss beamed over having just danced for the first time with 18-year-old grandson Anthony, son of Lee Radziwill.

The Auchincloss family, which owned Hammersmith Farm in Newport while Jackie was growing up, was to sell most of the homestead less than a month later to a group of New England real estate promoters. The estate, on Harrison Avenue near the famous Ocean Drive, was used the 1977 Cup summer as an enclave for the Swedish 12-Meter syndicate and crewmen. The main house and several caretakers' buildings were sold, but a smaller house edging the property and restored windmill were retained as part of the original Hammersmith Farm.

While the Auchincloss soiree was flitting about on the upper levels, most of the yachting types meandered among the five tents spread around the reflecting pool like a horseshoe. The syndicate heads stayed close to their tables, with men such as Lars Wiklund, manager of the Swedish syndicate, and Jorgen Blegvad, executive member of the syndicate's governing board, engaged in intense conversation at one end of the tent. On the opposite side of the pool, members of the *Enterprise* syndicate broke into tiny groups, moving from table to table, and occasionally throwing a glance in the direction of the teeming rain outside.

No one was thrown into the reflecting pool as in the late-night party in *Gatsby*. There was too much rain to make that thought seem appealing. But the *Gatsby* abandon was there—the 1 A.M. breakfast line in the rear of the tent, the slightly out-of-step swagger of a polished gentleman holding a "one-too-many" drink, and elegant ladies scooping up bits of wet grass on the hems of their ballgowns. The same elegant ladies who were later seen at 3:30 A.M. sweeping the tables clean of the floral centerpieces and bounding off with their trophies to their limousines which were impatiently waiting in the rain.

There had been a string of summer parties, from the more stodgy get-togethers of the New York Yacht Club elite to the commercial ventures of companies pushing everything from shoes to booze. There had been the syndicate parties—the bash at *Gretel II*'s summer home, "White Elephant," where French crewmen bellowed Gallic songs, Aussie beer was kept cold with ice stowed in dinghy sailboats on the front lawn, and party-happy crewmen weaved snake dances to the strains of "Waltzing Matilda." There was the party put on by the *Courageous* and *Independence* crews during which skipper Ted Turner turned the head of more than one guest with caustic words to arch-enemy Lowell North. There was the Australian challenger party in which a slide-show sequence sent the guests into gales of laughter when the commentator unwittingly described the *Australia* effort as "courageous." And, there were the Swedish parties held in tents adjacent to main house at Hammersmith, where everything from soup to nuts, New England clambake to Swedish smørgäsbord, was served to suit the occasion.

Yet, the America's Cup Ball stood out from all the rest. It might have been the location, or maybe the guest list. It could have been the time, when hopes were still high. Or, perhaps it was the size of the crowd. Maybe, it was the rain. It was a time for party lovers. And, for Newport, a slice out of the past. It was *Gatsby* . . . but it was *Gatsby* in Topsiders.

Chapter *VII* NARROWING DOWN THE CHALLENGERS

Never before had so many challengers been vying for the right to sail against the New York Yacht Club's defender in the America's Cup series in September. The fair selection of a challenger had become something of a challenge in itself. The system which was finally used was devised by Bruno Bich, son of the baron, and it was agreed to by all the competitors. The New York Yacht Club can select a defender by committee fiat but as the challengers all represent different interests no judgmental decisions could be allowed. The challenger would have to be picked on the basis of several series of elimination races.

The first series consisted of round robin races with each of the four potential challengers meeting each other as many times as the racing period would permit. Two sets of races were scheduled each day with the pairs rotating. It was agreed that the yachts with the best and worst scores would meet for the semifinal series of a best-of-seven races while the yachts with the second and third best scores from the round robin series would meet for the other semifinal best-of-seven series. The winners of these two would then be paired in a best-of-seven final match.

Spectator craft and 12-Meter tenders crowd close to the Coast Guard cutter *Point Turner*, waiting for the start of a race between *Gretel* and *Sverige*.

It had been rumored that Baron Bich was considering withdrawing from the round robin series in order to test his newly rebuilt *France I* against the disappointing *France II* so that he could then decide which yacht to enter in the eliminations. This would have meant settling for fourth seed out of the round robin. However, the baron was satisfied before the series that *France I* was his best bet, so she was entered.

Tuesday, August 2nd, the Coast Guard briefed the press on the patrol procedures for the challenger's series. The *Point Turner* (or other 82-footer) would take a position 150 yards outside of the starting buoy and in line with the starting line. No vessel can be closer to the buoy than the *Point Turner* nor to windward (ahead) of it. If the competitors come into the spectator fleet, the spectators are to hold their positions. After the start, the *Point Turner* peels off to the starboard side of the course. All spectators are to stay behind her and to starboard. The *Point Turner* keys on the starboard 12-Meter, keeping 200 yards from her and behind the other Twelve if the one on port is trailing.

Lieutenant Larry Craig seemed to have an excellent grasp of the finer points of 12-Meter racing. He appeared to know how far back to keep the fleet to keep them from interfering with the Twelves' wind on the first reaching leg. He also appeared to have an appreciation of the needs of photographers.

"I know you want to get into position to get both Twelves in the same frame," he told us. He said we could call him on channel 22 if we wanted to go in for a specific shot and then come right out again. The press was being relied upon to set examples for the other spectators. If we wanted to go to the reaching mark to set up for a shot, that was okay as long as we peeled off from the formation away from the course and circled around. In all, it seemed a very cooperative sort of thing with the maximum accommodation being made for the press without jeopardizing the competitors.

All the while, the Coast Guard emphasized that their function was to keep people from getting hurt—to protect the spectators (from themselves?) and the 12-Meters.

August 4th was the first day of the challenger's round robin series. *Australia* and *Sverige* were paired for the first start with *G II* and *France I* going 10 minutes later. *Sverige* was very aggressive and hooked up with *Australia* very early. At first it appeared that *Australia* might be turning faster, but *Sverige* ended up closer to the Aussies' stern. They broke off the circling about five minutes before the gun with *Sverige* underneath and in control. She did not force *Australia* over or to either side of the line, and it appeared that *Australia* was able to get far enough to windward to retain her ability to fall off clear ahead of *Sverige*.

Both yachts crossed the line late with *Sverige* ahead and to leeward. *Australia* tacked and *Sverige* covered.

The Coast Guard held the spectator fleet in position for the next start, so it was impossible to see what transpired with *Sverige* and *Australia* except that both yachts sailed out toward the starboard lay line and disappeared, for a time, into the haze. When they were about three-quarters of the way up the lay line, Alan Bond aboard his chartered yacht *Pat C VII* looking through his glasses shouted to us aboard Bruce Stannard's *Dancris* that *Australia* had crossed *Sverige*. As they rounded the first mark it was apparent that Bond had been right.

For a time it appeared that the Swedes would reach past *Australia*, but *Australia* was ahead at the reaching mark and then moved out on every leg thereafter. *Australia* won by a 1:18.

Meanwhile *Gretel II* was having her troubles with *France I*. The French crew, led by the baron himself, was very aggressive at the start. *France* maintained control over *Gretel* and took the start by quite a wide margin.

Everyone expected *G II* to grind down *France* and pass her early in the leg. It didn't happen. *France* maintained her control with a very tight cover. *Gretel* got closer on the reaches, but still couldn't get past. Then just after they rounded the leeward mark for the second beat, *France* caught her genoa on the mast for about five seconds. Her crew got it back quickly, and little damage was done to her lead. However, this looked like the time *Gretel* would make her move. She managed to get her tacks out of phase with *France*, but still couldn't sail through. They rounded the weather mark very close with *France* in the lead.

Gretel started a jibing duel, and *France* failed to respond—sailing off on port tack while *Gretel* went off on starboard. Whether by faster sailing, a better breeze, or by sailing a shorter course—perhaps a combination of all three—*Gretel II* was ahead by a considerable margin when the yachts came together at the leeward mark. She then lengthened her lead to two-and-a-half minutes at the finish.

The Australians had won the first two races.

Wind for these races was five to eight knots from the south-southwest. The haze was rather thick (not quite qualifying for the term "fog") in spots, but it burned off to provide about five miles visibility as the afternoon progressed.

After about an hour's rest, the Twelves went at it again. This time *Gretel II* met *Sverige* at the first start. The Swedes were again the aggressors, and easily controlled *Gretel II*, starting ahead and to weather. The official times showed them crossing the line even, but *Sverige* definitely appeared to have the advantage. Try as she might with tacking duels on each weather leg, *Gretel II* could not get past *Sverige*. She ground the Swedes down on the second weather leg, but could not get by. *Gretel* had to duck *Sverige*'s stern when they approached just before the mark, but Gordon Ingate drove *Gretel* close by *Sverige*, and when the latter tacked to to cover, Ingate drove her up with a luff, and the Swedes stalled. *Sverige* tacked away, and when they met at the mark *Gretel* had the advantage by seven seconds.

They remained very close together on the downwind leg and passed the leeward mark six seconds apart. *Gretel* maintained a covering position on *Sverige*, but she was not far enough ahead to give her disturbed air. As they approached the finish line it was impossible to tell which yacht would win, but *Gretel* just crossed *Sverige* a few yards short of the starboard tack line and forced *Sverige* to tack. *Gretel* continued on, making only one tack to the Swedes' two. That was

Approaching the finish line, the yachts were so close it was impossible to tell which would cross first.

Gretel was just able to cross *Sverige* and tack on her wind . . .

Forcing the Swedes to tack away and take an extra hitch to the finish line.

Sverige luffs across the line only 21 seconds behind *Gretel*.

enough to give *Gretel* the race by the slim margin of 21 seconds.

It must have been an exhausting day for all contestants, but a very satisfying one for the Australians. Gordon Ingate had told me he liked a good race. He had two come-from-behind squeakers, so he must have been ecstatic.

Both *France* and *Sverige* were impressive in defeat. Only when *Australia* got away from *France* early in the second race was there never a doubt about the outcome of a race. The Swedes were very happy that their yacht was able to sail so well (and they sail it well) in her first actual races. It promised to be an interesting couple of weeks.

As predicted, *Australia* came out on top of the round robin—being beaten only once, by *Gretel II*. It appeared that *Gretel* would be second by a substantial margin, however, she had to drop out of the series to be hauled for fairing between her hull and keel. This work had been previously scheduled in both Australia and the U.S. but problems, including inclement weather, had prevented the syndicate from completing the work before the start of the round robin series.

The baron sent out *France II* to replace *Gretel* so the other three challengers could all race on the final day of the round robin but the outcome remained the same as even with only six races sailed *Gretel* could not have finished worse than third. Therefore, the pairing for the semifinals was *Australia/France I* and *Gretel/Sverige*.

The yachts were holding true to form with *Australia* the most impressive, *Gretel* impressive in light winds—although she had to come from behind due to bad starts against both *France* and *Sverige*. *Sverige* improved with every race, and *France* failed to win a single race but came closer on at least two occasions than expected.

<hr>

It was no surprise that *Australia* beat *France* on August 11th, the first day of the semifinal trials. The margin was a convincing 5:53 at the finish. *Australia* was even able to overcome a premature start and still came out first at the weather mark. Had it not been for a 30-degree lift which favored *France*, the margin would have been substantially greater.

What did come as a surprise was *Sverige*'s win over *Gretel II*. This race, in what was reported to be nine knots but which appeared to soften considerably at times, was supposed to be *Gretel's* best weather. Officially, *Gretel* had the edge at the start by three seconds. However, she did not have a good position, and *Sverige* led at the weather mark by 1:04.

Gordon Ingate, *Gretel's* skipper, said later that the wave action —which was very severe considering the light winds—hurt *Gretel* considerably, particularly on the starboard tack. *Gretel* held even with *Sverige* for most of the first weather leg, but when they finally tacked onto port tack they could not cross *Sverige's* bow. It was all over for *G II* and she was a decisive 2:07 behind at the finish. Had *Gretel* won the start and had she been able to establish a lead from which to cover *Sverige*, very likely the result would have been reversed. However, it must have been a bitter pill for Ingate and his crew to be beaten by the Swedes in conditions for which *Gretel II* was designed to be at her best.

There was a long discussion aboard *Gretel's* tender following the race. Ingate, navigator Graham Newland, designer Alan Payne, and others of the brain trust went over the race, discussed sail selection, and generally looked like a beaten rugby team dabbing at cuts, bruises, and wounded egos.

A big issue of the day raised by the Australian press with Alan

Gordon Ingate, Alan Payne, Peter Campbell, and Bill Manning hold a postrace wake following their first-race defeat by *Sverige* in the semifinal elimination series.

Bond of *Australia* was the inclusion of an American as tactician and a twelfth member of the crew. The French had asked the other challengers if they would agree to having an additional crew member aboard for the challenger's series. They all agreed. The French rationale was that having an additional crew member could provide more depth in each boat and give the yacht which was ultimately named challenger a benefit even though only eleven crew members could sail in the final series. (The Americans had set a precedent for this in 1974.) *Australia* chose to sail with Californian Andy Rose who had been working with them throughout the summer. He had also worked with *Gretel II* and *Southern Cross* when they had been in Alan Bond's stable in 1974. Bruce Stannard and other Australian newsmen leaned on this question with some vigor at the press conference following the race. Alan Bond accused them of asking loaded questions to which they already knew the answers. No doubt he suspected unfavorable news reports back home for using an American in the crew. "We have nothing against Americans," quipped *Australia*'s skipper Noel Robins with a smile, but Bond was not pleased with where the questions were leading and suggested rather pointedly that if the press was going to ask loaded questions he was not going to come to press conferences.

Neither *Sverige* nor *Gretel II* sailed with the extra man. *Sverige* had twelve aboard before the start, but the extra man was left on the tender. *Gretel II* never considered sailing with a twelfth crew member. Ingate stated that *G II*'s deck layout was not suited for an additional man. He felt that allowing the extra man was a way for Baron Bich to sail aboard *France*, which he probably would not be able to do otherwise. Ingate said that the baron was a great sportsman and had done much to promote the cause of an international challenge and 12-Meter racing. The baron was 66 years of age, Ingate said, and the realistic chances of his racing aboard his own 12-Meter in three years time, at another challenge, were small. If he was not to sail, Ingate believed, the baron would have gone home, and the inclusion of a twelfth crew member while of no direct benefit to *Gretel II* would allow the baron to stay and sail.

Peter Clempner, who is in charge of running Ted Turner's 60' ocean racer *Tenacious*, asked me to join him to watch the races between the challengers the next day. As I walked down Thames Street on my way to Bannister's Wharf, I fell into step with Ted Hood, who was on his way there also. We exchanged the sort of idle chit-chat that usually passes between casual acquaintances who are deeply involved in separate enterprises. The conversation as we walked along went something like this:

"How's it going?"

"Well, it could be better."

". . . Things beginning to come together?"

"Yes, but we've got a long way to go."

"What sort of problems are yet to be solved?"

"Oh, I don't know, little things mostly."

I felt during our short walk together that Hood, who is usually taciturn, was even less communicative than usual. When I got to the dock I discovered the reasons.

Late the afternoon before, when *Independence* was practicing in Narragansett Bay, she ran down the aid to navigation buoy called "The Dumplings." They ran straight into it, never seeing it, and the boat came to a halt with the accompanying sound of metal smashing into metal. *Independence* suffered a few dents and scratches that were ultimately repaired, but no structural damage. The damage to *Independence*'s crew morale is harder to measure and harder to repair. While no direct accusations were admitted, it is not hard to imagine that relations between the workers up forward and the executives back aft, already strained, were strained even further. Even if no words were spoken there must have been thoughts such as "Why wasn't somebody up forward paying attention?" and "Why weren't the guys pointing the boat looking where they were going?" *Independence*'s crew was unquestionably shaken by this incident. Bell "11" continued to chime unperturbed wearing the white scars of battle proudly on its drab black framework.

After Hood dropped off to discuss details of the day with Jeff Neuberth, I saw *Independence* crew member Steve Lirakis. His passing retort to my "How's it going?" greeting with a rather telling, "You want a story or you want the truth?" Later, Steve was told he was being replaced and would not be sailing on the boat any more.

Ted Turner was in a different mood. "Only one thing worries us now," he told me as he scurried aimlessly up and down the dock, "and that's *Enterprise*. I don't know (if they are improving) but we're getting better all the time."

While he paced, Turner issued a stream of orders of details for the day. "We'll take the seven-ounce (genoa) today . . . and, leave the chutes ashore . . . just take the practice chutes . . ." and to no one in particular since it was obvious, ". . . no need to stretch the good chutes in practice."

Clearly, Turner had put out of his mind any possibility of a threat from his stable-mate *Independence*. Like the keen competitor that he is, he was focusing his attention on the primary problem of the moment—*Enterprise*. If outsiders could sense the self-destructive forces building in *Independence*, Turner, an insider, surely knew that he had nothing to fear from that quarter. Likewise, mention of the developing battles among the challengers was of no interest. Turner wasn't worried about them at this point, it was *Enterprise* he had to beat starting a couple of days hence.

Aboard *Tenacious*, when we left the dock, was a polyglot mixture of dedicated America's Cup fanatics and casually interested or mostly disinterested others. Three of Turner's children were aboard along with their black mentor Jimmy Brown who had played a similar role in their father's upbringing. Jimmy didn't set foot on deck all day even though he is an accomplished seaman. Piers Ackerman, an Australian journalist, was one of the few aboard beside Clempner, Brown, two paid crew, and myself who could handle the sails and lines aboard *Tenacious*. Richard McGinnis, his wife, and daughters formed the backbone of Turner supporters from Atlanta. Richard is the sales manager for Turner Advertising, and was coordinating the guests who would be aboard *Tenacious* for the final trials. The rest were associated with the Atlanta Hawks basketball team which Turner also owns.

Since the engine in *Tenacious* is about as effective as a brace of hamsters in a squirrel cage we set sail as soon as we had cleared Brenton Reef. It was hazy, and it was not readily apparent to the uninitiated where we were headed or why. A sprinkling of rain dampened spirits a bit, and soon Richard was making noises to Peter Clempner about meeting *Courageous* back at Brenton Reef Tower.

The fanatics among us included Peter who quietly sidestepped Richard's suggestion and kept *Tenacious* pointed in the direction of the race course. The challengers had already started when we arrived, and instead of following in the wake of the spectators we cut across the course, well behind and out of the way, to the wing mark to catch them rounding there.

As the Twelves approached it was clear that *Australia* was ahead of *France I*, which we all expected. However, *France* was only 57 seconds back. *Sverige* was a resounding 2:43 ahead of *Gretel II*. Adding to their misery, the Australians executed a sloppy jibe at the mark. That was it for *G II* as far as we could see. The finish would be predictable. *Australia* and *Sverige* would win, and the score would be 2-0 for each of them at the end of the second race. We chased them down the second reach ("shy run" in Australia) and—ho hum—kept on sailing toward Brenton Tower and our rendezvous with *Courageous*.

Courageous and *Independence* were tacking out of the Bay when we found them. I had been left at the helm with only non-sailors on deck. Peter and the rest were asleep below, but I passed the word for Piers. The two of us managed to maneuver *Tenacious* into position on the wind so that both Twelves would pass us as they tacked away from Beaver Tail toward Castle Hill. What a thrill as they came thundering up to us—not only for the spectators but for me at the helm of *Tenacious*, her "blast reacher" and mainsail pulling her along almost as fast as the 12-Meters. *Courageous* was ahead, which pleased Turner's entourage.

The grace and power of the 12-Meters was displayed at its best with them slipping effortlessly through the slight chop almost at our fingertips. *Independence* was so close that we couldn't tack until she had passed. When she had, I put the helm over, cast off the sheet, and Piers trimmed as the blast reacher filled on the other tack. Both Twelves tacked soon after we did, so our grandstand view continued on the other tack moving rapidly away from Butterball Rocks as we cleared the Bay. *Courageous* was now well ahead and to windward of *Independence*, and as if adding insult to injury, she bore off in front of the Hood Twelve to assume a leeward and ahead position.

Few among the three million who would visit Newport during the summer would be able to see 12-Meters sailing so close aboard. Fewer still would be sailing along with them aboard a similar size, close-winded ocean racer—particularly Ted Turner's own *Tenacious*. The folks from Atlanta had something to write home about, and I hope they got some photographs—I was otherwise occupied!

We woke Clempner as we approached Fort Adams and had to lower and furl the sails. Little boats, both sail and power, gathered around us as we motored in, and to those who asked we assured them that *Australia* and *Sverige* had won their respective races. We were safe in the first instance, but we were to learn later that we had missed a pair of very close finishes. *Sverige* had not won. *Gretel* pulled out a win in the last two legs, and *France* nearly passed *Australia* at the finish.

What had happened on the first leg which we had not seen but which Gordon Ingate later explained was a rather incredible botch by the Aussies. Approaching the weather mark, *Gretel*, which had lost the start to *Sverige*, was gradually grinding the Swedes down. Finally, *G II* was able to tack directly under *Sverige* and force her to tack. The Australian's joy was short lived, however. In their eagerness to catch the Swedes, they had forgotten to keep track of the position of the weather mark. When *Sverige* tacked away, they were already above the lay line. By the time the *Gretel* crew realized their mistake they had sailed almost three minutes beyond the mark.

This was the margin we had seen at the reaching mark, but contrary to our predictions, the race was not over. *Gretel* took seven seconds off *Sverige*'s lead on the second reach, 34 seconds more on the second beat, and passed the Swedes on the run. *Sverige* initiated a tacking duel on the last beat, which *Gretel* covered until Ingate realized that they were losing ground to the Swedish boat. "*Sverige* is the fastest tacking 12-Meter we have ever sailed against," said Ingate. He broke off the tacking duel, sailed his own course to the finish, and beat the Swedes by 58 seconds.

Australia squeaked out a win over *France*, but not without some difficulty. After being 3:37 behind at the last mark, a wind shift favored *France* which was able to come to within 19 seconds of *Australia* at the finish. When he came ashore the baron was so happy that one would have thought he had won the America's Cup itself. With virtually no chance to beat *Australia* in the long run, his elation was understandable. He had come closer to a victory than anyone expected he would.

The third race of the challenger's semifinal series should have established supremacy for *Sverige*, which seemed to be getting faster each day. *Australia*, it is assumed with a certainty even greater than that usually accorded the New York Yacht Club's defender, would win her series over *France I* in four straight. In fact, *Australia* won this day by a crushing margin of 8:54, and the action—of which there was plenty—was with the other pair.

Sverige won the start over *Gretel II*, as was becoming her style, and led at the first mark by 1:11. She increased her lead at the wing mark and was 2:30 ahead at the bottom mark starting the second beat. By now the wind, which was from the southwest at 16 knots at the start, was building into a full-fledged squall. The seas, which had been short and steep all day, built to threatening proportions. Shortly after rounding the bottom mark, *Sverige*'s jib, this one being used for the first time, began to come apart at the tack. Pelle Petterson sent foredeck crew forward to change headsails, and during this change *Gretel* took back most of her deficit. With *Sverige* slowed by the headsail change, she was overwhelmed by a giant wave. Pelle said he yelled to his foredeck man, who had his back to the waves, to hang on. *Sverige* lept over the wave—her bow pointing up at nearly 45 degrees before it smashed into the trough far below. "I should have watched out myself," Pelle said later, "because I got thrown by the same wave way back in the boat and landed on my back." He fetched up in the tailers cockpit about nine feet away from his normal position on the weather rail. The bow man was pitched far into the air, but landed on deck without being hurt. Petterson hurt his back slightly, but he regained control of *Sverige* quickly. They were still ahead of *Gretel II* when, about two minutes later, *Sverige*'s mast collapsed.

It was the severe stresses from the seas that caused the failure of *Sverige*'s mast rather than the increasing winds, which just before the dismasting reached a peak of 28 to 30 knots. *Sverige* had a small wire that connected the jumper struts (highest spreaders which face slightly forward of athwartships). This wire broke, allowing the spreaders to rotate aft. Unsupported in its highest section, the mast crumpled part way up, and the rest of it followed leaving a short section standing just above the deck. No one was hurt, but the race was over for *Sverige*.

"We sailed past within half a boat length," said *Gretel*'s skipper. They shouted over to ask if anyone was hurt, received a couple of weak smiles and a negative reply, and were waved on to finish the race alone.

Later the Swedes protested the Race Committee contending that it should have stopped the race when the conditions got so severe. I got the impression from listening to Petterson that they really didn't expect the protest to be upheld. Rather, they raised the point

Pelle Petterson directs the tuning of *Sverige*'s new mast following his yacht's dismasting in the third race.

of technicality to be sure that all factors were considered. The protest was disallowed, and the score was allowed to stand at 2-1 in favor of *Gretel II*.

The Swedes were allowed a day to replace their broken mast as is provided by the racing instructions. It was not charged against them as a "lay day." (Each contender is allowed to call two arbitrary lay days.) The French also asked for a lay day so there was no racing until August 16th when the final trials to pick the defender also began.

Australia and *France* started first. With a minute-and-a-half to go before the starting signal with both yachts sailing close hauled on the port tack, *France* bore away. *Australia* followed, but as *France* continued to bear away and jibe, she collided with *Australia*, hitting the Aussies bow on just forward of their port shrouds. *France* suffered a jagged gash in her stem, and *Australia*'s aluminum hull was dented. *Australia* continued on course and crossed the starting line 15 seconds after the gun.

After the collision, *France* lowered her genoa to examine the damage. Determining that it was primarily cosmetic, rather than structural, the French crew rehoisted their genoa and crossed the starting line 3:53 after *Australia*. Both yachts immediately flew protest flags.

Gretel won her start over *Sverige*, being positioned ahead and to leeward of the Swedes. Pelle Petterson immediately initiated a tacking duel, and about halfway up the first weather leg he forced *Gretel* to abandon her cover. The two yachts sailed on opposite tacks for some time, and when *Sverige* tacked to starboard to follow *Gretel*, the latter tacked to put the yachts out of phase with each other.

Sverige was clearly ahead when they converged, and when she tacked to cover, *Gretel* tacked away. However, as they approached the weather mark with *Sverige* on starboard tack with the right-of-way, they were exactly even. *Gretel* bore away under the Swedes' stern, but this put the Aussies in excellent position. By carrying her port tack out to the starboard tack lay line, she would be in a position to force *Sverige* to either take her stern or tack early. Incredibly, *Gretel* tacked before she could lay the mark, and in the ensuing two more tacks, *Sverige* got to the mark first. That was the race. *Sverige* lengthened her lead slightly on the two reaches, showing her superiority again on this point of sailing. *Gretel* fell further behind on the second beat but caught up significantly on the run and the final beat. *Sverige* won by 53 seconds, making the score even at two races each.

Ingate, who was acting as tactician while Graham Newland steered, discovered that the compass he used to sight the marks was ten degrees off. This had caused them to under stand the windward mark, and had probably caused *Gretel* to lose the race.

Australia increased her lead over *France* on every leg of the course and finished 10:16 in front. Pending the outcome of the protest, the series would either be over with *Australia* winning in four straight, or the score would be 3-1 in her favor.

Alan Bond charged the French with deliberately ramming *Australia*, and Barbara Lloyd, reporting in the *Newport Daily News*, quoted the baron as saying, "He (George Twist, tactician) told me to jibe, and then he told me to hit him (*Australia*)." In spite of the seemingly damning nature of this quote, what the French were attempting to do has long been considered a legitimate match-race tactic —lure your opponent into a situation from which he cannot escape without fouling you. Alan Bond is known to have a short fuse, but in this instance his accusation that the French had maneuvered in a dangerous way was upheld by the Protest Committee. They found that *France* had only been on starboard tack for about 10 seconds and by altering course so quickly, she did not allow *Australia* sufficient opportunity to keep clear. Each of the racing rules clearly states which yacht must prove its point, and in this case the burden of proof is on the right-of-way yacht to prove that sufficient room was allowed for the other yacht to respond to her new obligation to keep clear. *France* could not satisfy the jury on this point, and she was disqualified.[1]

Thus, Baron Marcel Bich's third attempt to challenge for the America's Cup came to an end just as those before it with a four-straight defeat at the hands of an Australian yacht. Because the outcome was clouded by an undecided protest, there was no fanfare, no farewell press conference, no blowing of horns, no three cheers for the victor and the vanquished. The baron returned to France two days later.

August 20th was do or die day for *Gretel*—the first of two, as it happened—and it didn't look too good for the Aussies. The weather promised to be in the 12–15 knot range, and the Swedes definitely had a psychological edge being one up on the scoring.

Fearing that this would be the last opportunity to take Bill Manning up on his offer to ride along with *Gretel* supporters aboard *Ursa Major* I called Bill Friday night and asked if he had room. Saturday, particularly as this day might be the last, was a tough day for Bill to fit in extra passengers, but he obliged uncomplainingly. It was a perfect day to be aboard.

The Race Committee postponed the start for 45 minutes while the breeze settled down in direction. This delay favored *Sverige* as the wind usually picks up later in the afternoon, and it already promised to be above *Gretel II*'s five- to eight-knot optimum range.

When everything was finally set for a start, both yachts came together with about six minutes to go. Both were near the Commit-

[1] See Appendix C.

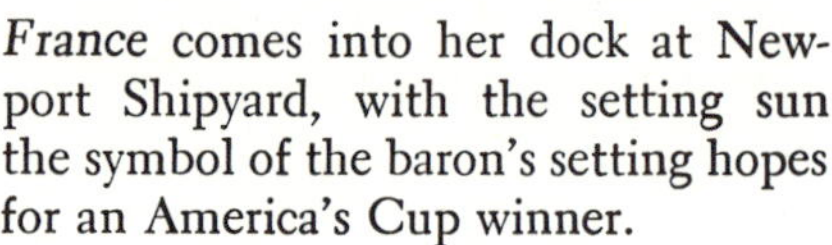

France comes into her dock at Newport Shipyard, with the setting sun the symbol of the baron's setting hopes for an America's Cup winner.

tee Boat end. *Gretel* was on port, and *Sverige*, on starboard and to leeward, tacked onto *G II*'s stern. The Aussies made no obvious attempt to keep the Swedes from establishing a controlling position. Gloom settled over the *Gretel* supporters on the bow of the *Ursa Major*. *G II* was going to blow another start—a start they needed desperately to win if the wind was going to favor their opponent.

The two yachts continued on port tack, headed up slightly toward the buoy end of the line with *Gretel* followed closely by *Sverige*. As they passed the buoy and continued toward the spectator fleet which was hiding behind the protective flank of the U.S. Coast Guard Cutter *Cape Horn*, we suddenly realized that *Gretel* was going to use *Ursa Major* to wipe *Sverige* off her stern. In they came, Graham Newland at the helm, Gordon Ingate dodging and weaving at his side as he simultaneously trimmed the main, looked for a hole among the spectators, and advised his helmsman of the possibilities. As they passed *Ursa Major*, accompanied by the shouts and cheers of its partisan passengers, Graham put his helm up and jibed *Gretel* around her own spectator boat.

Later, both Ingate and Newland explained that they were quite sure that Pelle Petterson would not follow them into the fleet because of his restricted midships view. (From the helmsman's position at *Sverige*'s tiller he cannot see to leeward of the genoa.) *Sverige* peeled off short of the spectators, jibing before reaching the *Ursa Major*, and when *Gretel* emerged, the hare had become the hound. She was now on *Sverige*'s stern.

The timing was perfect. *G II* chased *Sverige* up to the starting line with both yachts on port tack. Although she could have borne off clear ahead of *Gretel*, *Sverige* held on ahead of her, Pelle intent on giving his rival a dose of backwind. *Sverige* was early, and a recall signal was sounded with the start. *Gretel* was two seconds behind the gun, and she stepped off into the lead. When they recrossed the line properly, the Swedes were 32 seconds behind *Gretel*, and faced an uphill battle to try to catch the Aussies.

The prevailing southwesterly wind off Newport tends to veer, or change direction clockwise, as the day progresses. Using this knowledge, *Gretel II* maintained a loose cover on *Sverige* rather than attempting to sit on her wind tack for tack. By tacking on the Swedes' wind when they converged—*Sverige* on the port tack, *G II* on the starboard tack—Ingate forced Petterson to sail continually away from

Gretel (left) and Sverige head toward the spectator fleet with the Swedes firmly in control, close aboard Gretel's stern.

Finding a place to sail through, Gretel's skipper, Gordon Ingate, decides to try to wipe Sverige off his stern by turning through the spectator fleet. This was only the second time in America's Cup history that this maneuver had been attempted.

Ingate (at center, striped shirt) tails the mainsheet prior to jibing around the Ursa Major while starting helmsman Graham Newland carefully picks his way through the closely packed spectators.

Gretel jibes around Ursa Major (which happens to be her syndicate's spectator boat) and heads back out toward the Swedes, who did not dare to follow.

Gretel has now turned the tables. The hare has become the hound, and the Aussies are now in control of the Swedes because of Ingate's daring maneuver through the spectator fleet.

Newland, at the helm, blocks the Swedes from turning away from the starting line.

Sverige responds and heads up toward the line.

Both yachts near the line (the tugboat is one end) close hauled, just seconds before the gun.

At the instant of the starting gun, *Gretel* has timed it perfectly . . .

But the Swedes are too early and have to return and recross the line. This was the key maneuver that won *Gretel* the sixth race and evened the series.

the direction of the expected wind shift. The sequence was: yachts converge with *Sverige* on port, *Gretel* on starboard; *Gretel* tacks directly on *Sverige*'s wind, and *Sverige* tacks away. Instead of covering as soon as possible, *Gretel* continues on port toward the west and the expected shift until *Sverige* tacks or until there is danger of the yachts becoming too far apart whereupon *Gretel* tacks to starboard. When *Gretel* crosses in front of *Sverige* the sequence is repeated. There is no way for the attacker to avoid being forced to the wrong side of the course. If he remains on port tack he is forced to sail in turbulent wind which is disturbed by his competitor's sails. This is an unacceptable alternative to sailing on the wrong side of the course.

Gretel is at her best in these conditions—the wind not quite up to the 12-knot range where she begins to suffer slightly—and she reveled in it. Her combination of upwind speed and flawless covering gave her a lead of 1:29 at the first windward mark.

Sverige took a few seconds off *Gretel*'s lead at the reaching mark, but she lost them again on the second reach and was 1:30 behind at the leeward mark. But shortly after both yachts began their second beat, the first of several dramatic events took place.

Aboard *Ursa Major* the G II supporters were beginning to relax as they watched their yacht continue to stay comfortably in front of the Swedes. About a third of the way up the leg, *Gretel*'s genoa suddenly ripped from the leach near the lower spreader. The rip quickly spread until it went almost all the way to the luff.

"Thank God for the Gemini Foil," *Gretel*'s sailmaker, Peter Cole, said later. The Gemini Foil is a device which surrounds the headstay and provides two slots for attaching the luffs of the genoas to the stay. The ripped sail was, of course, in one of the slots, and the second slot (and an additional halyard) allowed *Gretel*'s crew to hoist a second genoa with a minimal delay.

There was a collective holding of breaths aboard *Ursa Major* as we waited for *Gretel* to set the new sail and take the ripped one down. Meanwhile, *Sverige* seized upon the opportunity to tack away, Pelle knowing that *Gretel* could not cover. During the period of perhaps two minutes that *Gretel* was without an effective headsail, *Sverige* was sailing approximately three feet to *Gretel*'s one.

When the new headsail was set and drawing it did not appear that *Sverige* had gained much ground. Gordon Ingate brought *Gretel* about to chase after Pelle, and the crowd aboard *Ursa Major* began to breathe again.

Then, "Oh no, not again!" Two tacks later, the second genoa ripped in the same way at the same place. This time they were a bit quicker to get up the replacement sail, but *Sverige* had tacked away. Possibly fearing that something in the rigging was cutting the sails, Ingate did not cover his rival this time. Instead, a man was sent aloft to look for the possible cause. He found nothing, but thereafter *Gretel* tacked as little as possible. Their lead had been cut to 55 seconds when both yachts had rounded the second windward mark.

Later on the dock, Peter Cole pointed to a couple of screws holding an inspection plate on the mast just above the lower spreaders. "Those screws," Cole said pointing aloft, "could have been burred the last time they were put in." Ingate had another idea.

"You may have noticed that *Gretel* is the only Twelve without patches on her genoas where they touch the spreaders," Ingate told the press later. "Peter Cole has insisted that we didn't need them, but I think you will see spreader patches on *Gretel's* genoas tomorrow."

Cole spent most of the night repairing the two ripped genoas and sewing on patches in way of the spreaders.

After rounding the mark and as if in sympathy for *Gretel's* problems, *Sverige's* crew dropped the inboard end of their spinnaker pole to the deck shortly after hoisting the spinnaker for the downwind leg. It took quite a while for them to get it back into position, and the spinnaker could not assume its most efficient shape until the pole was once again hoisted up the forward side of the mast. Not too many seconds were lost here, but as the yachts came together at the leeward mark *Sverige* was now surprisingly close. Only 22 seconds separated the yachts as they turned for the final beat to the finish. Could the mistake with the spinnaker pole have cost *Sverige* a chance to pass *Gretel* on the run? It surely didn't help!

By now the afternoon wind was at its peak, 15 knots. This was well out of *Gretel's* optimum range, and it was known that *Sverige* was faster in these conditions. It was tense aboard *Ursa Major* as lips were pursed, fingers crossed, and those aboard stepped up on tip-toes as if by having a better look they could will *Gretel* on.

The Swedes did not initiate a tacking duel as expected. Pelle Petterson said later that it was their observation that *Gretel* had improved her tacking so there was no advantage for the Swedes to initiate a tacking duel. Nevertheless, *Gretel* was still nursing her genoas—not knowing what had cut the other two and if this one might also rip. With *Sverige* so close astern and the wind more to her liking, *Gretel*

Steve Ingate (at right, wearing sunglasses) leads a group of young *Gretel II* supporters in song to celebrate their sixth-race victory over *Sverige*.

could not afford to rip another headsail. Petterson missed a great opportunity.

Gretel was able to hold her lead throughout the final leg, and she finished 45 seconds ahead of *Sverige*. The series was even at three wins for each yacht. *Ursa Major* erupted in a spontaneous cheer, and *Gretel* came by to take her bow before her supporters. The old men in the old boat had taken a series to seven races for the first time in America's Cup history.

Gretel's win over *Sverige* in the sixth race demoralized the Swedes. *Gretel* had won the start decisively. They had overcome serious difficulties on the second weather leg when their genoas tore. They had been able to lengthen their lead on the last leg when, in theory, *Sverige* should have been faster. Sunday "looked like a perfect *Gretel* day," as Pelle said later but the Swedes could not afford to call for a lay day, because if for some reason the seventh race could not be completed by Tuesday the series would go to *Gretel*. The rules called for a discard of the first race if this situation arose, and *Sverige* had won that race.

Conversely, the Aussies were high following their dramatic win and with the prospect of their weather for the last race on Sunday. They were entitled to a lay day, but they chose to sail. It was a fateful decision.

The Race Committee postponed the start for an hour and three-quarters waiting for a light south-southwest breeze to fill in. When they started at one-forty-five, *Gretel* was over the line early, but she quickly dipped back and was clear (later both Ingate and Newland indicated that they had not seen the recall signal but had dipped the line because they thought they were over). This cost *Gretel II* valuable position and the possibility of backwinding *Sverige*. The yachts split tacks, and when they came together, *Sverige* was able to cross just ahead of *Gretel*. Petterson tacked, but too late. *Gretel* was able to drive through the Swedes' lee to a safe leeward position. Pelle thought it was all over—that *Gretel* would be able to suck up underneath him, pointing higher, and backwinding his sails. It didn't happen. *Gretel* could not point up, could not drive through the Swedes' lee, and *Sverige* gradually, inexorably drove over the top of *Gretel* and pulled into the lead. The race thereafter was close—as all of their races had been—but *Gretel* was unable to make a serious threat to *Sverige's* leading position.

The selection of the wrong genoa may have cost *Gretel* the race and the series. Opting for their three-and-a-half-ounce genoa at the start, they found it too light for the wind they encountered on the first leg. When they came together with *Sverige* the light genoa did not provide them with the power to stay with *Sverige*, and with its draft pulled aft because of the stronger than optimum (for that genoa) wind they were unable to point high enough to backwind the Swedes. Both Ingate and Newland admitted later that this was the turning point of the race. Both knew at that moment that it was all over. Later during that first leg they changed to their six-ounce genoa, but it was too late. A bobble when Gordon initiated a tack before the windward sheet was attached—forcing him to bear away again briefly—did nothing to help either morale or position.

In victory, the Swedes were about as jubilant as other crews are in defeat. A handful of people—almost all having direct connections to the *Sverige* effort—gave three cheers as *Sverige* coasted into the basin at Fort Wetherill. Pelle smiled a lot, but that was the extent of the joy exhibited. *Gretel* sailed by under her spinnaker, but her gesture of sportsmanship—if that is what was intended—went unseen by the Swedes.

In defeat, the Aussies were about as sorrowful as other crews would have been in victory After passing Fort Wetherill, *Gretel* flew her spinnaker all the way into Newport Harbor. Their dock was edge-to-edge people. They were greeted by a rousing cheer. Champagne corks popped, and virtually everyone within reach went for a swim. They are a happy bunch, great sportsmen, the underdogs, the darlings of the summer, but now they were out. But defeated? Never!

Later, at a press conference Gordon Ingate and Pelle Petterson traded compliments:

"First of all," Ingate began, "many congratulations to Pelle Petterson for a fantastically fine series. He's obviously designed and produced and organized a fabulous boat, and I would like to pay my respects to the Swedish challenge. They've obviously put something together, for the first time, in very, very good order indeed.

"And I say thank you, Pelle," Ingate continued. "It's been a good series—fantastic, and as I've said to this conference before, he's not world champion for nothing.

"In respect to the race today, I suppose that the best way it could happen was that we were very fortunate to take it right down to the wire, as the Americans say, and we sat around there (at the start) for an hour or so probably hoping that we wouldn't get a start—at least I was hoping that we wouldn't get a start—maybe it would be fog tomorrow (laughing) and all sorts of wonderful things. Then the breeze started to slowly drift in and I thought that this was going to be it. This was what *Gretel* has been designed to do . . . (Ingate was interrupted by one of *Gretel*'s crew members riding a bicycle in front of the stage which temporarily broke up the press conference.) The wind was ours, the sea was ours, it was smooth water, everything was in our favor. It was exactly the way we had planned it to happen. Alan Payne, our designer, Peter Cole, our sailmaker, and our syndicate people—I pay my full respects to them—they produced every single thing that they said they would. Generally, I'd like to pay respect to the crew. They never put one single foot wrong. It was probably the best crew handling we've seen. But there was something that went wrong somewhere along the line, and I think that we, in the best Australian vernacular, we blew it.

"It was a good series, other than the last race, it's hard to be able to put exactly the reasons we lost, but I think probably we were beaten by a better boat, a better skipper, and a better organization."

Peterson summed up by saying:

"I'm really flattered by all the nice words from Gordon, and whatever happens in the coming races, we're truly grateful for a perfect match we've received from the *Gretel*. They've been perfect matches—and, well there shouldn't be a loser in races like this.

"To be honest," Pelle continued, "this morning, I wasn't very optimistic. The day looked like a perfect *Gretel* day, like Gordon said, smooth water and not much wind. I was very fortunate and thankful to all the guys behind me, sailmakers and others, who spent last night making some new sails for us. We tried some new things today, and we were just fortunate that they worked. I guess last night I must have felt something in the direction of what Gordon feels now. I blew it. Yesterday was my chance, I thought—fresh winds—we just couldn't make it. I guess in these races so much happens in the start or just after the start that it decides the whole race. You get a little bit ahead of your competitor, you get the cover right, then it's a lot easier to sail. So I know exactly how you (Ingate) felt today. That's exactly how I felt yesterday. It just so happens that we switched days, and we're so grateful. I don't know who decides these races, but they just happen. Someone wins, and the other one is the loser. We're the fortunate ones, and that's the way I feel. Thank you all."

It was interesting in hindsight that the next three days of racing for the New York Yacht Club final trials were cancelled because of adverse weather conditions. Later it was revealed that the *Gretel* syndicate had discussed the probability that this would happen, based on the weather forecasts that they had heard. They considered taking the lay day to which they were entitled. If the series could not be continued, they would win three races to two on the basis of the first race throw out. If it didn't blow hard enough to cancel racing on Monday, they would be at a disadvantage. Sunday promised *Gretel* weather, and most of the feeling among the decision-makers was that they wanted to win on the race course, not in the "rule book."

Ingate said later that he could feel disaster in the air as they waited for the start. The crew was cocky—overconfident. They had victory in their hands and were mentally drinking the champagne before the start. Ingate worried about it, ". . . but you can't say anything to them," he said.

What if the wind had failed to fill in until later on Sunday. What if the *Gretel* afterguard had decided to start with the six-ounce genoa instead of the three-and-a-half. What if they had called a lay day Sunday instead of agreeing to race. There were these and many more "what ifs" for *Gretel*'s supporters to think about regarding this series and those that were to come. However, the "what ifs" do not count. They do not register on the scoreboard, they only register in the hearts of those whose judgments have caused them. "What ifs" are the bitter memories of defeat.

Australia (left) leads *Sverige* as the yachts approach the finish line—typical of the closeness of their racing in the final elimination series.

It seemed, following their seven-race series with *Gretel II*, that the Swedes had perhaps reached a peak in their crew performance and in the development of *Sverige*'s speed. Except for their dismasting, they had had little gear difficulty, their sails looked good, their tactics were okay, and their crew work was nearly flawless. Although most dockside experts thought *Australia* would win, it was beginning to appear that *Sverige* could upset the favorite. After all, *Sverige* had the advantage of a difficult seven-race series to hone her to her peak while *Australia* had a romp over the French followed by a week with no competitive activity. Surely this final elimination series would be close and provide exciting racing.

The first race started in a fading northwester which had come in following the three days of foul weather. *Sverige* had a slight margin of three seconds at the start, and she lengthened her lead on the first beat into fading breezes. The Swedes got the better of the wind shifts and moved into an impressive lead of 3:12 at the first mark. This was extended at the reaching mark, but *Australia* moved to within 1:47 at the beginning of the second beat.

If *Sverige* covered *Australia* on the two remaining beats she was virtually assured of a victory in this important first race. However, the Swedes covered the east side of the course—an unpardonable sin in a northwester to those with local knowledge—and the Aussies sailed into the inevitable header. Petterson, seeing the mistake, tried to get on top of *Australia*, but it was too late. When they crossed *Australia* had a slight lead. Pelle attacked immediately, tacking on the headers and trying to force Noel Robins to tack at unfavorable times, and the boats were very close going into the weather mark—*Australia* leading by a scant 13 seconds.

Rounding the mark, *Sverige* jibed and the crew set her spinnaker with perfect timing and precision. *Australia*, holding to the west, was caught, and the Swedes regained their lead.

Noel Robins attacked from close behind on the run and both yachts moved to the east side of the course on port tack. *Sverige* held onto her lead and may have increased it slightly.

About three-quarters of the way to the bottom mark *Australia*, which had gotten to windward in a fruitless attempt to pass, jibed onto starboard toward the course centerline. To the amazement of the spectators, *Sverige* maintained her course which took her farther and farther away from the line between *Australia* and the mark.

The basic match-race tactic is to stay between your competitor

As *Australia* and *Sverige* rounded the windward mark and headed off on the run . . .

The Swedes turned inside *Australia* . . .

Jibed . . .

And surged . . .

Into the lead.

and the next mark. If that principle is adhered to and your boat has sufficient speed to maintain this position, there is no way your competitor can beat you. However, here was Petterson violating this principle for the second time in this race.

Predictably, *Australia* found more wind on the west side of the course than *Sverige* had on the east. When the yachts converged near the mark, *Australia* had regained the lead and rounded with a 1:09 advantage. That was it! Noel Robins did not make the mistake of not covering his competitor. He controlled *Sverige* closely on the final beat and won by 51 seconds.

The Swedes called for a lay day to work on their rig. They had installed a new mast between the semifinal series with *Gretel,* and they said they were having trouble controlling the spar.

The second race, sailed in a typical sou'wester, was extremely close but *Australia* led all the way. This was a classic match race. *Sverige,* the yacht behind, attacked *Australia,* the yacht ahead, but unlike his opponent the previous day, Robins covered Petterson precisely. The Swedes never had an opportunity to get ahead although the finish time of 25 seconds was extremely close.

The Swedes were still having difficulty with their mast and sails. The mainsail looked terrible—worse than it had all summer—and *Sverige* called a lay day so her crew could try to do something about it. With the score 2-0, time was running out.

Sverige took the start from *Australia* at the gun of the third race. However, they failed to capitalize on their advantage. Incredibly, *Sverige* sailed off by herself on the starboard tack, leaving the Australians the favored port tack taking them toward the west and the expected wind shift.

I had been watching this race from aboard the *Ursa Major* with the *Gretel* group, and I was so surprised by the Swedes' tactic that I sought out Graham Newland, *Gretel's* navigator and tactician, to confirm my belief that the Swedes were making a gross tactical error.

"I don't believe it," said Newland. "We have always covered the west side of the course because you usually get a header over there." Later *Sverige's* Magnus Olsson said that the Swedes believed that the wind shifts more often favored the yacht on the east or south side of the course. Those with more experience in the area would not agree.

The result was that *Australia* led at the first weather mark, having erased their 30-second deficit at the start. The finish time of 50 seconds was still quite close, but close doesn't count. The score was now 3-0 with a minor miracle needed to save the Swedes from a disaster.

The following day I was invited to watch the racing from *La Costa Brava*, a luxurious 98-foot motor yacht the *Gretel* group had chartered. (Gordon Ingate said that they had had to make a commitment to the charter before they knew whether or not they would be in the finals—so why not enjoy it.) In addition to the *Gretel* syndicate there were many of the *Australia* syndicate members aboard. I also met two delightfully attractive, young Australian women who said they were friends of Alan Bond. Allison Reid and Chris Ingate, daughters of *Gretel* syndicate members John Reid and Gordon Ingate, plus several other slightly more matronly beauties lent an appropriately sexy air to the opulent atmosphere of *La Costa Brava*'s wide decks, comfortable saloons, gold-plated bathroom fixtures, electronic organ, and uniformed crew waiting to be of service. Adding to this beauty and opulence I was surrounded by one of the largest assemblies of Australian yachting dignitaries ever to sail on a single ship. In addition to the Ingates and the Reids there were Sir William Northam, Australia's Gold Medalist in 5.5 Meters and Commodore Bill Fesq of the Royal Sydney Yacht Squadron and navigator of *Gretel II* in 1970, to name just two.

This was, without doubt, the best way to watch a dull sailboat race—and dull it was! *Australia* escaped a move by *Sverige* to put Robins over the line early. Instead it was Petterson who found himself behind by 28 seconds at the start. From that point on it was downhill for *Sverige*.

Since *Sverige* had been able to beat *Gretel II* several times in the light winds that *Gretel* was supposed to excel in, and since *Gretel* had decisively beaten *Australia* in their only light air meeting, most people—including the Swedes—thought that *Sverige* would do much better against *Australia* in a light air race. When confronted with this logic the night before the last race, *Australia*'s co-designer Johan Valentijn simply smiled and said "We'll see."

We did. The last race was very light. It started with only seven knots true wind, and at times it was so light that there was a fear that it might not be finished before the time limit of five-and-a-half hours expired. The end was punctuated by an approaching rain squall which knocked out the wind after *Australia* had finished and left *Sverige* with drifting conditions. To make matters worse, a wind shift

Sverige and *Australia* circling each other in prestart maneuvers . . . (*Lucia Carpenter photo*)

From which *Australia* barely escaped being forced over the line early. (*Lucia Carpenter photo*)

Sverige's crew was eager and fought hard at the start of the fourth race . . . (*Lucia Carpenter photo*)

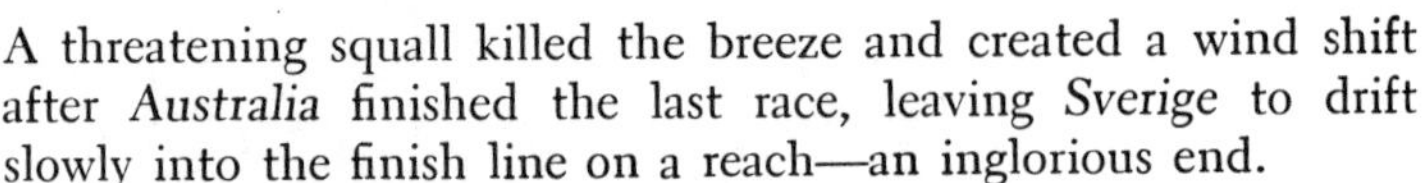

But the fight was taken out of them as they drifted dejectedly across the finish line well behind the victorious Australians. (*Lucia Carpenter photo*)

A threatening squall killed the breeze and created a wind shift after *Australia* finished the last race, leaving *Sverige* to drift slowly into the finish line on a reach—an inglorious end.

caused *Sverige* to overstand the finish line so that she limped home in a gathering haze with eased sheets and slatting sails. It was an inglorious finish. Aboard *La Costa Brava*, however, there was a joyous celebration. *Australia* had won the right to challenge for the America's Cup, and whether those aboard were *Gretel* or *Australia* supporters they were still Australians. The champagne flowed, the bar's hard liquor locker was opened, and several loud (quantity replacing quality) renditions of "Waltzing Matilda" and "Tie Me Kangaroo Down, Sport" wafted across the water accompanied by Allison Reid picking out the cords on the organ.

While we had stayed close to the challenger's match all afternoon, we kept in touch with what was going on with the New York Yacht Club's defenders. *Independence* had been eliminated the previous day, and when Norrie Hoyt told us over radio station WADK that no second race had been started following *Courageous*'s first-race victory over *Enterprise*, it was virtually certain that *Courageous* would be named the defender.

When we docked at Newport Shipyard and went over to welcome the victorious *Australia*, *Chaperone*, the *Enterprise* group's tender pulled up with a disheartened crew from the eliminated defender. They were saddened and bitter in their disappointment, but they gave the Aussies their congratulations. The celebration was enthusiastic but relatively sober. Asked by Barbara Lloyd why nobody got thrown into the water, Johan Valentijn replied, "We're only halfway there. When we win the Cup, that's when we'll jump in the water."

The victorious *Australia* crew backs their 12-Meter into her dock at Newport Shipyard following their defeat of *Sverige*.

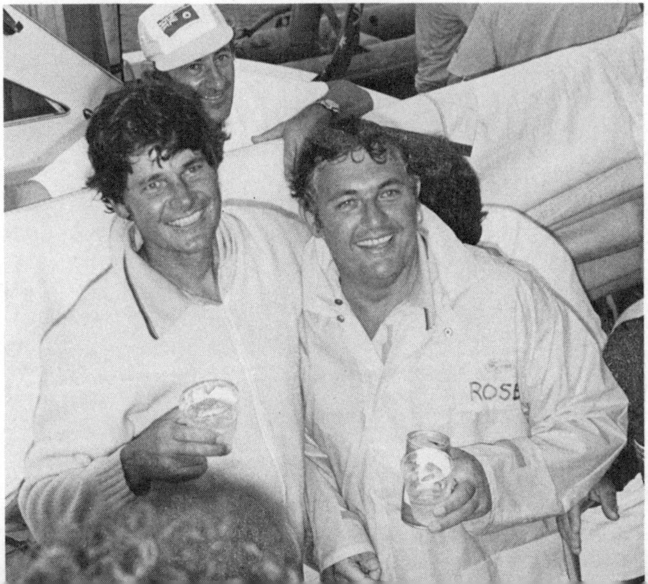

Noel Robins (at left) and Alan Bond (at right, wearing Andy Ross's foul weather jacket) toast their victory following the last race against *Sverige*.

During the elimination series, the *Gretel* syndicate had two excellent spectator craft at their disposal. *Ursa Major* was loaned to them for the summer by her owner/skipper Jack Armstrong.

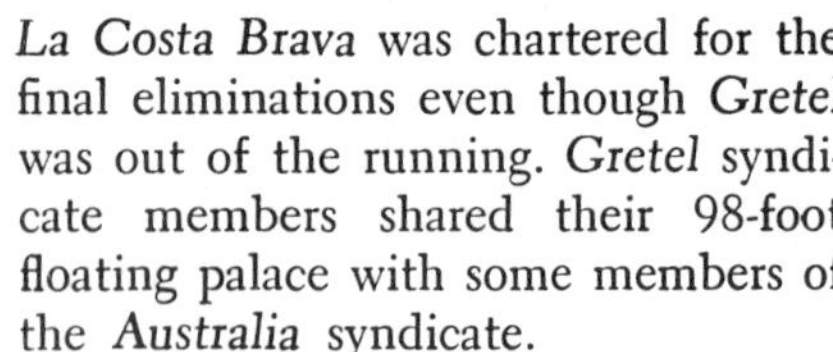

La Costa Brava was chartered for the final eliminations even though *Gretel* was out of the running. *Gretel* syndicate members shared their 98-foot floating palace with some members of the *Australia* syndicate.

Sally (at left) and Chris Ingate watch nervously from *Ursa Major* as husband/father takes the Swedes to an exciting seven-race series.

Hanne-Marie Bense, who handled protocol and press relations for *Gretel*, and sailmaker Peter Cole watch intently at the rail of *Ursa Major* during *Gretel*'s match with *Sverige*.

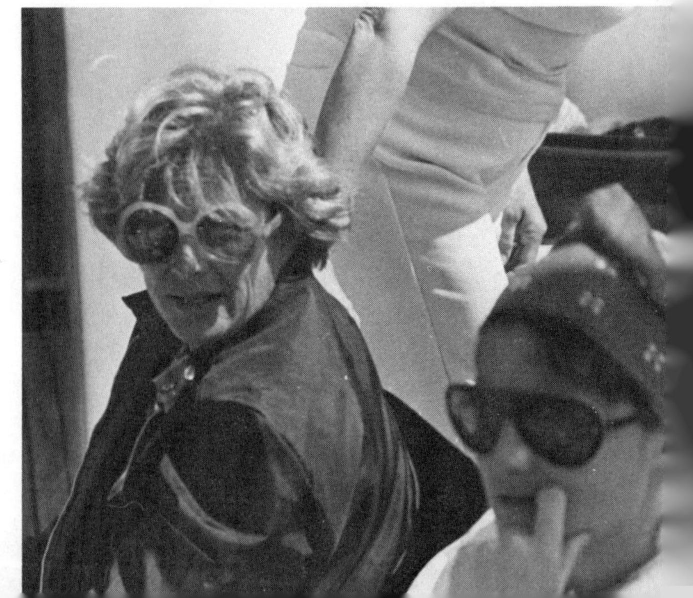

There are compensations for those crew members who don't get to sail.

The captain of *La Costa Brava* is caught at a time of understandable distraction talking with Allison Reid, daughter of *Gretel* syndicate member John Reid, during an otherwise dull moment on the race course.

There are other diversions for those spectators who would rather sunbathe or doze . . .

Or play backgammon.

Sally Ingate (at left) leads a happy group of Aussies in song following Australia's victory over *Sverige* . . .

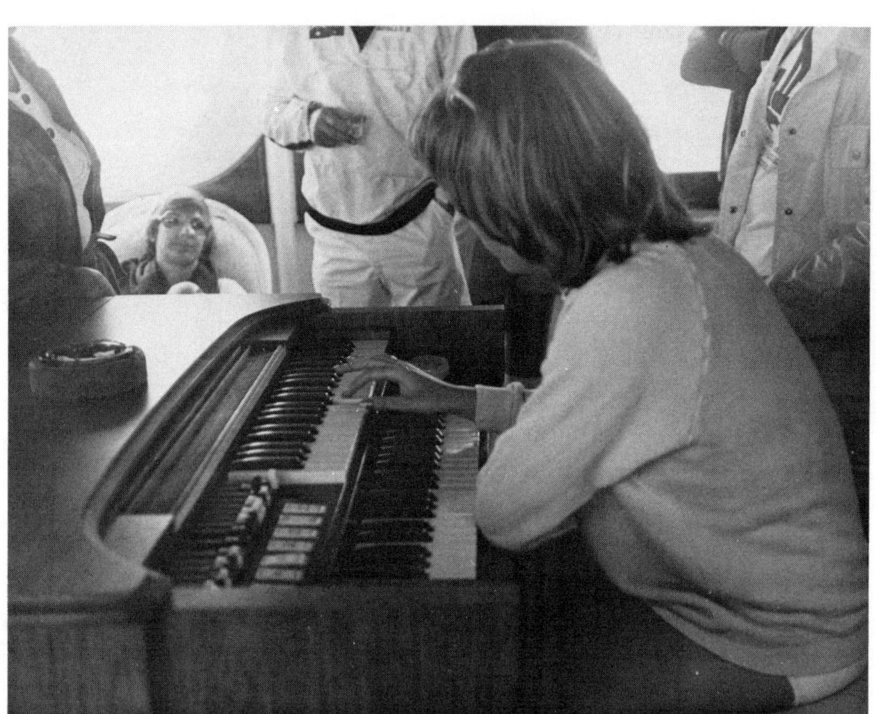

To the one-handed accompaniment of Allison Reid on *La Costa Brava's* organ.

Chapter IX   UPSTAIRS, DOWNSTAIRS ON THE "TUB DERRIÈRE"

by LUCIA CARPENTER

It is not possible to be everywhere at once, and this particular America's Cup it was more difficult than ever to keep track of everything that was going on. There were not only seven (eight if you count *France II*) 12-Meters and crews, there were also the various other necessary groups such as the New York Yacht Club's Race and America's Cup Committees, the International Race Committee, and the International Jury. Normally, the working functions of these committees are "off limits" to all but their members. However, it turns out there were a couple of "spys" aboard the International Race Committee's chartered tugboat *Pilot*. Lucia Carpenter and Gene Sieck formed the backbone of Ida Lewis Yacht Club volunteers who provided the International Race Committee with victuals for their days on the water. Lucia Carpenter worked with the author on a previous America's Cup book, and she provided this account of her days on the tugboat which became known as the "Tub Derrière." Lucia also had an excellent vantage point for close-up photographs which appear with this chapter and elsewhere.

Here is Lucia Carpenter's report from an unusual and exclusive vantage point:

The Yacht Club d'Hyeres, as challenging club of record, was responsible for running trial races which would determine the challenger for the America's Cup. While the French had the option of bringing their own boats and race committee to this country, Bruno Bich, acting for the Yacht Club d'Hyeres and his father, Monsieur le Baron, asked the New York Yacht Club if they would be willing to assist France in setting up the trials and in organizing a race committee.

Early in March, Bruno met with NYYC Race Committee Chairman Fred Scholtz and Bob Conner and Robin Wallace, commodore and vice commodore of the Ida Lewis Yacht Club. These men were most helpful to the French in planning the best-of-seven race semifinal and final series that had been agreed upon by the foreign challengers.

Next, the International Race Committee was formed. It was felt the chairman of the committee should have no involvement with either the challengers or defenders and John Morgan, a Canadian who had assisted in the 1976 Olympic Race Committee, agreed to occupy the chair. Wallace, a transplanted Englishman, was named vice chairman and Bill Thomson from Noroton, Connecticut, became liaison man to work with Bruno. They worked long exhausting days (and nights) during the entire challenge series assisted by twenty-one other committee members from the United States, Bermuda, Canada, Sweden, and Norway who worked on a rotation basis to man the three boats. In addition to running the races, the committee worked closely with the four syndicate representatives who were on board each day as observers.

Dr. Robin Wallace, Chairman John Morgan, and Bill Thomson, on the bow of the "Tub Derrière" under the burgee of the Yacht Club d'Hyeres, celebrate the end of their duties as the International Race Committee for the challenger's series. (*Lucia Carpenter photo*)

Hatterascal and Tortog, the mark and stake boats that would be used for the final Cup races, were offered to the International Race Committee and Harry Anderson, vice commodore of the New York Yacht Club, suggested Pilot, a tugboat, as committee boat.

The committee's fleet and the "upstairs" slate of "Tub Derrière" was complete.

Also in the spring, volunteers were solicited from the Entertainment Committee of the Ida Lewis Yacht Club. Gene Sieck and I eagerly raised our hands. We heard nothing more about what we'd volunteered for until Gene received a phone call in late July from Bill Thomson. He said Gene had been highly recommended to the committee and he would like to meet with her that afternoon. Gene, with dreams of being the first woman to serve on an International 12-Meter Race Committee, said, "I had an instant case of euphoria. I couldn't believe that on just one try someone—a woman—was actually going to make it." Within five minutes of their first meeting, "Reality set in and I realized it wasn't going to be that at all. It was going to be 'vittling' and that the woman's traditional role was not to be changed." After agreeing to her "downstairs" role of chief vittler, Gene went with Bill to look at Pilot. With pleasant thoughts in her head of Bobarra, the New York Yacht Club committee boat (ninety-eight feet long, thousands of brush strokes of brightwork, deep pile carpeting, crystal ashtrays, and a permanent uniformed crew of four), Gene was startled to find herself climbing over the rail of a tug boat. Jim Perkins, the cigar-puffing owner-captain, was dressed in a well-worn khaki cap, jeans, and a T-shirt emblazoned with a picture of Pilot and the message "The Great Newport Towing Company." Pilot was painted in traditional tug boat red and black, had little if any brightwork, linoleum on the combination main cabin/galley floor, and dime store ashtrays. Traces of her crew were strewn all over the cabin and the dream of plush committee boat grandeur evaporated in cigar smoke and diesel fumes. The condition of her "downstairs" working quarters really appalled Gene, but affable Captain Perkins assured her the refrigerator would be emptied and the cabin spotless before the first working day.

The next afternoon, the entire committee that would be running the round robin series met in Pilot's main cabin ("downstairs"). As chief vittler, Gene was told she was in charge of having someone on board each day to serve morning coffee, luncheon, and afternoon

The committee boat of the International Race Committee, the retired tugboat *Pilot*, which became known as the *Tub Derrière*. (*Bob Foley photo*)

snacks, to keep downstairs in good working order, to make sure the syndicate members were happy, and, above all, to have the food on Pilot before the 8:30 A.M. departure time. I later asked her what would happen if the supplier was late with the food. She said, "I was told that Pilot leaves at 8:30. Not one minute before or after. Hatterascal (one of the stake boats) leaves ten minutes later and could transfer the food. After that, we charter a boat at our own expense or lose our heads." After Gene's duties were outlined, instruction sheets were passed around and the contents discussed. Then everyone went above (upstairs) to the committee work area to get down to the serious business of the day—the distribution of the official International Race Committee uniforms. Each member got a Yacht Club d'Hyeres necktie, a navy blue cap, and a blue windbreaker. After much trying on to determine proper sizes, it was explained, with apologies, that the

The New York Yacht Club's *Bobbara*, race committee living as it is supposed to be.

cap and blazer emblems and tie tacks (replicas of the America's Cup) had not arrived but would be along soon. They really had wanted to be in full regalia for the trial run on Wednesday. The trial run was to make sure everything was running smoothly before the round robin started on Thursday, the first day the observers would be aboard.

Robin Wallace had made arrangements with the restaurant that was supplying the luncheons for Bobarra to prepare a similar buffet for Pilot, with box lunches for her crew. But there the similarity between Bobarra and Pilot ended. Bobarra had a luxurious saloon and afterdeck in which to be served by four girls using proper cutlery, china, and linen. Most days Pilot had one vittler who set up food on a dropleaf, plastic-topped table using disposable everything and who prayed the fourteen people she was responsible for that day would not want to eat at once as there was only room to seat seven in any comfort. Gene planned Wednesday's menu with the restaurant and learned they were only preparing the buffet so she went to the grocery store with an extensive list of necessities to get them through . . . coffee, coffee cake, fruit, cookies, ice tea, paper cups, roller towel, etc.

The day of the trial run Gene picked up the food at 7:45 and drove to Pilot where she was met by a helpful crew who unloaded her car, stowed the food, beer, and soft drinks, filled the portable ice chests, and even backed her car off the dock and parked it for her. Sadly, this chivalry lasted only two days. From then on it was grab help where you could—most often from the syndicate representatives.

The cabin, that was supposed to be spotless, was still a mess. The refrigerator was half filled, newspapers, dirty coffee cups, brimming ashtrays, and the remains of doughnuts covered the table, and filthy cat box was still under the stairs. After some quick cleaning, Gene served coffee and coffee cake and then sat down to plan the most efficient way to organize lunch. Much of the morning the captain was with her apologizing for not cleaning up and trying to be helpful, but from Gene's point of view his good efforts were undone by his cigar. And, as the diesel fumes got stronger and Pilot's roll increased, Gene found herself less and less able to think about food. "I'd set the table after a fashion (everything slid all over the plastic top) and I realized I just couldn't do it. I was seasick and mortified. John Morgan told me to stop working, Kim Collins (the committee's signal man) coped with the food, and Robin and Bill coped with me. I was put in a bunk in the crew's quarters and strangely enough in the horizontal I was fine. They closed the door and opened the ports, and the cigar and diesel fumes were missing. Midafternoon I was offloaded onto a stake boat and I guess a couple of them thought I'd never be back." When she got ashore Gene had that awful hung-over-from-seasickness feeling but feminine honor was at stake and out she went, shopping for things she now knew were needed, and she managed to get it all back to Pilot and stowed. Thursday the round robin series started and the syndicate representatives were aboard. Upstairs the committee was working smoothly and efficiently, and downstairs there were signs of improvement. Gene was fortified with seasick pills and a linen tablecloth helped anchor the food platters to the table. But the cat box was still there and the kitten—as kittens will—was all over the place. Gene said, "I'd set up the table for lunch and there was the cat in the middle of it. I'm a cat lover but enough's enough. I'd pick it up and put it on the cabin sole and a minute later it was back in the food. I finally told Bill Thomson that I could not tolerate this kitten walking all over the food after being in the filthy cat box and between it and the damn flies that had invaded the cabin we were all going to die of the plague." Bill is unflappable but he'd had it, too. He grabbed the cat and box and went tearing aft. For a moment Gene thought both had gone overboard. They had not, but they were taken off Pilot for good when they docked that afternoon.

Friday was my introduction to Pilot and, although I'd been filled in thoroughly by Gene, I was still expecting the fat, jolly "Little Toot" that was my childhood passion. Instead, I found "Big Soot." Gene had warned me to wear dark clothes but, through vanity, I arrived in clean light blue pants and later went home with a seat full of grease and rust stains that took three hours of lemon juice and steam treatment to remedy. Peter Geddes, the committee gunner, commented, "When Pilot's running at slow speed she sounds like she's saying, 'Pollute, pollute' . . ."

As this was my first day, Gene was going along to help. I quickly learned the briefing she had given me was accurate. The crew had already backslid and no one was waiting helpfully to unload the car when I arrived with the food. My introduction to Bill Fesq, the Gretel syndicate observer, was made as he was kindly taking a tray of cold cuts and a bowl of chicken salad off my hands so I could climb aboard. I was a bit bewildered and very relieved when Gene came aboard. We cleaned up the usual debris left by the crew (later learned

Pilot was a nighttime drinking spot for some of the local fisherman which explained some of the untidiness) and served coffee to the committee and observers.

In addition to Bill Fesq, John Fitzhardinge, Australia, François Giriud, France, and Pelle Gedde, Sverige, were on board. The observers were busy with their stop watches and tape recorders at the start, at turning marks, and the finish but there was much time for conversation, reading, crossword puzzles, and other idle amusements. During one of these lulls on Friday, before everyone felt completely at ease with each other, François was studying a small plaque on the forward bulkhead. In his quiet French accent he said, "Oh, that should be the baron's motto." It read, "The difference between men and boys is the price of their toys." What had been a rather stilted atmosphere instantly turned to one of hilarity and we all began to feel more comfortable with each other.

The Swedish observer the first day was Göran Pettersen who alternated this duty with Pelle Gedde. He was quite uptight and told Gene he was very nervous about the whole thing and she said, "Well this is your first trial and your first attempt at the Cup and I think your nervousness is completely understandable." But he said no, that was not what was troubling him. It was the fact that he is secretary of the Royal Göteborg Yacht Club and when they took the Cup to Sweden he would be responsible for running the whole Cup race over there and he had not realized the enormous amount of preparation that went into the defense. That day, and through the round robin series, he was sure the job was going to be his! Later he stopped worrying about 1980.

Sometime during the first few days, Pilot started being referred to by the committee upstairs as "Tub d'Hyeres." She was a marvelous platform for all the committee equipment but she was much too slow to cover all the turning marks and hard to get into position for the starts and finishes. When John Morgan told Gene the new name it came across to her as Tub Dernier (for the living end) and in the end, she was known as the ultimate end, Tub Derrière and Gene and I became the Derrière Guard.

When Bruno Bich first came aboard there was some nervousness about his reaction to the "Tub" and the upstairs work of the committee but he's a real pussy-cat and said, "Everything's just purr-fect, purr-fect."

Bruno did, however, find room for improvement downstairs and greatly civilized lunch by keeping us well stocked with marvelous red, white, and rosé wines and sometimes a pâté en crôut made by his French chef. Not to be outdone, the Australians kept the coolers well stocked with Tooths KB and Swan Lager, to the delight of the beer drinkers. Gene had the weekend duty and I went for my second run on Monday. The day was routine. Clutter in the cabin and the head a place to be avoided if at all possible. Bobarra had bathrooms with gold dolphin faucets and bidets. The Tub's head was equipped with a bucket of water to goose the recalcitrant flush system and a can of Lysol spray.

By now I was resigned that it was going to be a month of long, hard-working days and absolutely no luxurious pleasure boating, but there were compensations: the starts and finishes were observed from a vantage point not even the press had, the lovely sight of the baron's three-masted schooner, Shenandoah (generously made available to friends and wives and relatives of the International Committee members), the rare opportunity to be with and learn from the observers and committee members the inside workings of a 12-Meter campaign.

. . . And that very special Monday when we were coming in after the day's racing, Independence and Courageous had been practicing and as we entered the East Passage to Narragansett Bay they came abeam of us with spinnakers flying. Independence was on our port side and Turner ducked Courageous underneath our stern to starboard. You could almost hear Turner and Hood's minds working,

Independence (at left) and **Courageous** staged a spectacular display **of** seamanship jibing back and forth in **front** of the International Race Committee and the challenger's representatives coming into Narragansett Bay **after** a day of sailing: "Göran's eyes were popping, the Australians were awed with respect, and the rest of us **were** literally gaping in our excitement." The Swedes suddenly realized how difficult it is to win the **America's** Cup when the Americans are so **proficient.** (*Lucia Carpenter photo*)

"Aha, the foreign observers, let's show them what this racing is all about." And with that we slowed down and they forged ahead in what was one of the most spectacular downwind jibing duels any of us had ever seen. At one point, both boats seemed to be heading right up on the lawn of Hammersmith Farm. This was the summer home of the Swedes and they came flying out of the house with binoculars at the ready. On board we watched almost in disbelief as they flipped the the 12s from one jibe to the other as if they were racing dinghies. Göran's eyes were popping, the Australians were awed with respect, and the rest of us were literally gaping in our excitement.

Independence and Courageous were bow to bow on different jibes heading directly for a small yawl close to shore. You could see that skipper's confusion as he tried to decide whether to try to sail away or to stop when, prudently, his sails went limp. Hood got the edge on the next jibe and there was no way Turner could get through him. From then on it was Hood all the way as they rounded Fort Adams and headed for Bannister's Wharf. It looked as if they had every intention of carrying their spinnakers right into their moorings, but wiser heads on the tenders put a stop to the fun and games. Kim Collins and I had our cameras clicking constantly and we hoped that his telephoto lens was getting great color close-ups and I'd have the backup black and white shots with my simple Kodak. We do have the black and whites but Kim's photographic triumph was shot with an empty camera.

Judy O'Neil had the lunch duty on Tuesday, the final day of the round robin series. We'd had rumblings that the caterer was not altogether pleased with things and when Judy returned the platters to them that evening they said, "Thank you, we quit." Starting work at 5 A.M. to prepare our food was just too much for them when they had a restaurant to run and Bobarra and their regular marina customers to cater for. We knew it was difficult, particularly when lay days were called late in the afternoon and we'd have to cancel an entire order at the last minute. Later in the month we even had to resort to the police to contact one of our suppliers. He was closed when we got in and had an unlisted phone number the police could not release. They very kindly offered to cancel the next day's order for us.

I called Gene and found she was sick—and, of course, Judy's news didn't help. Five straight days on Pilot, shopping when she got in, plus the day-to-day chores of her own household had laid her flat and the thought of finding a new caterer by Thursday made her sicker. After many phone calls I arranged to meet Robin at a new supplier the next morning. Bill Thomson was also in charge of finances and we needed his okay. With more phone calls I located him on the tennis court at Bailey's Beach. He was delighted when we reported the new caterer would supply luncheons, breakfast, fruit, and afternoon snacks for a figure well with in our budget. The new caterer would also deliver everything to the boat each morning and said the lay days would be no problem. When we got in, we could go home instead of shopping and running to the caterer. Downstairs on the Tub Derrière was still in business.

Upstairs, under John Morgan's leadership, the Tub Derrière was a model of efficiency. Special navigational equipment had been installed including Loran, courtesy of Raytheon, a large compass donated by Ritchie, and an anemometer and relative wind indicator from Kenyon Marine. The position of the starting mark was checked by Loran using a Northstar 6000 and the legs of the course were then established using specially prepared Loran C charts. Each member of the committee had specific duties and they were carried out with precision. Starting lines were proper, shapes went up and down on time, the cannon always fired, and voices were never raised. From the first moment on board the committee got along and worked as if they'd been doing it together for years. They demonstrated their team spirit the day the electric anchor winch conked out and they all joined the crew to manually haul the bow anchor aboard. No easy job in 16 fathoms of water. By the time they got it in they decided the stern anchor could damn well look after itself.

The final races between Sverige and Australia started on August 25 and everyone (excepting, of course, the partisan observers) hoped for and expected a close series. However, it quickly became evident that it was likely to be four straight for Australia. After Australia's third win Gene and I decided to ship out together for the next, and probably final, race and the last day on the Tub Derrière. Sverige got the start but didn't cover and that was the end of the challenge series. Australia steadily increased her lead and finished in a rain squall that quickly passed leaving Sverige several hundred yards from the finish line with her sails slatting. Göran Pettersen looked close to tears and I had a large lump in my throat at the sight of lovely Sverige limping across the line with her dejected crew.

Bruno, Göran, and John Fitzhardinge boarded tenders for a quick trip back to Newport while the committee and the derrière guard had a toast to the summer as *Tub Derrière* made her stately way into harbor. John Morgan asked us if we were going with the committee to Fort Wetherill. When we looked blank he explained their wives were all meeting them there to take part in the official "thanks for a great effort" ceremonies and they hoped we'd join them.

Pilot dropped us off at the Fort where everyone commiserated with the Swedes, watched the crew get tossed overboard, and even boarded *Sverige* for a close-up look. From there *Tortog* took us across the harbor to *Australia* where spirits were high and the boat low in the water with every inch of her deck covered with embracing bodies. They saved the dunkings until after the Cup races and let their joy out in loud refrains of "Tie Me Kangaroo Down" and the heretofore rather serious John Fitzhardinge was leading them all with a mile-wide grin on his face and a very dark drink in his hand.

We went with *Tortog* to her dock space at Goat Island and as we disembarked Fred Scholtz, the New York chairman, invited us on board *Bobarra* for a drink. Gene and I didn't start the challenge series in luxury but we certainly ended it that way.

The days on *Tub Derrière* were mostly work but evenings on shore were something else. The International Race Committee probably dined at every good restaurant in Newport and there were numerous private parties. The America's Cup Ball was a spectacular mob scene and a party unto itself, but particularly memorable to me were Kim Collin's "cookout" and Bruno's final dinner for the International Race Committee on board *Shenandoah*.

Kim's party was held at his parents' lovely seventeenth-century farmhouse "Cajacet" in Jamestown overlooking the lights of Newport. The informal "cookout" (I was expecting hot dogs and hamburgers on the lawn) turned out to be a fabulous roast beef dinner for thirty-odd guests. The roasts were smoked over an open fireplace in the living room and then cooked over coals to a delicious rare stage. Informality was the keynote and we sat on the floor in small groups getting to know each other better in a few short hours than we had after days on the Tub. Göran Pettersen, who was now much more at ease, said he would move to America if only he could live in such a beautiful spot. Bill Thomson gave International Race Committee badges to everyone at the party and Gene and I even got our ultimate reward, Race Committee tie tacks.

Bruno's dinner on Shenandoah was the last official gathering of the International Race Committee. As we drove across the bridge to Goat Island a light rain stopped and the lovely schooner appeared in full dress ship with lights twinkling everywhere. It was an evening of champagne, superb French food, final reminiscences with new and old friends, and toasts for all. Speeches were given, praise heaped on all the deserving, and, as a final accolade to the three men who really made the Tub d'Hyeres (Derrière) work, Bruno presented enormous Yacht Club d'Hyeres burgees to Chairman John Morgan, Vice Chairman Robin Wallace, and the indispensible Bill Thomson who kept upstairs and downstairs together on the redoubtable tug Pilot.

 HANGING OUT
IN NEWPORT

Ludwig and Connie Becker were classmates of mine in high school.
When I was spending fall Saturdays sailing, they were cheering for the
MHS football team. As far as I knew they never were near a sailboat
until our paths happened to cross many years later. Lud and Connie
are now sailors, they own a 40-foot fiberglass auxiliary in which they
cruise from Long Island Sound to Cape Cod.

One afternoon I was looking for suitable photographic subjects
on Bannister's Wharf when I was hailed from The Moorings, the
next pier to the south. It was Lud Becker. He and Connie were
aboard their boat and they asked me to come aboard.

Lud and Connie are, perhaps, typical of the many millions of
people who visited Newport in the summer of 1977. They are
America's Cup fans. This was their third week in Newport—they had
found a berth for their boat on the eastern end of Long Island (rather
than sail it back to their home in Centerport so it wouldn't be so
long a sail to get to Newport—and they would have stayed all summer if they could.

The Beckers had planned their vacations to coincide with the
America's Cup trials. This week they had been out every day follow-

ing the Twelves, watching the races. A 40-foot auxiliary which can power at a little over six knots on a calm day is not an ideal vehicle from which to see the races. The Coast Guard keeps all spectators a safe distance away from the Twelves, and the only boats which get a good view are the powerful cruisers and sport fishermen who can stay ahead of the pack and jockey for position next to the protecting Coast Guard cutter. People with auxiliaries, like the Beckers, have a tough time of it—their boats don't have enough power to maneuver with the faster spectator craft, and they are too close to the water to be able to see over the three- and four-decked floating palaces that invariably get into the front row. In addition, the trailing boats are forced to wallow in the wash of the others' wakes. That alone can make it a nasty ride with those aboard hanging on for dear life in the confused seas. At best these people can putter up to the reaching mark and watch the Twelves as they come by. Then they can move leisurely to the windward mark and catch the end of the second beat and the finish. Is it really worth it?

Lud and Connie think so. Obviously, they love it—otherwise they wouldn't come. They don't really know anyone involved with the America's Cup. They don't have a chance to see the Twelves at their piers. They don't get to see the crew members while they work on the Twelves, and they probably wouldn't know any of them if their paths crossed on the street. The attraction for the Beckers is just to be there, to bob around in the ocean all day, to sit in the cockpit sipping a gin and tonic and watch the sun go down beyond Goat Island, and to have a lobster for dinner at the Pier.

The Beckers arrive in Newport "first cabin" in that they have their own boat, they can enjoy getting out on the water, they can stay ashore and wander the shops and tour the mansions. They are not bound by the tight schedules of hotel reservations, and they can depart when they please and head where they please. Their land-bound counterparts are more restricted. Why do they come, these people standing on Bannister's Wharf licking ice cream cones who point to Ted Turner's *Tenacious* and ask if that's one of the 12-Meters?

Knots of them crowd into the dead end of the wharf and try to peer through the latticework fence which separates them from Loomis, Hood, Turner, and their crew members. They sit, sipping beers under the Cinzano umbrellas at the Black Pearl's outdoor terrace. They wander the boutiques and shop for knickknacks. These people are not inveterate America's Cup fans, yet they are an intrinsic part of the whole scene.

The tourists nurture the scene. They are at the same time the reason for the scene and a part of it. At night Bannister's Wharf becomes a circus—complete with musicians, jugglers, and mimes. The 12-Meter crews would surely not put anything in the hats that are passed. In fact, the 12-Meter crews have been home in bed for hours when all this nightlife is going on. Yet, in a way it is all for the crews' benefit. It is a part of the America's Cup just as much as the America's Cup Committee, but the masses have little or no appreciation for what is going on beyond the lattice fence, nor do they normally have an opportunity even to see the Twelves sailing.

Among the throng on any given afternoon one might see Janie Turner with her mother and Ted's mother, but they would be indistinguishable from the rest unless one happened to know them. Also among the crowd you might see an older lady who would also be indistinguishable from the rest. She could be Mrs. Hardy, Jim and Tom Hardy's mother—looking more like 65 than her 83 years— and she would probably be scampering over the cobblestones more spryly than most.

While neither Jim nor Tom Hardy were in Newport for the 1977 America's Cup, that did not stop Mrs. Hardy from coming. Jim had been in England racing in the Admiral's Cup, and she had been there. She loves to travel, so what would be more natural than for her to come to the America's Cup, see the races, and visit old friends on her way home to Australia?

An irrepressible woman, she could be seen scrambling up the

America's Cup fan and mother of two-time challenger Jim Hardy, Mrs. Hardy journeyed to Newport even though her son was not involved this time. (*Dan Nerney photo*)

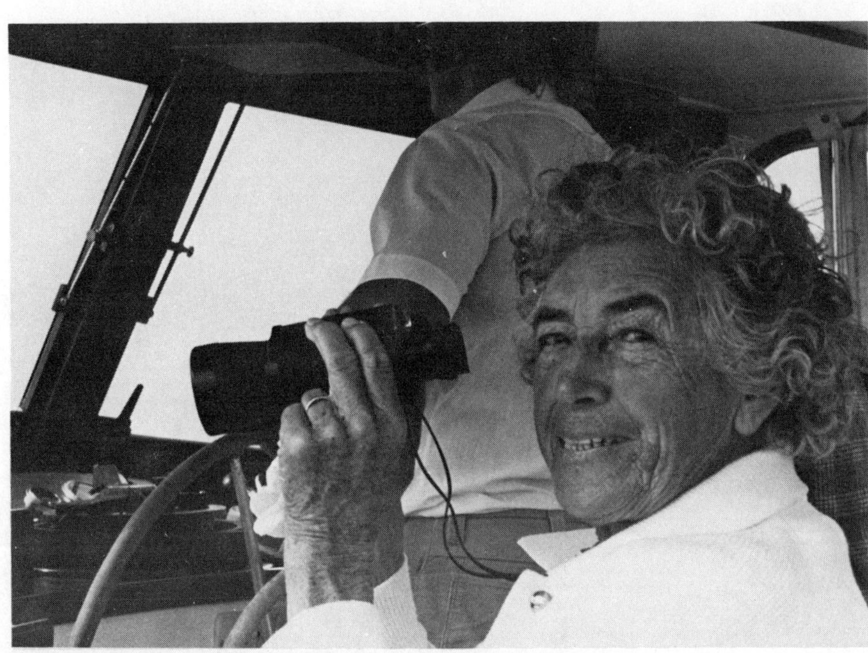

ladder to the flying bridge of one of the spectator craft on the race course. She was out there every day, took a more active interest in the races than most, and she was an ardent fan of *Australia*. Right to the last tack of the last race she was positive that *Australia* would win. Alas, for her, it was not to be. Still, that did not stop Mrs. Hardy from climbing up to the microphones at a press conference and extending greetings from her son, the skipper of *Gretel II* in 1970 and *Southern Cross* in 1974. Rather a special America's Cup fan, one might say.

Jack Walker is another special America's Cup fan—not typical at all. Jack and his wife Dianna have been to every America's Cup series since 1962—having been turned on to the scene by their friend Bob Harris. The Walkers live in Montreal. Jack is a commercial artist with his own studio, but for two or three weeks every three or four years, everything stops while the Walkers go to the America's Cup. Invariably a client will have a rush job just about that time, but Walker puts him off. He will work his butt off all summer. After the America's Cup? Okay, but a commission from the Queen of England would not keep him away from Newport.

Walker was so taken by the enthusiasm of his Australian friend, Bob Harris, who extolled the excitement of the 1958 America's Cup with such glowing accounts that Jack vowed to find out firsthand. Observing the antics and the wild enthusiasm of the Aussies in 1962, Walker was hooked for life. He is an entertaining fellow, with a picturesque manner of speech which was made famous in a previous America's Cup account. When I first met Gordon Ingate he had hardly said hello when he asked "Where's Jack 'F—' Walker? I have to meet him." They met in due course. In fact, the Ingates and the Walkers dined together on their last night in Newport.

Walker is no longer an automatic fan of the Australians, and in 1977 he made the full conversion to rooting for *Courageous*. Perhaps he realizes that should the Australians win the America's Cup it will

Canadians Jack Walker and Paul Paquin, rabid America's Cup fans, plan three years in advance to assure a good view of the races. Not even a commission from the Queen of England would keep Walker in his Montreal graphics studio during an America's Cup match.

Bruce Stannard, Jack Gale (mainsheet trimmer on *Gretel* until she was eliminated by *Sverige*), and Ray Martin broadcast the "tack by tack" account live to Australia where fans stay up into early morning hours to hear what happened.

cost him a great deal more to go to Australia for an America's Cup match than the $2,000 he spends now to go to Newport.

Bob Harris hasn't been to an America's Cup match since 1970, but in a way he was present in 1977. Harris had returned to his native Australia in 1973, and it was not possible for him to go to Newport in '74. It was rumored that he was to take responsibility for the Hardys' public relations, but when their effort collapsed for lack of funds so did Harris's chance for a trip to Newport in '77. However, Bruce Stannard and Ray Martin, broadcasters for a Sydney radio station, discovered that Bob was the "guest expert" in the studio back home, and Harris got to talk with some of his friends on the race course via satellite. So in a way, he was involved.

Suzanne Landrieu is a lawyer—admitted to the Bar in the State of Massachusetts, but she does not practice law. She hangs out with the sailing crowd, sailing frequently, and one is certain to see her at any important sailing function—particularly the America's Cup. Suzanne, a foxy red head, knows everybody involved with sailing, and vice versa. She is as outspoken as she is independent. Once, sitting at dinner with Ted Turner and his crew, who were discussing the virtues of size in a woman's breast, Suzanne, who has nothing to be ashamed of in that department, turned to Ted and said, "Anything more than a mouthful is a waste of time."

For Suzanne, coming to Newport for the America's Cup is ". . . a necessity of my life because that's what I've been involved in so heavily for the past four or five years. It's on a different level (than offshore racing) which is amusing, interesting, and of course you have that great bullshit element which adds a little intrigue—Lee Loomis, Alan Bond—although it all seems so much more quiet this time around."

Landrieu longed for the intensive competition between *Courageous* and *Intrepid* which went down to the wire in 1974, but she admits that the foreign challengers added some spice that she felt was missing from the U.S. defenders. "It's like you were waiting for the U.S. to come," she said, "and they never came."

Earlier all the excitement of people coming back to Newport had Landrieu turned on. Seeing the crews getting together—the camaraderie—working together, drinking together. "But you've done it so many times before that that's not going to keep you going all summer."

For a while Suzanne dated one of the crew members from *Australia*. She was also close to some of the guys with *Enterprise*, and she is an old friend of many in the *Courageous* camp—Turner, Marty O'Meara, Bunky Helfrich—guys from Turner's ocean racing crews with whom she has sailed. She also knew Australian newsman Piers Akerman, so she saw the action from all sides.

"It was interesting to see the Australians," Suzanne reminisced. "They knew they had a good boat (*Australia*), they had some good crew, they felt they had the potential, but most of the more experienced guys realized that it would never come together. They were talking a month ago (a month before the final series) with some of the *Gretel* good guys about organizing the next challenge."

"I was quite close to some of the *Enterprise* people," said Landrieu. "They had a good group, people who could get along with each other—so they thought in the beginning. It was all very loose. We'd go up there for hot tubs after drinking down at the bars. No one would mind. You'd smoke a joint, drink some wine. That was a good feeling that I guess everyone realized couldn't last. It ended quite quickly, and it just disintegrated from there."

The biggest enjoyment Landrieu had all summer, she said, was seeing Turner do so well. "He's an incredible person."

"His game plan after he wins the World Series," Landrieu told me, "is to work his way up in politics to the presidency. You know, he says that, and you laugh. But when you look at him you realize he's not kidding. I talked with him about an hour on this. He knows how much a part the media plays in politics in the U.S. and being a media man now he's progressing along. It all makes sense. He has a lot of 'Elizabeth Rays' and people in the closet that I don't think he'll get away with. He said he was going to make Russ (Russell Hoyt, one of Turner's ocean racing competitors with whom Landrieu sails) secretary of the navy. I was going to be the first woman on the Supreme Court, and he was going to have Marty (O'Meara)as chief of protocol. Piers was going to be one of his political writers . . ."

Later, when Turner had returned to his business empire in Atlanta, I asked if he had politics in his future. He just laughed and said, "What I'm trying to do is preserve my sanity."

Suzanne admitted that if she's going to be the first woman appointed to the Supreme Court she'd better quit fooling around with boats and boat people and begin practicing law.

One afternoon during the observation trials I was wandering around Bannister's Wharf after having been frustrated in an attempt to get aboard one of the King's Point Fund's tenders. Piers Akerman was standing on the foredeck of a magnificent motor yacht, Mount Gay rum and tonic in his hand, beckoning me to come aboard. With him was Peter Clempner who was in charge of Ted Turner's *Tenacious* for the summer. The vernacular for "in charge" in this case is "boat nigger," and Clempner is a king among boat niggers.

The yacht, upon which Akerman and Clempner stood, was a 1960s vintage Feadship. It was in Newport for charter work to serve the affluent, avid spectator, one of the hundred-odd such "floating gin palaces," a term of envious derogation invented by poor sailors. It was owned by someone we'll call "Bob Smith."

How Akerman and Clempner came to be aboard, I didn't quite know, but they had brought their own bottle and were doing their best to consume it when they became aware that someone aboard another boat was eyeing them through binoculars. Their reaction:

pull the curtains in the saloon where they sat and continue drinking. The binoculars belonged to Bob Smith, who was aboard one of his other yachts on an adjacent pier.

While I was talking with Piers and Peter, Smith came over, obviously agitated but not knowing quite how to handle Akerman. Piers introduced himself as if he had just laid out several grand for a charter (Smith has two partners which his continual reference to "my yacht" did not admit). We chatted for a bit, and Piers invited Smith to come to the reception given by the city of Newport for the Swedish crew which was then under way. Smith was torn between associating with this ruffian who had preempted his expensive yacht and meeting the Swedes to whom he had chartered it for the following weekend, and I could almost see the wheels of dismay churning inside his head.

Subsequently, Smith excused himself and went below with the crew. We followed into the pilothouse after a suitable interval and heard him below berating the captain for allowing us aboard. Peter called down, "Hey, are you coming to this party or not," and muttering something about his wife and kids on the other dock and, "leave VHF channel 68 on I'll call you," Smith departed.

Another Mount Gay and tonic later and following an unsuccessful attempt by Piers to locate a joint, Smith called on the radio with the surprising news that they would join us. Would we please wait for them at our dock?

Meanwhile, a sizeable black cloud had been forming to the northwest. This was the promised cold front that would break the week-long spell of 100-degree weather. I gave it 20 minutes before it hit, Piers suggested a considerably longer time. I think it split the difference.

Smith, his wife, and their three daughters (the youngest in a stroller) met us on the wharf while the lightning was already splitting the sky. When we got to America's Cup Avenue, the wind was blasting the sand into our eyes. Smith had taken a detour to the Clarke Cooke House (Akerman right behind him to introduce him to the maître d'), and Clempner had excused himself to make a phone call. Mrs. Smith, the girls, and I headed for the Colony House but were driven to shelter by the windblown sand.

A period of indecision ensued during which we all could have made it safely to Colony House. After some pulling and hauling we made it to the middle of the intersection opposite the Treadway Inn when the rain began. It didn't start with a trickle. One minute it was blowing sand, the next minute it was blowing water—lots of it! The Smiths retreated in disarray to the Clarke Cooke House, and Piers and I took off at a run for Colony House.

We got part way down Thames Street, and I chickened out, pulling up soaking wet in front of a toy store. I looked out to see how far Piers had gotten, but he was nowhere to be seen. On second thought, I did not want to spend the duration of the storm standing in a store front. I was already wet anyway, so I struck out again into the rain in search of Piers. I did not have far to go—he was relieving himself on a cardboard carton in the next store front. (The store was closed.)

When Piers had finished his chore, we bolted out into the rain and headed for the party. Down Thames Street, up Broadway, take a breather under the theater marquee, through the park under the trees aHA, aHA, aHA—breathlessly up the steps to the party. The party was over. All the Swedes had gone home.

One morning in July I met Bruce Stannard, in the post office. Bruce told me that both *Australia* and *Gretel II* were hauled at Newport Shipyard and that Alan Bond was painting the deck of *Australia* along with the rest of the crew. Since Bond was once a sign painter (according to Stannard) he intended to hand letter the various deck markings once the deck paint was dry. I went over to see if I could get a photo but missed it.

While there, I met a couple who appeared to be in their seventies. The woman said that she really didn't know that much about 12-Meters, but that she did know quite a lot about "shape." As far as she was concerned *Gretel II* was the nicest shape of the three (*France I* was nearby). "I'll bet that one wins," she said, pointing to *Gretel.*

They said that they had been coming from Fall River to the America's Cup races since Sir Thomas Lipton's last challenge. That was 1930, the first year the America's Cup was held in Newport.

While taking photographs I also chatted with Alan Payne and Gordon Ingate. They had lunched with Willy Carstens, who was one of two professionals aboard *Vim* in 1958 and who went to Australia with *Vim* when she was sold to Sir Frank Packer, Australia's first challenger with *Gretel I* (also designed by Alan Payne). Willy goes back to the J-boat day also, having sailed aboard *Ranger* in 1937.

Later I had dinner with American measurer Bob Blumenstock and Swiss measurer Oskar Weber. They had also seen Carstens and remarked on his excellent physical condition. "Strong enough to have a good 'snoot full' by lunch time," said Blumenstock.

After dinner, which was served by candlelight because electrical power had been interrupted throughout Newport, we adjourned to the Candy Store's top-floor porch bar. As had become usual for a weekend night you could hardly find room to stand. Peter Cole was there in the crowd as was "Kiwi Jill," the cook from Bob Smith's Feadship. We said the inane things one says in a crowded bar—shouting above the babble—and I told Jill about running in the rain with Piers and missing the party. Jill, in turn, told me some choice vignettes about her "owner."

Peter Cole and I hoisted a toast to the absent Bob Harris, and then Peter told me the story of Hugh Treharne, one of Australia's best known yachtsmen and crew member aboard *Gretel II* in 1970 and *Southern Cross* in 1974. According to Cole, Treharne was arrested earlier in the year for stealing *Vim*'s transom. It seems the *Gretel II* syndicate wanted to charter *Vim*, the Twelve with which the Matthews family almost beat *Columbia* in 1958, as a trial horse. But *Vim*'s present owner, who I gathered was not too highly regarded in the Royal Sydney Yacht Squadron, had cut about six feet off *Vim*'s stern, rendering her useless as a trial horse. It should be explained that *Vim* is considered something of a national shrine in Australia. She was the first 12-Meter ever seen in Sydney, and was the trial horse for all the Sydney-based America's Cup challengers. To alter her classic beauty by so gross an act was an unpardonable sacrilege. Adding insult to injury, the truncated stern kicked around on the hard next to the Royal Sydney Yacht Squadron clubhouse gathering dust. It was rumored that a local restaurateur was going to use it as a bar, or perhaps, burn it. This was too much for the incensed Treharne—he stole it. *Vim*'s owner, equally incensed, brought charges and had Treharne arrested and taken to court, but the charges were later dropped. Cole didn't know what finally happened to the stern. Hopefully, Treharne still has it, perhaps hanging in his den.

Sober reflection suggests that a form of madness compels otherwise sane people to cram themselves into places like the Candy Store's upper porch bar. This night was just like so many others with barely

T-shirts and sweatshirts proclaim partisan support . . .

And frank admissions. (Dan Nerney photo)

room to stand. People were constantly coming and going, and it was almost impossible to carry on a conversation. Someone was always trying to squeeze between you and the person to whom you were shouting.

Besides Peter Cole there were several other *Gretel II* crew members there—Jack Gale and his son ("have you met my brother?") Geoff. Oskar Weber found someone from France and was jabbering away happily in one of his more familiar trilingual tongues. Others? One could only guess at who they were, where they were from, or why they were there. It was a great mixing pot of people from all over the world, literally. Some were conservatively dressed—the men in jackets and ties, the women in dresses—most were in informal attire—sport shirts and halter tops. What people had on below the waist was impossible to tell. There was lots of exposed skin among the young women who stood around in groups of two looking bored and expectant. All of this was going on by candlelight, as the electricity was still out all over the town.

Finally, the lights came on, accompanied by a great cheer from the patrons. The dining tables were cleared away on the second level porch, the musicians plugged in their electronic instruments, and the night began in earnest.

It was not after this night, but after a similar one—a Tuesday—that the following item, by David Coor, appeared in the *Newport Daily News*:

GIRL IS NUDE, DOG IS MUM

The HMS Rose's watchdog, Jagger, usually is very efficient and vicious. But he's a sucker for a pretty face.

Early yesterday morning a young woman who found her clothing an unconscionable burden took advantage of Jagger's one weakness, and by 11 A.M. was providing an "unusual extra exhibit" for 35 visitors touring the replica of the British Revolutionary War vessel moored at former King's Dock.

"The night watchman is still trying to figure out how she got past him," ship manager John Millar said today.

Most of the tourists apparently spotted the young woman lying nude in a hammock held up between two of the frigate's cannon before someone casually made note of her presence.

The woman, who was not reported to police and whose name was never asked, told Millar she had fallen into the water after the waterfront bars closed. She somehow got aboard the ship, removed her wet clothes, and fell asleep in the hammock.

Turner began feeling the hot breath of his competitors in the observation trials. Lowell North had beaten him several times, in July, and the score was not nearly as lopsided as it had been in June when Turner lost only one very close race to North, but Turner had ended on a high in late July, winning his last race against North and winning the Demitasse dinghy racing as well. The big question for the final trials to answer: was Turner still hot?

Normally, the aim of the America's Cup Committee has been to find the two weak boats early in the final trials, eliminate them, and have a good series of head-to-head racing between the two remaining. However, this time with only three Twelves racing the Committee's job was narrowed down to finding one weak boat. Instead it found two.

From the start of the final trials it was clear that Turner and *Courageous* were still hot. The first racing on August 16th pitted *Courageous* and *Enterprise*. *Courageous* got the start, and covered *Enterprise* tack for tack up the first windward leg. *Courageous* rounded the first mark with a 52-second lead, and that was about the margin all the way around. Obviously, both boats were extremely even in these brisk conditions with winds over 15 knots, as the margin at the finish was 56 seconds. This was the largest margin at any mark.

The America's Cup Committee called for another race even though the first race had not finished until four P.M., and *Courageous* won this one in similar fashion. It was a shortened windward/leeward/windward with a finish time difference of a mere 33 seconds.

In 30 seconds a 12-Meter covers a distance of approximately 400 feet sailing upwind in average conditions. This means that they were separated by only about five boat-lengths of open water throughout the race.

The next day *Courageous* met *Independence* with the same result. This race was sailed in a 15-knot sou'wester, but a prediction of severe afternoon thunderstorms caused the race to be shortened at the third mark. *Courageous* won by 50 seconds, and the yachts returned to the harbor by three P.M.

Courageous had the next day off, and if *Enterprise* could beat *Independence* twice, that might have given the America's Cup Committee an indication of their weak boat. However, while *Enterprise* was able to get the start and hold *Independence* throughout the first race—which was finished at the bottom mark—North was not able to contain Hood in the second race. *Independence* won the start and held off *Enterprise* to finish a windward/leeward/windward race with a 58-second lead.

The race on August 19th between *Courageous* and *Enterprise* started in very light winds (from the southeast at six knots). Cou-

Courageous and *Enterprise* approach windward mark very close in light air on August 19.

Courageous hoists her spinnaker.

Enterprise has her pole up as if she were going to set her spinnaker as well . . .

But she carries on with her "garbage bag" (green genoa) and will subsequently sail right over the slower moving *Courageous*.

rageous won the start, and covered *Enterprise* carefully to the first weather mark. The yachts had seesawed back and forth in the light and variable winds, but Turner's yacht had stayed ahead—if sometimes only barely—by keeping between *Enterprise* and the windward mark. As the yachts rounded the mark *Courageous* set her chute but *Enterprise*, rounding only 23 seconds later (barely more than a boat length in the light wind), held high, maintained her speed, and sailed right around *Courageous*. Turner headed up to catch North's breeze as *Enterprise* went by, and soon the tables were turned—*Courageous* swept past *Enterprise* to regain the lead.

Going into the reaching mark, both yachts were forced to tack downwind to maintain steerage way. First one, then the other, would appear to be ahead, but it was *Courageous* which won out with a 25-second lead. Again, *Enterprise* caught a fresher puff, and she sailed through *Courageous* to windward. *Courageous* responded by sailing above *Enterprise* in an attempt to pass. *Enterprise* luffed to keep *Courageous* from passing, and Turner attempted to force North to curtail the luff by calling "mastline" (indicating the mast of the leeward yacht was abeam of the helmsman of the windward yacht). This call was disputed by North, and a protest ensued which was later disallowed (see Appendix C). *Enterprise* rounded the bottom mark with a lead of 32 seconds, but she sailed into a hole on port tack which *Courageous* was able to avoid by tacking soon after clearing the mark. The wind and the race fell apart from that point, and was finished at the end of the second beat with *Enterprise* a dismal, but representative, 8:21 behind. There was no second race due to the lack of wind.

Courageous had a resounding win over *Independence* the next day in what could only be described as pleasant summer sailing weather. The wind was in the 8- to 12-knot range for most of the

The lead changed several times during the first reaching leg, and *Courageous* rounded the wing mark ahead of *Enterprise*.

Lowell North's unusual appearance with his wife Kay (partially hidden, left) and a few friends at the Black Pearl's terrace bar presaged the announcement that he had been removed as the skipper of *Enterprise*.

race, finishing in a brisk 15 knots. Once again, *Independence* appeared to be doomed. However, Hood got the start from Turner in the second race and went on to win by 43 seconds.

Stormy weather forced the cancellation of racing until August 25th when *Courageous* and *Enterprise* were to meet for the third time during these final trials. Meanwhile, the word was out that the America's Cup Committee expected to see some action with *Enterprise* and *Independence*. Perhaps some drastic changes were in order. It was during this period that Lowell North was replaced as skipper of *Enterprise*. Malin Burnham, who had been *Enterprise*'s helmsman for starts and upwind, was named skipper, and Halsey Herreshoff, grandson of the famous "Wizard of Bristol" Nathanael Greene Herreshoff who had designed and built many Cup defenders, went aboard as tactician.

Enterprise also made crew changes. Steve van Dyke, who had sailed as tactician aboard *Intrepid* in 1970 replaced Scott Perry. This was only the latest of crew shake-ups aboard *Independence*. Hood's son Teddy and Steve Lirakis had been replaced before the final trials by John Wright, a veteran of *Courageous* in 1974, and Bob Connell, who had sailed on *Constellation* and *Intrepid* in '64 and '67.

Changes of this sort, made in desperation, seldom work. The notable exception was in 1974 when Hood stepped in at the last minute to relieve Bavier. But Hood had inherited a going concern.

The first race between *Courageous* and *Enterprise* on August 25th was extremely close in a fluky northerly. (This was also the first race of the final series between *Australia* and *Sverige*.) *Courageous* took the start from *Enterprise*, but the latter got a break on the wind shifts on the first windward leg and came from behind into contention.

They were nearly overlapped at the reaching mark, struggling for the advantage which *Enterprise* was able to attain.

Enterprise was over a minute ahead at the end of the second reach, but *Courageous* managed to grind *Enterprise* down by playing the shifts to better advantage and maintaining speed. At the end of the second beat *Courageous* had gained the lead by 44 seconds. She maintained approximately this margin to the finish.

After a grueling full America's Cup course, the America's Cup Committee asked for a second race which did not start until four-thirty. Turner completely outfoxed Burnham at the start, forcing *Enterprise* to make a premature start. That was it. *Enterprise* never recovered, and lost after three legs by 1:11 at which time the race was halted at the third mark.

There was now no question that Turner was still hot. The America's Cup Committee would have difficulty selecting anyone but Turner. Still, the rumors persisted that the conservative New York Yacht Club would rather go with one of the other two. This was understandable. Turner had, in the past, been unpredictable. He had previously had differences with George Hinman when both were involved with ill-fated *Mariner* in 1974—Hinman had replaced Turner as *Mariner*'s skipper—and now Hinman was chairman of the America's Cup Committee. Whatever their private thoughts, the Committee kept its own counsel, and no outward signs were ever given that they would lean toward anyone but the boat that was best suited to defend the Cup. Likewise, Turner never showed any impatience or outward sign that he might think he was being discriminated against. Although sometimes vocal ashore, he was doing the job with cold precision. *Courageous* had, up to this point, been beaten only once by *Independence*. While the other two crews were continually beset with problems, *Courageous* was a smooth-running machine. The final outcome was beginning to be obvious.

Courageous lost the start to *Independence* in their race on August 26th, but Turner and his crew went to work and were in the lead by over a minute at the first mark. Steve Cady, writing in the *New York Times* on August 27th, described it eloquently:

> In a westerly breeze of six knots, Turner scratched and clawed his way up to windward, playing the lifts and headers and coaxing his boat to point higher into the wind than *Independence*. Within 10 minutes, *Independence*'s advantage to windward had shrunk to a boat length or two. After 15 minutes, with *Courageous* beginning to feed his boat bad air, Hood tacked away. Turner quickly covered, and that was the boat race.

The finish was close for a light air race with 48 seconds separating the yachts after a four-and-three-quarter-hour struggle. However, it was another significant victory for *Courageous*. *Independence*'s days were numbered.

Courageous had the day off on August 27th while *Enterprise* and *Independence* battled it out for what was becoming a poor second. However, if either crew was ready to concede defeat, it was not apparent in either of the two contests.

Independence won the start of the first race. Both boats were even until a bobbled tack gave Hood a slight advantage. *Independence* rounded the first mark with a 14-second lead—the yachts almost overlapped. However, *Enterprise* passed the Hood yacht at the reaching mark and Burnham was able to hold the lead from there to the finish of a slightly shortened (19 miles) America's Cup course. The greatest margin in this race was 42 seconds, and the finish was nine seconds. It was the closest race of the summer, perhaps the closest race ever between two 12-Meters.

The second race was even more exciting. *Enterprise* maintained a slim lead on the first beat and the two reaching legs, then *Independence* came back on the second beat to pull virtually even with *Enterprise*. As they went for the windward mark, Malin Burnham shot head to wind to coast around. Hood was forced to go up with him, and the two yachts rounded the mark overlapped. *Enterprise*, having the inside at the mark, came out of the rounding slightly ahead, and she maintained her lead on the downwind leg where the Committee ended the race. The margin was 15 seconds.

Enterprise and *Courageous* were to meet on August 28th, but a broken toggle on *Enterprise*'s headstay forced cancellation of the races. She was given the day off to effect repairs.

Courageous met *Independence* on the 29th and that spelled the end for the Hood boat. *Courageous* gained the lead on the first weather leg, increased it steadily on every leg, in the 15- to 18-knot sou'wester, and went on to win by 1:23. Rather than starting another race following the finish at one fifty-five, the America's Cup Committee sent the yachts back to the harbor. Shortly after their arrival, the Committee paid its fateful visit to *Independence* to thank the crew and tell them their services were no longer required.

It was a solemn occasion. The America's Cup Committee in their double-breasted navy blue jackets, straw hats with red, white, and blue bands, and Yacht Club ties shaking hands with the *Independence* crew members. There was, of course, surprise in the Hood camp. There always is. Even though the outcome is recognized as inevitable, the skipper and the crew always think there will be one more chance. There was not.

As Hood accepted the handshake of America's Cup Committeeman Bob Bavier, the man he had replaced in *Courageous's* cockpit three years before, Ted Turner watched from a respectful distance on the deck of that same *Courageous* which he now captained. Three years ago, Turner had stood where Hood now stood, and there were tears of compassion in Turner's eyes.

"It was bound to happen," Hood said to me later, "we couldn't take *Courageous.*"

"I think what they'll do is knock them out tomorrow," said Lee Loomis, referring to *Enterprise.* And then he added, "It's been a helluva long summer."

Loomis was right. The same pattern was repeated the next day. *Courageous* beat *Enterprise* by taking the start, gaining her lead on

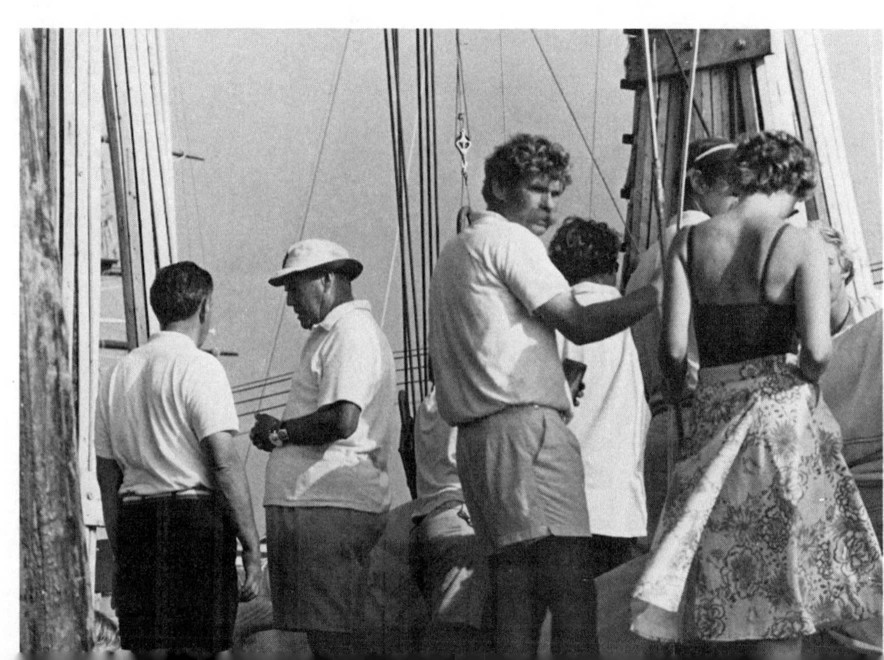

Independence's skipper Ted Hood receives condolences from a disappointed A. Lee Loomis following the America's Cup Committee's fateful visit to tell Hood that his yacht had been eliminated from contention as a Cup defender. Navigator Pete Lawson clutches a beer can in one hand and holds the starboard shrouds in the other as if for support for the woeful burden of defeat.

the first weather leg, establishing her cover, and staying ahead. *Enterprize* closed up on the last windward leg in a fading breeze, but the outcome was never in doubt. After the race, the Committee sent the yachts back to the harbor, and the drama of the previous day was repeated on *Enterprise*'s dock except that it all happened in the middle of a horrendous downpour. As the Committee waited for the rain to stop, then went over to Bannister's Wharf to tell Turner and his crew that they had been selected to defend the America's Cup, the clouds parted, and the sun shown down on the victors. It was an omen!

This same day *Australia* defeated *Sverige* for the fourth time thereby wrapping up the challenger's series. After the *Enterprise* crew had gone to Bannister's Wharf to congratulate *Courageous*, their tender, *Chaperone*, stopped at Newport Shipyard so they could congratulate the crew of *Australia*. There was bitterness among the *Enterprise* people over their elimination. There had been a running battle going between Turner and North all summer, and it came to a head with open hostility expressed here on *Australia*'s dock. There were offers of help for the Australians, which would have shocked the America's Cup Committee, but fortunately, nothing ever came of it. After champagne and/or a few beers and much back pounding, *Chaperone* backed away with a few dying, "go get'ems" directed toward *Australia*.

The preamble to the America's Cup was over.

The end of a long, tough summer.

Chapter XII LETDOWN

The day after *Australia* beat *Sverige*, and the New York Yacht Club Selection Committee chose *Courageous* to be the defender, virtually everything in Newport came to a sudden stop. It was like the end of a play. One minute there is plenty of action; the climax is reached; there is the applause (as the victors are congratulated by those who have lost), then the curtain falls, and those left looking on are met by silence and a sense of bewilderment.

The end of long ocean passages are similar. One is used to day after day of the same routine. Then there is heightened excitement as landfall is made. But after one is in port and the boat tied up, there is a sense of loss. The goal has been achieved, but the routine to which one has become so accustomed has been broken. What do we do now?

Like the theater when the audience has walked up the aisles and out through the exits, by Thursday Newport was practically deserted.

I left too, having some business to attend to out of town Wednesday afternoon, and when I returned Thursday morning, I happened to meet Hanne Bense (who had handled press relations with the *Gretel* group) who was browsing through the antique shops on Franklin Street. "Hi, what's happening?" I asked.

"It's very quiet," she said. "A lot of the crew has already left and we're having a meeting tonight to decide if we can sail *Gretel* any more."

"It's very sad," Hanne said. "There's a great sense of let down. We're closing the White Elephant tomorrow, and those who are left will move into the smaller houses."

When I checked into the press room to see if there were any developments while I had been away, there was a sense of finality there as well. Steve Cady and Judy Lawson were the only ones there besides Erika Brigham who was faithfully holding down the information desk with no information to give. The big news was that Alan Bond was having difficulty bringing off his five-race series with *Sverige.* (Bond had said he considered *Sverige* was a much better boat than their 4-0 score had indicated. He proposed an Australian/Sweden Cup to be raced for in a five-race series before this America's Cup.) The Swedes were losing crew, and it would be difficult for them to race in a series with *Australia.* However, they would stick around for the weekend and would race as many races on Saturday and Sunday as could be gotten in.

My son, Doug, was leaving for college in a few days so I suggested on Thursday evening that we go out to dinner. We ambled down Thames Street at about 7:00 to the Bavarian Restaurant. Out of two dozen tables in the front room, only two were taken. We not only sat down immediately, but were able to quibble over which table. We were there until 9:00, and maybe two other tables were occupied in that whole time. Newport was deserted. I happened to glance down Bannister's Wharf as we passed by. There was hardly a soul to be seen. There was no line in front of the Clarke Cooke House. There was no one sitting on the curb outside the Black Pearl—no overflow from the terrace bar into the street. Nor was there anyone in front of the Hot Dog Annex. I could see all the way to the lattice barricade that has kept the public away from *Courageous* and *Independence.*

Friday morning at Williams & Manchester, *Enterprise* was having her mast unstepped. Pelle Petterson was there, camera in hand, having a look at *Enterprise's* details, and I stopped to ask him how he was.

"Oh, okay," he replied with a decided lack of enthusiasm.

"Will you be back to try again?" I asked.

"Yes, I hope so," he replied. "It would be a shame to waste all the experience we have gained." He said he would be going home to Götteborg after racing against *Australia* on Sunday. I asked him if he would come back for the America's Cup races themselves, and he said no, he had many things to attend to at home. And then he added as an afterthought, "I have to earn some money so we can come back again."

As I looked past Mack's Clam Shack, I saw activity aboard *Gretel*. Before going home, I went over to check out what had been happening over there. Peter Cole, Jack, and Geoff Gale were busy on deck removing fittings. Gordon Ingate and a couple of the others were below removing fittings from the mast.

"I assume from this that *Gretel* is not to sail again," I said.

"You assume correct," Jack Gale said looking up from a compass he was removing from the deck.

"We decided not to sail," said Peter Cole, "then we changed our mind, then we changed our mind again."

Gordon Ingate stuck his head out of the forward hatch. Ingate, normally a cheerful man win or lose, had the look of a whipped cocker spaniel. The work of disassembling *Gretel* so that she could be shipped back to Australia was clearly a joyless enterprise. Ingate had promised after *Gretel* was eliminated from the series by *Sverige* that *Gretel* would sail in the Ida Lewis Yacht Club consolation race for 12-Meters on September 10, but here she was being dismantled. Ingate would stay for the America's Cup, he said, but the *Gretel* syndicate people didn't know what they would use as a spectator boat. *Gretel*'s tender, *Island Gypsy*, had already gone to Boston to be sold, *Ursa Major* had other commitments, and their charter was up on the palatial *La Costa Brava*.

Nor was there much joy among the winners. I had run into Ted Turner quietly strolling down Thames Street with a friend Thursday evening, and for the first time in weeks, Turner failed to say anything worth quoting. The letdown was unmistakable. Virtually everyone in Newport was acting as if they had just come from a funeral.

Chapter *XIII* INSIDE THE SYNDICATES

It can be well understood that the manager of a 12-Meter syndicate has his hands full enough with internal problems that he doesn't need any extra difficulties. If, for instance, the docks at Williams & Manchester, Newport Shipyard, and Bannister's Wharf—the three areas where all the Twelves were berthed—were open to the public there would be endless difficulties with people getting in the way, asking countless inane questions, and possibly even getting hurt. Therefore, all docks were closed to the public. Only authorized people were allowed inside the restricted areas.

The syndicates have a bit more difficult time with the press. Most realize the legitimate need of reporters to be informed although, of course, they should not be privy to any secrets that the syndicate wants to keep from the competition. All registered press people were issued cards by the Rhode Island Yachting Committee—an arm of the state administration. However, these only got one into the press room. Each syndicate and the Newport Shipyard also issued passes, which were good for various—and sometimes capricious—states of entry.

Barbara Lloyd, writing in the *Newport Daily News* after the series mused, "I, for one, will be happy to toss my wrinkled passes into the drink. No more having to think about sticking the red, white, and blue *Independence-Courageous* card in my hip pocket before breakfast. No more traveling the sticky path between walking out on the 12-Meter dock and getting thrown out on your ear."

Early in the season magazine editor Mike Levitt was winding up last-minute details for *Nautical Quarterly*, which was doing a special issue on the America's Cup. Levitt had received permission from project manager Jeff Neuberth to take some photographs aboard *Independence* to round out a sequence he had taken weeks before. Previously, he had been run off the dock, but this time as he stepped aboard *Independence* he was told by one of the crew. "No pictures, Loomis's orders." Rather than argue the point, Levitt left the boat and went in search of Lee Loomis. As he was walking down the dock Levitt spotted two crew members carrying a sail. Thinking it might be an interesting photo, Levitt brought his camera to his eye only to see a huge hand blocking the lens. It was Loomis. Levitt spun away— lowering the camera—only to be grabbed by Loomis who attempted to eject him from the dock.

" I was never so close to hitting someone in my life," Levitt said later. It was a good thing he didn't try; Loomis is a big, powerful man who must outweigh Levitt by 80 pounds.

A. Lee Loomis, who earned the nickname "The Big Loom," is of the old guard who believes firmly that the America's Cup is the private domain of the New York Yacht Club, that the public—and therefore the press—has no right to be involved. The press was barely tolerated, and the general public was absolutely prevented from getting anywhere near the Twelves or their crew members. Shortly after the Levitt incident, the following was issued:

KING'S POINT SYNDICATE PRESS INFORMATION

Due to the small size of our dock facilities and the ever-present confines of time, we ask that the members of the press cooperate with the following precedures.

Press Passes
1. Applications for Syndicate press passes should be left for Richard Sayer at the dock office. He is handling press organization and press admittance to the dock area and will be at the dock every afternoon from approximately 5 P.M.-6:30 P.M.

Eligibility

2. Syndicate press passes will be issued to members of the working press on a publication/organization basis, with a limit on the numbers issued per organization. As such we require a letter from your organization or publication authorizing you as their representative.

Press Hours

3. Members of the press with Syndicate passes will be admitted to the press area at 5:15 P.M. every evening for a post race or post practice press conference.

Designated Press Area

4. When admitted inside the main gate, it is requested that all press remain *off of the dock itself*, that is, remain in the designated press area behind the gas pumps at the head of the pier. Please keep clear of all crew members and their work. PRESS WILL NOT BE PERMITTED ON THE 12's, THEIR TENDERS, OR THE DOCK ITSELF AFTER RACES OR PRACTICE SESSIONS.

Press Conferences

5. The skippers and their afterguards will be available to talk with the press *in the designated press area only*, as soon after the boats dock as is practicable.

Cameras

6. Please, *no pictures* of either boat's afterbody when she is hauled.

Interviews

7. Personal interviews with the skippers or crews or working rides on the tenders must be arranged in advance through Richard Sayer who will schedule them on a case by case basis and as time, space and sailing schedules permit.

Crew's Residence

8. Press are NOT permitted at the crew's residence, Conley Hall, at any time, unless personally invited by Mr. Lee Loomis.

Some of these requests are reasonable, but others clearly are not. Any tourist with a 150-mm lens could get as many photographs of both Twelves' sterns from Bowen's Wharf as he wanted, and someone in a rowboat or one of the crews of the fishing boats coming in and out of Aquidneck Lobster's dock could get enough to draw a set of plans. A crew member from one of the foreign Twelves could do the same, yet a press photographer was threatened with expulsion from the dock and removal of his "Syndicate press pass" if he was caught trying it.

It was not a happy place, and Loomis was not a popular man with the press. One Australian newsman, who had covered several previous America's Cups, complained about Loomis's attitude. "He's the sort of man who gives the New York Yacht Club a bad image," he said. "I'm sure 90 percent of the members aren't that way, but it's the minority who are like Loomis who give the overall impression of stuffiness."

It is difficult to fault the dedication and singleminded effort that Loomis put into his syndicate. He raised the money—putting a lot of his own into the pot—and saw to it that everything that was needed was obtained. "Loomis has been obnoxious at times," said one of the crew members, "and the place has been like 'Stalag 17', but he did raise all the money and stay out of the inner workings. He gave us a free hand to buy whatever we wanted. We never had that (in other syndicates) before."

It was no secret that Loomis and Turner did not get along—although to the credit of both, their differences were never public. Hood was Loomis's "fair-haired boy," and when *Independence* was eliminated and *Courageous* selected Loomis had faint praise for Turner and lavish praise for Hood. Several times he stated publicly that the real credit for *Courageous*'s success belonged to Hood.

The *Independence/Courageous* syndicate, officially the King's Point Fund, had all the right ingredients. Hood, the skipper who stepped in at the last minute and saved *Courageous* in the 1974 trials before going on to win the America's Cup, had all the makings of success. He started early, avoiding the problems of last-minute changes that had plagued virtually every new 12-Meter previously. He had *Courageous*, unquestionably the fastest Twelve in the world following the 1974 series, and he had available to him the best crew members to be had. What went wrong?

Loomis's determination to do anything that would put *Independence* in the winner's circle carried over into crew selection and other things. Going into the spring, they knew they had a boat that was, at best, only marginally better than *Courageous*, and perhaps it wasn't as good. This put everyone on the defensive. Instead of settling down and working to perfect what they had, *Independence* kept looking for the magic panacea—whether it be a new sail, a new piece of equipment, a new method of doing things, or a new person to do them.

"Loomis thinks that Hood is next to God," said one crew member. "Probably one of the weaknesses of this whole thing was that Loomis was unable to criticize Ted Hood."

Some of the crew had asked to set up a training program, to go out and do a hundred tacks a day for a week, then do a hundred jibes. "If you have 11 guys but they haven't worked together," said one of the 11, "you don't have much. If somebody has always sailed a Finn (single-handed Olympic dinghy) and you put him on a Twelve he's not going to integrate very smoothly until everyone gets some practice together."

The crew work wasn't bad, it was just that there are several ways to do most jobs, and because the *Independence* guys never settled down and practiced together they never knew exactly how things were going to happen. It was a matter of poor communication.

In contrast, Turner, who by contract with the syndicate was

Jeff Neuberth, former starboard tailer aboard *Independence*, reverted to full-time project manager early in July. The importance of the project manager's job was no substitute for sailing, but Neuberth took the change with good grace and probably functioned more effectively with only one job to do.

guaranteed full control over *Courageous*, stuck with what he had. Few changes were made in equipment and no changes were made in crew. It wasn't until late in the observation trials that *Courageous* had any new sails of her own, and these were painstakingly made and refined by Robbie Doyle. Turner's group observed the experimentation that went on aboard *Independence*. They copied what worked and ignored what didn't. They did very little pioneering on their own.

Crew members aboard *Independence* were not secure. First to go was Jeff Neuberth. It was said that Jeff was having difficulty handling both a crew assignment (starboard tailer) and the job of project manager, and it was true that he was probably too busy to do both effectively. However, it was a bitter disappointment to Neuberth—after having worked for three years on *Independence*—to find himself beached, and the reasons for it were probably related more to friction between the crew members handling the sails and the afterguard in the cockpit.

"They were hacking up the tacks," Neuberth said, "and we were getting the blame." Tacking a Twelve is a delicate maneuver. If the helmsman isn't in tune with his crew and their capabilities, he can make them look terrible. But Neuberth was not bitter about it. "Hood is human, just like everyone else," Neuberth added, "and he's under a tremendous amount of pressure."

Neuberth said he was "pretty upset" at first when they took him off the boat and made him full-time project manager. He'd still rather have sailed even though the job of project manager was more important. He acknowledged that he was having difficulty doing both.

As project manager Neuberth was responsible for all the bits and pieces. He made sure all the parts were available, that tools were obtained and returned when they had been used. He was in charge of purchasing everything, and with his background working with *Mariner* in 1974 and since then for Hood on both *Courageous* and *Independence* he was able to save the syndicate considerable amounts of money. He knows how much things should cost and what discounts are available through various sources. He knows the best sources of supply and how to get parts sent in as quickly as possible.

With so much importance placed upon Neuberth's job, why was he unhappy not to be sailing? "Who ever remembers the name of the project manager?" Jeff asked. "Indeed," I asked him, "who ever remembers the name of the starboard tailer?"

It was important to Neuberth as project manager to have sailed aboard *Independence* in the early stages. That way he was able to know the boat and know what the needs were.

"This has been a good learning experience," said Neuberth who has been involved with *Independence* and *Courageous* for almost all of the time since he graduated from college. "I managed a $1.3-million corporation that went into the ground. That looks good on a résumé. People, like friends of my parents, meet me and ask me what I'm doing for a living, and I tell them I'm driving a corporation bankrupt."

Independence was an uptight ship. One of the reasons could be read in the newspapers every day. Daily reporters, anxious for stories, continually sought out the skippers for comments about their performance. Hood often was quoted as saying that they were having this or that problem or that the crew wasn't as good as he had hoped. The same reporters quoted Turner as saying that his crew was the greatest, his boat was great, the sails were great, Robbie Doyle was doing the best job of anybody, Gary Jobson was the greatest tactician in the world. Conley Hall may have been like "Stalag 17" to some, but they did get to read the newspapers.

A symptom of this uptightness was running into the buoy. This sort of thing could have happened to anyone except that it happens more often to losers than winners. A cohesive crew would have been able to shrug it off as one of those things, but aboard *Independence* it had a devastating effect on morale.

Early in the summer after a particularly bad practice session, a 10 P.M. curfew was imposed on *Independence*'s crew. While, accord-

Sign on the wall in Neuberth's "office" on Bannister's Wharf.

ing to some observers, there had been some laxity in crew performance perhaps stemming from lack of sleep, others would have handled it differently. Here was one lesson the Hood organization did not learn from past defense efforts. The winning crew has almost always been the more relaxed crew. It may be a chicken and egg—which comes first—proposition, but a crew of adults does not function at its best when they are treated like preppies.

Conversely, Turner was much looser with his crew. They had the same standards of performance, they were worked just as hard, but they were not asked to do unreasonable things and they were not constantly in fear of losing their jobs.

In April '77 Steve Lirikas received a letter from Jeff Neuberth asking if Steve would like to sail aboard *Independence*. Lirikas is a boatbuilder by trade, and he had worked on such past 12-Meter projects as *Heritage* in 1970 and *Courageous* in 1974. He lives in Newport, he had the time—more or less—and who wouldn't jump at the chance?

Everyone makes sacrifices to sail on an America's Cup Twelve, and Lirikas was no exception. He had just bought a house in Newport, a do-it-yourself project with three apartments that needed renovation before they could be rented. Lirikas was counting on the spring months to get things ready for summer rentals, but with the chance to sail on *Independence*, his schedule became rather hectic. He would leave for Marblehead at 5 A.M. on Friday mornings, sail and work on the boat for four days, and then head home Monday night. When he got there he would work until 2 or 3 A.M. on the house—putting in 18-hour days until it was time to go back to Marblehead.

When *Independence* moved to Newport, Steve and his wife Bernadette could not move into Conley Hall because they had an 18-month-old daughter. Ironically, while they would have preferred to be with the crew, the fact that Steve was the only crew member not subject to the disciplines imposed at Conley Hall caused some jealousy among those who had to live there.

Just prior to the final trials, Lirikas was relieved of his job as *Independence*'s bow man. Why was kicked off the boat?

"No one ever really spoke to me," he said. He had started off the season trying to establish communications between the bow and the afterguard—developing hand signals for various things, trying to find out what was wanted in the way of information. Nobody seemed interested. Lirikas also tried to seek out Hood to find out what he wanted in the boat, how he wanted things to operate, but Hood was either unwilling or unable to communicate these things to Lirikas.

"I don't really know," Steve mused about his dismissal. "All I can infer is that because I talked back or because I asked a lot of questions that I was relieved of my duty. That's really all I know."

He thinks he's a good bow man—better than some others who were highly touted—but as far as the world knows he was kicked off the boat because he wasn't any good.

"I think that I'm pretty good," Lirikas said. "I still feel I'm pretty good, and I don't think that it's made me feel less good about myself, but it can create an image that I'd prefer not to have to bear. Hood reported in the papers that he replaced people because they weren't good enough for the job." Lirikas thinks that was unfair.

Speaking of *Independence* Jeff Neuberth said, "Everyone who walks down the dock is a potential crew member. We're going to put up a sign over this thing (work shed) that says 'former crew members only.' "

So many people had been kicked off one 12-Meter or another that Neuberth thought they should have a new Twelve with the crew composed of rejects. It was an impressive list. Neuberth decided to call the boat "Maybe Something."

Turner, kidding Neuberth one day, said, "How's the boat coming?" "We're going to paint it tomorrow and put it in the water," Neuberth told him, "and then it's all over for you guys."

Turner wanted to know if that was where all the spare parts were going. "I want to know where my spare mast is," he quipped.

Courageous did not get the same service from the syndicate as *Independence*. *Courageous* did not have a spare mast until they were selected to defend the Cup. As mentioned, they did not get new sails until well into the summer. "Don't get me wrong," Turner said, "we got everything we needed, but sometimes we had to pay for it ourselves."

The secret of *Courageous*'s success was a combination of factors. Turner has an ability to evaluate the strengths and weaknesses of people. Once he is confident that a crew member knows his job, he leaves him alone to organize it. When asked about the crew organization he obviously didn't know that much about it and referred all such questions to the team coach, Marty O'Meara.

O'Meara was originally a part of the crew aboard *Courageous* in the slot later filled by Robbie Doyle. It was always intended that Doyle should be there if he became available, and O'Meara, who is 50, left the boat in June bowing to the younger, stronger sailmaker.

O'Meara became team coach. He is the sort of person who makes a contribution no matter what he is doing. In the past he had done most of Turner's logistics—shipping boats to Australia for the One Ton World Championships, for example—and he takes care of a lot of the protocol which Turner often overlooks. In the words of one crew member, "He is the grease in the gears behind the scenes."

O'Meara was on the tender every day taking notes about tactics, sail selection, sail trim, and a hundred other details that he had observed. He would spend hours with Turner and Jobson after races and practice sessions going over these notes, helping them to spot potential weaknesses or suggesting better ways of doing things. He was a constant source of input.

An *Independence* crew member complained, with obvious admiration for O'Meara, "*Independence* never had anybody to do that."

O'Meara is high in his praise of Turner and his ability to get the most out of people who work and sail with him. "Over the years part of his strength has been not only his own determination and aggressiveness and his ability to learn—I would underline the latter—part of his success has been his ability to pick out good guys, maybe not people who you'd recognize as super stars, but really solid, sound sailors that recognize the importance of keeping themselves in physical trim and mentally the right attitude and going out and just plain working. I would say the foundation of our efforts are people that Turner had enlisted over a period of years. Our crew list didn't change one whit since the very first day when we started sailing in March.

"We felt that all the boats would be doggone even on boat speed," O'Meara said regarding the philosophy of sailing *Courageous*. "We hoped that *Courageous* would still be competitive. We didn't feel that we could expect that *Courageous* would have any particular edge on boat speed. So, therefore, we felt that we had to set the boat up to be easily handled in multiple tacks and many maneuvers. We had to train the crew to be better than the next guy because we felt it would come down to the way the boats would be handled and, of course, how successful the sails would be. Our fundamental philosophy was, make the boat functional but not fancy with no fiddly gimmicks or tricks that are going to go wrong and cost you."

Hood had done a good job of upgrading *Courageous*. There was, of course, the deck layout to be rebuilt to conform to the new 12-Meter rules. Also, *Courageous* had to be modified to shorten her waterline to make her rate in with the increased displacement (which had not been discovered until after the 1974 series). When she had been sailing against *Independence* in the fall of 1976, *Courageous* was not at 12-Meter.

"The stuff he (Hood) did to the stern was really good," Jeff Neuberth thinks, "taking the crease out and just cleaning things up. I'm not sure the stuff we did to the bow helped . . . that we did for the measurement. The other stuff cleaned the boat up, and moving the rudder didn't hurt any. Unfortunately (for *Independence*), the changes we made to *Courageous* made her faster." And then by way of an afterthought Neuberth added, "I don't think *Enterprise* is an improvement on *Courageous*, I think those guys are living in a dream."

Enterprise was, unquestionably, a disappointment. Preseason thinking was that surely if Hood had not designed a better boat than *Courageous*, Olin Stephens would be able to. It is difficult to tell—even for Stephens—whether or not *Courageous* was improved by Hood and if so by how much. Also, it was hard to tell if *Enterprise* was being sailed up to her potential.

If Hood was too uptight in the way he handled his crew, Lowell North, skipper of *Enterprise* for most of the summer, was too loose. There seemed to be no rules of conduct in the *Enterprise* camp. Everybody was happy-go-lucky, buddy-buddy. It was California dreamer stuff. They developed pet names for their various experimental sails—the green jib was called the "garbage bag." A special two-ply mainsail which showed scalloped panels running vertically near the leach was called "jaws." There is certainly nothing wrong with that sort of loose informality, but they didn't have the discipline that was needed. It was almost too cutesy to be a serious effort.

Like Hood, North continued to fiddle with his boat well into the summer. They finally decided to settle down and give the crew some consistency, after several of North's key crew members held a pow-wow with him, suggesting it was past time to settle down. However, it would appear that by then it was too late. *Enterprise* had many innovative features which might prove useful at some point, but there is a great deal to be said for the *Courageous* philosophy of keeping things simple and making them work. It seems there are lessons yet to be learned from the America's Cup.

North was replaced as *Enterprise's* skipper late in the August trials. It was a time of desperation, and desperate measures were taken. North had an unusual method of skippering a Twelve. Malin Burnham was the starting and upwind helmsman, and North steered very little himself. North is a born tinkerer, and he felt he was most useful concentrating on the things that made the boat go fast. The syndicate decided, under pressure, that something drastic needed to be done to produce a winner, that getting North off the boat altogether might work. It didn't.

Both North and Hood were under tremendous pressure to win. Not only did they have pressure of defending the America's Cup— that was a long-term pressure gnawing in the background—they also had the prestige of their businesses at stake. Surely, when each made his commitment to get into the America's Cup defense, neither entertained the thought that he would lose.

For Hood, who was the first to commit, it was natural to follow out of the success of 1974, seeing all the problems that could have been overcome if he'd been able to exert his influence completely from the beginning with a defender of his own. Particularly with Lee Loomis offering his complete support, Hood thought he could overcome any obstacle.

Actually, it was not North who initiated the plan to build and campaign *Enterprise* but when offered the helm, the chance to sail to glory against one of his chief business rivals was irresistible.

There were those who were not happy that the two sailmakers were dedicated to separate efforts. Turner was quiet when it came to Hood because he was his syndicate mate, but he was very outspoken against North. Turner accused North of backtracking on an offer to supply sails for *Courageous.*

"They are liars," Turner said of Lowell North and John Marshall (who runs North's East Coast loft and sailed aboard *Enterprise*). "They promised to let me have some sails and they didn't."

Understandably upset by this blast, North countered by saying that Turner had made his request while sailing in Europe the summer before. North thought it was a casual request, something like, "Hey Lowell, you guys are gonna sell me some sails, aren't you?" To which North replied, "Sure, Ted," and went on to concentrate on the race.

North thinks he shouldn't be held to a casual comment like that when other pressures later dictated that another decision should be made.

But Turner was adamant, "There is a lot of unsportsmanlike conduct in this series which I don't like. Commercialism. I'm putting stuff into this sport. They're taking it out." And again, "Their future as sailmakers is at stake. They may not eat for the next three or four years."

One of the more significant contributions to technology in this America's Cup came from *Independence*. Navigator Ralph (Pete) Lawson had at his disposal one of the most sophisticated navigational instruments ever used in a sailboat. It was a computer.

Computers are not new to sailing or to the America's Cup, but this one licked several problems of previous systems. Computer technology has reached the point where no sailboat condition is immune to emulation by a computer. However, the problems involving miniaturization and the availability of sufficient electrical power were not overcome to the point where this potential could be realized until the system used by *Independence*, and to a lesser extent *Courageous*, was developed.

Lawson was the one who designed the requirements of the system, but the programming of the software (instructions allowing the computer to operate with specific input data) was done by Scott Garon, a Digital Equipment Corporation (DEC) design technician. The central processing unit (CPU) of the system is a DEC LSI-11 microprocessor, a standard commerical component adapted by David Shanin. Input to the system was fed by Signet instruments—standard yacht equipment providing speed of the boat through the water, magnetic (compass) heading, wind direction, and wind velocity. Control of the computer was provided by a Termiflex hand-held terminal—a keyboard and digital display slightly bigger than a hand-held calculator.

With this system, Lawson could position *Independence* at Bannister's Wharf when they left in the morning, and the computer would automatically keep track of their position all day. Naturally, this necessitated very accurate calibration of the input from the Signet instruments. Lawson learned to trust the computer implicitly. Invariably he would provide a bearing and distance to a mark from the computer and the information would be proven absolutely accurate from visual observations. He said that after a while he just didn't bother looking.

Not only would the computer provide Lawson with accurate navigational information, with it he could tell the helmsman what heading to steer for optimum speed made good to windward and the best angle and speed for tacking downwind. "Best of all," said Lawson, "the information was based upon the wind direction and speed prevailing at the time. It was constantly updated from the input from the instruments." In addition, by pushing a couple of buttons, Lawson could ask the computer how far it was to the lay line on either side of the course. Information about wind shifts—angular change, duration of shift, and velocity differences—could be provided by pushing another set of buttons. This information was very useful in deciding tactical maneuvers as well as optimizing speed made good.

Courageous had a similar system, using the same hardware, but Lawson and Garon were continually updating the software, adding new wrinkles as they learned about the equipment and gained confidence in it. Only after *Independence* was eliminated did *Courageous* have the advantage of the same software that Lawson used. Lawson's policy was to add small things one at a time so as not to disturb the basic workings of the system. A small glitch in a computer can put down a whole system if drastic revisions are undertaken frequently, and Lawson was anxious to avoid that sort of problem.

Sufficient power to run an extensive computer system has been a problem in the past. Modern technology, squeezing more and more capacity into smaller and smaller components—helped accomplish this, but Garon's and Shanin's efficient planning of software and efficient use of memory minimized the time, and hence the electrical power, requirements of the various functions. The microprocessor has a capacity of 16K (16,000 "words") of memory and the programs were fed into memory every morning through a paper tape reader.

The system has wide application possibilities, according to Lawson, for navigation and offshore racing. The system is expensive (an exact figure, including hundreds of hours of development time, cannot be determined, but it is several thousand dollars) but the technology used is not exotic. Basically the same sort of things could be done with a hand-held programmable calculator for several hundred dollars—only it would take much longer and be more subject to operator errors.

A buddy of one of Ted Turner's sons fishes unconcerned on the work float beneath *Courageous*, oblivious to the hordes outside the lattice gate who would have given almost anything to stand where he stands.

Chapter *XIV*   SAILING *GRETEL*

Two days after *Gretel* had been eliminated from the semifinal round Peter Campbell asked if I would like to take a sail aboard her. They were going out the next day, and I would be welcome to join them. I could think of several reasons why I shouldn't, but they were all overwhelmed by this single opportunity to actually sail a 12-Meter.

I have done enough sailing in a lifetime to be thoroughly jaded: Transatlantic, Bermuda, Fastnet, Jamaica, Mackinac—all ocean races on a great variety of yachts. I have even logged 1,200 miles aboard a 12-Meter, but this was a sea delivery trip of *Heritage* in 1970 with a small mainsail. Never had I sailed aboard a geared-up America's Cup contender. Of course I went!

One can stand on the dock and look for hours at the deck layout, winches, turning blocks, tracks, stoppers, halyards, spinnaker pole, backstays, mainsheet, vang, Cunningham, outhaul, and imagine how it all works when the sheets and guys ("braces" in Australian), are rigged. However, the most vivid imagination—even to the experienced eye—is no substitute for actually working with the gear while the yacht is sailing. All the little details go unnoticed until they are actually put to use.

The many faces of *Gretel's* skipper Gordon Ingate.

Consider *Gretel's* mainsail halyard locking system, for example. Most small one-design racers use some form of halyard lock if their class rules permit. Offshore racers do not use them because they can be cantankerous and unreliable, often jamming and invariably requiring the yacht to be head to wind before they will release. An ocean racer also must have a reefable mainsail—all of which make halyard locks on large yachts rare. However, the Twelves are not restricted by class rules or the need to reef or lower the main quickly. Therefore, the advantage of a locking system—which relieves the compression of the halyard from the mast—has not been ignored in modern Twelves. *Gretel's* is rather a marvel of ingenuity. A ring riding on the headboard of the sail engages a pin when the sail is fully hoisted. The ring swivels to allow the headboard to assume its proper angle to the wind on various points of sail, but the swivel must be immobilized when the sail is hoisted. Before hoisting, a size #10 knitting needle is inserted through holes in the swivel to hold the ring perpendicular to the mast while the sail is hoisted. After the lock is hooked, the knitting needle breaks, and the headboard is free to swivel. With this system the main must be hoisted with *Gretel* precisely head to wind, but the sail can be lowered (reliably) at any angle—a vast improvement on previous halyard locks. This is but one example of the myriad innovative gadgets and ideas that go into all America's Cup contenders but which are seen or appreciated only by those who actually use them.

Below, *Gretel* is a maze of wires, sheaves, tubes, and struts. Her new aluminum deck and deck beams look incongruous attached to the wood frames of her hull. Since the new rules required that her deck be rebuilt, *Gretel's* designer Alan Payne opted for an entirely new deck of aluminum which would be lighter, stronger, and easier to fabricate than a modification of her old wood deck. There is no "habitable" space below except for a cramped navigator's work area aft of the helmsman's cockpit. Even in this space one must be careful to keep hands, elbows, and odd bits of clothing from mixing with the steering cables, but then, no one is meant to relax on a racing 12-Meter.

Our crew for this outing was made up mostly of members of the press. *Gretel's* father and son team Jack and Geoff Gale were, besides Gordon Ingate, the only regular crew members aboard. Peter Campbell, who was one of *Gretel's* press liaisons as well as a radio and magazine reporter, was the only other person aboard who had sailed *Gretel* before. Tom Clagget, a member of the *Enterprise* syndicate; John Morgan, chairman of the International Race Committee; Bill Thomson, International Race Committee member; and myself were the only others aboard with much sailing experience. The rest ranged from neophyte down to "first time" sailors. However motley the crew, it made up for ineptitude with unbounded enthusiasm. Jack and Geoff showed how to work the winches, tail the sheets, and haul on the halyards, and allowed everyone enough scope to make mistakes but not to get hurt. Gordon Ingate was a model of patience. He cringed a lot but only raised his voice for the benefit of Peter Campbell's tape recorder. For a man who was forced to watch while a bunch of ham-fisted journalists butchered his delicate baby, Ingate was surprisingly calm.

The first surprise was the way *Gretel* sat in the water while we hoisted the mainsail. Her great weight and deep hull is not easily buffeted. Where a smaller boat would be blown sideways, threatening to wipe out boats in the nearby anchorage, *Gretel* sat motionless as if fastened to the bottom. However, the slightest amount of drive derived from the leach of her mainsail pushed her forward and provided

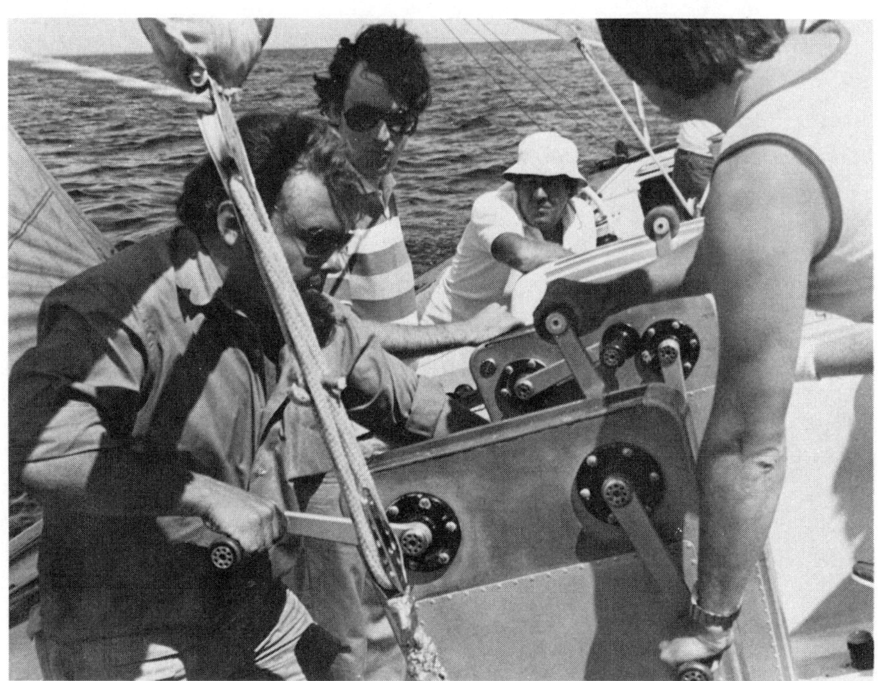

Australian newsmen Piers Akerman and Ray Martin strain at *Gretel's* coffee grinders.

a surprising amount of control for the helmsman. It is this characteristic which allows match-racing helmsmen to lie head to wind for minutes at a time to keep an opponent from getting on his stern. An occasional filling of a portion of the mainsail leach is enough to maintain control.

We filled away and headed out of the harbor under mainsail. *Gretel* ghosted along in the smooth water with only a hint of motion although we were making between four and five knots. Then it was up genoa as we passed Fort Adams, sheet in on the wind ("no, crank the handle the other way . . . that's it, now push down on the button on the floor when it gets too tough . . . okay that's good, stop . . . STOP ferchrisake!"). We got lifted by the current coming out of Narragansett

Bay past the Swedes' base at Fort Whetherill, and ssswooshhhhh—away we went like sultans on a magic carpet.

A couple of tacks—not bad for a crew whose most recent exercise consisted of pounding typewriters and holding down mike buttons—had us past Castle Hill and buoy R "2" in no time. Two immediate impressions: *Gretel* slips through the water with no apparent effort—the motion is an easy lope in the slight ground swell coming in from Rhode Island Sound—and even with our novice grinders and tailers the genoa sheets in with lightning-like speed. The silent power of the Twelve is a symphony of grace. She makes almost no noise (Ingate says he listens to a boat to tell how good she is—"noisy boats are wasting energy," he says) and the water slips past her hull without the slightest argument. No doubt winching in the genoa is more difficult on a windy day or during a tacking duel when it must be done every 50 seconds, but the coffee grinders on a modern Twelve are a marvel of efficiency.

I was to appreciate this later watching the competitors tack on their upwind legs. The genoas seem to flow around the mast and rigging and come home with hardly a flutter—much more quickly and effectively than on my 30-footer. Having done it aboard *Gretel*, watching these maneuvers later was much more meaningful.

Tom Clagget steered as we sailed out toward the America's Cup course where *Courageous* and *Enterprise* were racing in the fourth day of the final trials. They were on the first weather leg when we arrived near the starting line, so we followed the practice of most casual spectators and sailed out to the wing mark to meet them on their way down.

Gordon turned the helm over to me as we passed beyond the wing mark. *Gretel* is a marvel to steer to windward. Except that there

The motley-looking crew enjoying the sunshine and a couple of cans of beer is not *Gretel*'s regulars, but representatives from the press and the International Race Committee out for an afternoon sail.

is a considerable lag in the response time, she handles with the preciseness and feel of a dinghy; yet there is the solidness and stability of a granite cathedral. She will go where you point her yet, give her head, she will track with her luff strings just lifting (indicating perfect airflow on the genoa) as if on rails. Steering a 12-Meter on the wind is one of the ultimate sailing experiences.

Gordon wanted to arrive at the reaching mark about the same time as *Courageous* (which we could see now was in the lead) and *Enterprise*. "Ready about," I called to our stalwarts forward. "Hard alee." Trying to remember the Mosbacher technique, I eased *Gretel* into the wind, accelerating the turn as it progressed and then slowing it as she came through the eye of the wind.

Gordon told me to come off on a reach, but this was a one-shot chance for me to feel how a Twelve tacks and accelerates onto the new tack. I held her about where I thought she should be if we were to continue to windward, and our efficient winch grinders sheeted the genoa in. I had only a second or two before Gordon said, "Come on, Ted, head her off," and I reluctantly turned away from the wind and called for an easing of sheets.

"Okay, Geoff," Ingate called forward, "let's see the chute."

"You mean you want us to set the *spinnaker*?" came a plaintive voice from the grinder's cockpit.

"We're got to show these guys what *Gretel* can do," was the reply from our determined captain.

The spinnaker pole crashed to the deck at one point in the set, but the chute went up and filled with relative ease. We were close reaching toward a rendezvous with the racing Twelves on an intersecting course with the growling spectator fleet—diesel engines smoking and thrusting aside a million gallons of white froth in the quarter wakes of *Courageous* and *Enterprise*.

Ingate commanded that we hold course, and as the Twelves jibed around the wing mark we were right there with them. The USCGC *Point Turner* passed us to windward, and the rest of the spectator fleet took our stern. Gordon was ecstatic. "Now you'll see what we mean by 'Gretel weather,'" he said.

The spectators gawked and waved, pleased with the unexpected novelty of having a 12-Meter in their midst, and we waved back, each of us with "Walter Mitty" thoughts—"look at us, guys, we're sailing *Gretel II*." To his credit, Ingate did not hide in the navigator's com-

International Race Committee member Bill Thomson looks competent as he trims *Gretel*'s spinnaker on the run back to Narragansett Bay.

partment while we were on public display, and in spite of our mishandling and the wallowing spectator wash, *Gretel* stayed even with the other two Twelves 100 yards to windward. And when the spectator wash subsided she gained on them. No slouch, this one!

Unable to resist the charms of his mistress any longer, Ingate took the helm, ordered the spinnaker doused as the other Twelves reached the leeward mark, and put *Gretel* on the wind again in the wake of the spectator fleet. This was *Gretel* weather for sure, and we stayed with *Courageous* and *Enterprise* tack for tack just outside the race course. Surely we were catching them—although it must be admitted that they were more interested in their own tacking duel than what we were doing. Here for the first time all summer, *Gretel* was in her element, sailing in conditions for which she was designed, and loving every minute of it.

Ingate's face seemed to cloud over as someone thinking introspective thoughts. "Do I sense a certain amount of frustration?" I asked him.

"Oh, Ted, if you only knew," was Gordon's sad reply.

The rest of the day was pleasant but anticlimactic. We broke off about halfway up the second beat and headed back toward Newport. Suddenly our interlude, our day in the sun, our momentary glory as *Gretel*'s masters was bowing to reality. Gordon had a six o'clock meeting with Alan Bond, the rest of the crew had deadlines to meet, and I had several days' writing to catch up on. But we had all had a unique experience, learning the meaning of "*Gretel* weather" firsthand.

Chapter XV THE AMERICA'S CUP RACES, SEPTEMBER 1977

September 13, 1977—This is the day that all of the previous activity has led to. This is the climax of months of effort. It is "put up" day for the volumes of written and spoken words. It is the bottom line on the ledger of millions of dollars spent. It is the last frame of miles of exposed film. It is the day we see if the challenger is worthy, if the defender is ready. This day arrives to each America's Cup with a heightened sense of suspense. Surely *this* time the match will be even. Surely *this* time the challenger will at least shake the foundations of the New York Yacht Club.

The Twelves leave their respective docks. The cannon booms from Bannister's Wharf. There is a loud and enthusiastic salute for each as the people lining the docks cheer and wave and the yachts in the harbor blast their horns. The Committee boat *Bobarra* leaves Goat Island, the Coast Guard cutters move out, and the spectator fleet begins filing past Fort Adams. Hundreds of vessels of all shapes and sizes crowd through the narrow passage between Beavertail and Castle Hill heading out Narragansett Bay. The big cruisers forge ahead pushing white bow waves and trailing chevrons of rolling wakes. The auxiliaries plod along under power and roll in the confused water.

The big cruisers forge ahead, pushing white bow waves and trailing chevrons of rolling wakes.

The large Coast Guard and navy ships glide effortlessly down the bay picking their way through the multitude of spectators. The Coast Guard's proud square-rigged ship *Eagle* moves incongruously under power, her yards squared up, her sails furled. Her silhouette is matched in miniature by the brigantine *Black Pearl* and the topsail schooner *Shenandoah*, and a touch of history is added by the replica of the Revolutionary War sloop *Providence* under full sail. Amid the throng is the red-hulled catamaran *Hel-Cat* with 85 reporters, pencils and cameras poised, waiting to tell the world—what?

The Twelves arrive at the starting area, hoist mainsails, and drop tows. The *Bobarra* sets the line and drops anchor on station. The Coast Guard and navy ships form a protective diamond around the course area. The privileged spectators, with their red and orange numbered flags, form up behind the USCGC *Point Turner*, and the small boats buzz back and forth chasing wayward spectators out of the restricted area.

Aboard the *Hel-Cat* people stake out places at the rail. Turner steers *Courageous* close aboard and doffs his cap to the press. Minutes later *Australia* crosses *Hel-Cat* and Robins waves.

At eleven-fifty there is a horn from the *Bobarra*. Simultaneously the Committee breaks out the course signal and the two mark boats spring to life as they roar off on diverging courses to set the windward and reaching marks. There is a babble aboard *Hel-Cat*. "What's the course?" "Who can read the code flags?" "What's a blue flag with some white in it ?" As if they themselves were responsible for locating the first mark, there is an eagerness to know all there is to know. Then *Hel-Cat*'s Captain Glas bellows over the loudspeaker that the course is ". . . two, two, five. Two, two, five degrees to the first mark."

Turner steers *Courageous* close aboard the press boat.

Minutes later, *Australia* crosses *Hel-Cat* and Robins waves.

At noon *Bobarra* fires a gun and hoists a yellow shape. Aboard *Hel-Cat* dozens of thumbs punch dozens of stopwatches, all with a fervor equal to that of the navigators aboard the Twelves as if each observer were making the start himself. Those without stopwatches pester their neighbors, "How much time now?" "Ah, nine minutes, fifty-four seconds."

The Twelves come closer to each other, circling like gladiators measuring each other's steps. The Twelves lock together, probing for a weakness. "Robins is turning faster!" "Look, he's gaining . . ." "What's he doing now?" "How much time left?" "Ah, seven fifteen."

As the seconds tick away, ten thousand minds wonder which yacht will be ahead when the gun goes. Which will have the advantage? Can he hold it? Will he be faster upwind? ". . . FIVE, FOUR, THREE," someone counts down the seconds, "TWO, ONE, GUN!" The defender is to windward. The challenger is falling behind. The challenger tacks. The defender covers. The challenger tacks again. The America's Cup is all over. . . .

This time it was to be no different. The yachts came together well below the starting line, and as they did so, *Courageous* tacked to windward and ahead of *Australia*. With approximately 2½ minutes to go, both boats headed toward the line on starboard tack. *Courageous* killing way slightly so as to fall just aft of abeam of *Australia*. As they got nearer the line, with about a minute to go, it became apparent that if they went for it, they would both be early. Both boats slowed slightly, and at about 30 seconds, *Courageous*, on *Australia's* weather quarter, tacked onto port. *Australia* bore off down the line on starboard, and when they crossed the line, *Australia* was 12 seconds behind the gun and *Courageous* 28 seconds behind. *Courageous* was off to the westward, the favored side of the first beat, however, and soon *Australia* tacked to sail after her rival to windward and behind. Gradually *Australia* seemed to fall down closer to *Courageous*, with *Courageous* pointing up higher underneath. Five minutes after the start, it looked like *Courageous* could cross if she were to tack. They kept on on the port tack sailing toward the starboard tack lay line, toward the west, *Courageous* protecting herself against the expected header.

At 10 minutes, they were still on this tack, *Courageous* ahead and to leeward still, but now definitely being able to cross. At 15 minutes it was even more apparent. *Courageous* had been moving closer to the wind and moving out ahead of her rival.

The reason for this is hard to say, except that *Courageous's* genoa appeared to match her mainsail much better than *Australia's*. The Australians had allowed the head of the genoa to fall off up high so that it didn't seem to have the drive of the other boat's. At about 17 minutes, *Courageous* tacked and crossed *Australia*. *Australia* tacked in a safe leeward position, but she was too late and *Courageous* ground over her to blanket her. *Australia* tacked away and *Courageous* let her get away to the west now covering the eastern side of the course. And that's the way it went for the balance of the leg up to the weather mark, both boats nearing the lay line, but not quite getting there, *Australia* tacking to the west, *Courageous* tacking to the east with *Australia* tacking out of phase on opposite tacks.

At the weather mark, the margin was 1:08, and it appeared that the race was in the bag for the defender. The first reach was uneventful, and at the wing mark, the margin was 1:16. At the leeward mark following the second reach it was 1:23. *Courageous* rounded the mark and continued on port tack toward the starboard tack lay line, and did not tack until *Australia* did, both boats going to starboard. This time they worked more toward the port tack line working toward the east, and at the second weather mark the margin was 1:12.

On the downward leg, it was thought that *Australia's* longer waterline would enable her to catch up. Both boats headed straight downwind, jibing only before reaching the leeward mark. There was no attempt by *Australia* to outmaneuver *Courageous*, and at the end of the run the margin was 1:18. Turner continued his loose cover, protecting the east side of the course on the final beat to the finish where the margin was 1:28.

The wind appeared to pick up at the finish to about 12 to 15 knots. The sea was quite rough mostly due to the spectator fleet. Jack Walker, aboard the press boat *Hel Cat* looking through the windows in the cabin said, "When you can see one boat out one window, and the other boat out the other window, you're in big trouble." About halfway through the course, we were talking about the possibilities of a *Gretel III* challenge. Walker said, "The race isn't half over, and you're talking about next time. I've been suckered in again. I've got to save another $2,000 for 1980."

Reports of this race in the press emphasize that *Australia* was ahead at the start because she crossed the starting line before *Courageous*. This would have been significant had they been on the same tack, but since they had split tacks, the fact that the times were different is of very little, if any significance. Granted *Australia* would have been closer to the windward mark (assuming a perfectly set starting line) but whether she was better or worse than *Courageous* cannot be judged by the time alone. The fact that *Courageous* was headed in the direction her crew wanted to sail (to the west) and the fact that *Australia*, after crossing the line on the starboard tack (heading south) came onto the port tack with *Courageous*, would indicate that the challenger wanted to be on that side of the course also.

Therefore, the advantage is one of position, and on that basis, one would have to say that *Courageous* had the better start although she crossed the starting line later than *Australia*. *Courageous* ended up in a position going toward the breeze—toward the direction of the wind shifts—and she was able to work up underneath *Australia* from that position. Seventeen minutes after the start, *Courageous* was able to tack and cross the Australian boat. That was the boat race. Thereafter there was nothing *Australia* could do to pass unless *Courageous* made an error, and she did not. *Australia*'s only error was the selection of the wrong headsail. Her skipper, Noel Robins, said they had left the sail that they should have had "in the box" making it sound as if they did not have the sail they would have liked to have had on board with them.

At the press conference following the race, Ted Turner started out being much more sedate and straightforward than he had been earlier in the summer. But later he loosened up a bit with a couple of good quips. Somebody asked him if Bowe Kuhn (baseball commissioner) was coming to Newport, and Turner said, "I hope he does, and I'll push him in. Seriously, I have heard that he might come to Newport, but I think it will take a lot of courage."

The second race began with a fever pitch of excitement and ended that way as well. But between the first weather leg and the finish, it was a dreadful ho-hum affair with *Courageous* having a commanding lead. Both boats hooked up early at the start, *Courageous* switching the positions from the first race, positioned herself to leeward of *Australia* and was able to get well in control. It was too early for *Courageous* to push *Australia* above the line, and at about the five-minute mark, she bore away, with *Australia* bearing away on her stern. There was a series of tacks and jibes and when they came out once again, heading for the line on the starboard tack, *Australia* was underneath and *Courageous* was on top. They reversed position again with *Courageous* to leeward and slightly ahead as the boats went for the line. *Courageous* was a bit early and was forced to run down the line. Both boats had waited until about 30 seconds before falling off, and it appeared that *Australia* accelerated more quickly and drove over the top of *Courageous* well to windward.

It didn't look good for the defender. *Australia* moved out to windward drawing almost abeam of *Courageous*, and it appeared for a while that she would move into the lead. But then suddenly *Australia* tacked and in light winds, fell way off. *Courageous* continued on the starboard tack and appeared to get a lift. The wind was shifty. At first it would appear that one boat was ahead and then the other. Just when it looked like *Courageous* had a commanding lead, *Australia* tacked and took it all back. *Courageous* moved into a new breeze and pulled away. She tacked to consolidate her position, and then tacked again just to leeward of *Australia*. From then on it was a parade to the mark, but very close. The Twelves would first be lifted, then headed. At times they would converge, the windward boat would be headed so that it appeared that they would come together. Then they would head in opposite directions with the windward boat lifted and the leeward boat headed.

As they approached the mark, it was crucial for *Australia* to just lay and *Courageous* not to. A lift would favor *Courageous*. She would get to the mark ahead, although the distance would be closed slightly. A header would also favor *Courageous*. She could then tack and cross ahead of *Australia*. The best situation for *Australia* would be that she could fetch the mark and *Courageous* could not. For a while it looked as though that is exactly what would happen, and there were quick bets being made among the press on the *Hel-Cat* as to who would be ahead and what the margin would be. Two bets that I heard were *Courageous* by three seconds and *Australia* by seven seconds. Just as *Courageous* approached the mark, she got the lift that allowed her to fetch, and within about five boat lengths, you could see that her spinnaker pole was raised and she was assured of being able to lay the mark. *Courageous* rounded first, set her chute, followed 49 seconds later by *Australia*. When they rounded the mark, *Australia* jibed, the wind had shifted so that instead of the leg being a starboard tack reach, it had become a run, and most of the leg was sailed with the spinnaker poles well aft on the port side.

Australia seemed to get the better of the situation coming to the wing mark, and when they rounded, now taking down their spinnakers and going for the leeward mark on their genoas, she was very close, being only 22 seconds behind. It was a parade to the bottom mark, and when they got there, the Race Committee signaled a course change to 110° representing a wind shift of about 60°. *Courageous* rounded with a comfortable lead, and headed up close hauled on the port tack which was not very much further from the direction she had been sailing to the mark. *Australia* rounded and tacked. *Courageous* covered. For a while it appeared that it would be a similar situation to the first leg, with *Australia* being very close, the spectators not knowing from one moment to the next which boat would cross the other if they were to converge.

For a time *Australia* was well off on the port tack, and *Courageous* on the starboard tack repeating a pattern we had seen earlier in the trials in the racing between *Sverige* and *Australia*. But suddenly there was a wide margin. *Courageous* moved well ahead, and as the leg proceeded very, very slowly, it became apparent that the defender was either much faster, or had taken advantage of wind shifts much better. At the weather mark, the margin was a whopping 10:45. But as *Courageous* rounded, her speed dropped considerably, and she was up to almost 45° off course in order to get her spinnaker filled. Aus-

tralia rounded, set her chute, and went off on the starboard tack. They paraded down the course first on one jibe and then the other, with *Courageous* in front covering each move *Australia* made.

The question was raised as to whether the boats would finish within the time limit (they had to finish within five-and-a-half hours). But it would seem they had plenty of time. Once they got down to the leeward mark, the boats would move quite a bit faster, and we felt sure that *Courageous* would be able to preserve her lead and to finish the race. For the last half of the last leg, the wind was extremely light, and while *Courageous* was well ahead, it became a race to the finish. As the countdown got into minutes . . . three minutes, then two-and-a-half minutes . . . it looked like *Courageous* could fetch. No, she didn't make it. Finally, as if it had been a photo finish, with everyone on their feet, the Committee fired two guns. The time limit had expired. A great cheer went up from the *Pat C VII* with Alan Bond's contingent aboard, and they went over to congratulate *Australia* for having waited out the clock.

The second attempt to run the second race was started with winds from the south at eight to ten knots with a light rain starting just before the hoisting of the course signals. As they had done before, the two boats came together at about the 10-minute gun dead to leeward of the Race Committee boat. *Courageous* was able to get on *Australia*'s stern as they reached away from the line on port tack. Then *Courageous* jibed away and *Australia* followed, coming on the wind just to windward of Turner's yacht. *Courageous* assumed a position of about a boat length to leeward and slightly ahead, just enough to keep her wind clear.

At the five-minute gun, both boats were stalled about 150 yards to leeward of the Committee boat. They jogged slowly toward the line, just maintaining way with the leaches of their mainsails; as they approached closer to the line, *Courageous* was in a position to force *Australia* over early. *Australia* crossed the line with about a minute and forty-five seconds to go, tacked to port, and dipped down back to the line just short of the Committee boat. *Courageous* followed, and the two sailed underneath the Committee boat. *Courageous* jibed, *Australia* tacked, and the two boats apprached the line, crossing almost exactly even, *Courageous* to leeward and ahead, *Australia* to windward and behind.

The yachts were about even for about half of the first weather

As they approached the line, *Courageous* was in position to force
Australia over early . . . (*Dan Nerney photo*)

When they converged, *Courageous* was able to clear
Australia by about two lengths. (*Dan Nerney photo*)

Courageous led *Australia* as they headed down the first
reach for the wing mark. (*Dan Nerney photo*)

leg. Then *Australia* tacked to port. Turner held on for a while and then followed. *Australia* tacked and they converged once more; this time *Courageous* tacked to leeward of *Australia*. *Australia* tacked away. After a short interval, *Courageous* tacked to port and when they converged, *Courageous* was able to clear *Australia*, which was on starboard tack with the right-of-way. *Courageous* tacked directly in front and about half a boat length to windward, and *Australia* tacked away. They split for about five minutes, then Turner tacked to port and *Australia* continued on a port tack. After a five-minute interval, the wind began to lighten considerably.

Suddenly it was clear that *Courageous* had a substantial lead. When they reached the weather mark, *Courageous* was two minutes ahead, and it appeared that the race was over. The lead was two minutes at the reaching mark, and the boats remained substantially even througout the second reach and the second beat. *Australia* closed the distance considerably on the run, and was 1:04 behind *Courageous* at the bottom mark. But there was very little the Australians could do to break away from the close cover put on them by Turner in the final beat. The boats never were very far apart, and *Australia* finished 1:06 behind *Courageous*.

The outcome of the race was never in doubt, and it was not a very exciting one to watch. Perhaps some of the dampening effect came from the skies which were cloudy all day and sprinkled the course with intermittent rain. The spectator fleet, which was quite large at the start in spite of the inclement weather, had dwindled to less than 100 boats at the finish. The fact that *Australia* was able to pick up time on the run, and did not lose anything on either the second or the third beat, was an encouraging sign for her. But up to this point, she had not been able to put together a winning combination on the first weather leg. If they could only manage to be ahead at the end of the first beat, it appeared they could stay there and win a race. However, at this point most observers felt that it would be another four to nothing America's Cup.

The third race started on a cloudy, foggy, drizzly September 17. The wind was from the south-southwest at about eight knots at the start. *Courageous* and *Australia* came together about six minutes before the start again to leeward of the Committee boat. *Australia* on starboard forced *Courageous* about, then Turner jibed slowly, Robins letting him go, and Turner tacked underneath *Australia*. In about five minutes, the two yachts were about four lengths apart heading slowly toward the line on starboard tack. With three-and-a-half minutes to go, *Australia* tacked. *Courageous* luffed and didn't tack. Thirty seconds later, *Australia* tacked again and Turner tacked to starboard. The two yachts went for the line to cross on the starboard tack with *Courageous* ahead and to leeward. Just at the gun, but before crossing the line, *Australia* went off on port tack. *Courageous* held on starboard tack for about forty-five seconds, and then tacked over to port on *Australia's* weather quarter. At that point, both boats seemed to be lifted, giving a substantial advantage to *Courageous*. But six minutes later, both yachts were headed, and *Australia* looked like she could tack on starboard and cross *Courageous*. She did not. She held on. The yachts sailed into an increasing header seven-and-a-half minutes after the start, but again, *Australia* failed to tack and take advantage of her position. This was the crucial turning point of the race. In spite of the header, *Courageous* continued to point and foot well, and just 10 minutes after the start, the two yachts were lifted back toward their original heading and *Courageous* was in a commanding lead. Approaching the lay line, *Australia* tacked, and *Courageous* crossed with a substantial margin and then covered the Australians. The yachts were lifted again on starboard tack so that *Australia* was pointed above *Courageous's* starboard quarter. Nevertheless, as they were very near the lay line, this wind shift did not help. *Courageous* was in perfect position so that neither a header nor a lift would favor the yacht behind. That was virtually the yacht race.

The wind lightened on the first reach and swung more to the southwest, so that both yachts jibed at one point and took the reaching mark wide. The wind returned for the second beat, and the two yachts fell into a pattern very much like the previous race.

The margin at the end of the second beat was over three minutes. Once again, *Australia* appeared to take about a minute off her rival on the downwind leg. But this advantage is largely an imaginary one. In the light airs that prevailed, the yachts move very much faster sailing to windward than they do downwind.

Once again the Australian yacht appeared to be almost as fast as her rival, but the race was lost in a tactical decision in the first windward leg. Noel Robins failed to take the race to his opponent. He failed to capitalize on the only opportunity presented him in the race and thereafter there was no contest.

Prior to the start of this race, the skipper of the Coast Guard cutter *Cape Cross* met Ted Turner. "If you win," he told Turner, "I'll play the 'Theme from Rocky' as you cross the finish line." No doubt Turner forgot about the conversation, but as *Courageous* approached the finish, there was the *Cape Cross* guarding the leeward end. Her loud hailer was cranked up full blast, and the stirring music blared out over the water sending shivers down the spine. *Courageous* crossed the line, the gun sounded from *Bobarra*, and Turner circled *Courageous* around the *Cape Cross*, bowing and doffing his cap to the cheers of the surrounding spectators.

By missing his opportunity to take the initiative in the third race Noel Robins conceded the America's Cup to the defender. At the press conference following that race, Robins said that the header which favored *Australia* just after the start was not sufficient to allow him to cross *Courageous*. Aboard the *Hel-Cat* it appeared certain that *Australia* was ahead about seven-and-a-half minutes after the start, but it must be understood that a spectator cannot tell what will happen in a crossing situation as well as the competitor can. Besides, Robins would have to say that he couldn't cross, otherwise what excuse was left for not tacking at that time. However, he is still subject to the same criticism for not tacking on the header whether he could cross or not. By tacking when headed, Robins would have positioned *Australia* much closer to *Courageous*. *Courageous* would have had to make a covering tack if she crossed or a tack to leeward if she couldn't. Either way it would have been better than holding on hoping for an additional header. Even if the shift continued after she tacked, *Australia* would have been in position to take advantage of the further shift. Whichever way the wind shifted, Robins would have had the initiative which would have allowed him to force *Courageous* into unfavorable positions. By failing to take the initiative, *Australia* settled for a miracle to give them the Cup. However, it's easy to be a "Monday morning quarterback."

While the fourth race was held in weather the Australians kept hoping would be better for them, there was little doubt in anyone's mind what would happen. If *Australia* could ever get into position where she could blanket *Courageous*, things might be different, but Turner and his crew were too good. The yachts were even at the start. *Australia* was ahead and to leeward as they crossed on port tack in the moderate westerly wind. Both yachts tacked to starboard shortly after the start with *Courageous* assuming the ahead-and-to-leeward position. Perhaps fearing that they would fall down in the defender's wake, *Australia* tacked again to port, *Courageous* held on for about two minutes. When the yachts converged—*Courageous* on port tack, *Australia* on starboard—*Courageous* was ahead by two lengths. She rounded the windward mark with a lead of 44 seconds, which was extended to 56 seconds at the bottom mark. By the end of the second weather leg, *Courageous* had a 2:11 lead, and she finished 2:25 ahead of *Australia*.

While the record book will show this series as another four to nothing rout, it was close in many ways. The boats were very close in speed. Gordon Ingate said later that he was sure the hulls were equal, that the difference was in the crew and the sails. Whether or not this is true, the races followed the pattern of the summer. Times and distances were very close throughout the series, just as they had been among all the contenders. However, the challenger proved to be just a trifle slower in the all-important opening moments of each race.

During the America's Cup, ads for another event said of Olympic Gold Medal gymnast Nadia Comaniche, "In an imperfect world, only she has attained perfection." However, *Courageous* sailed a perfect series. Her crew did not make a single mistake that was discernable to her competitor or to the spectators. The "only slightly imperfect" Australians had no chance.

Any similarity between Nadia Comaniche and Ted Turner ends there, however. Following the race, pandemonium broke out among the spectator fleet. They crowded around *Courageous*, and their hero—whom Barbara Lloyd said had ". . . rocketed from famous to superstar . . ."—stood on *Courageous*'s aft deck to receive their adulation.

The victors doused their genoa—as Turner and Jobson waved to the converging crowd—and *Courageous* ducked behind the protective flank of the Coast Guard.

Australia's crew arrives by Whaler to give their congratulations to *Courageous* following the final race. Noel Robins acknowledges cheers with a wave. *Australia's* co-designer, Ben Lexan, is in front of Robins (in white shirt).

An hour later, as both Twelves moved slowly into the harbor surrounded by spectator craft and protected by a phalanx of water-spouting Coast Guard cutters, a crowd of thousands awaited Turner and his crew. The channel in front of Bannister's Wharf was choked with boats which had to be moved back by the Coast Guard and the Harbormaster to allow *Courageous* and her tender to enter the dock area.

The crowd went wild, cheering and waving. Horns blared from all over the harbor. Small boats rammed toward Bannister's Wharf until you could have walked across them from Aquidneck Lobster Company to *Courageous*. As soon as *Courageous* was secure, the crew started going into the water—Turner, Jobson, Doyle, and the rest by one's, two's and three's. Alas, nobody pushed "the big Loom" so he jumped in himself. The *Courageous* crew had agreed on the way into the harbor that they would not throw Loomis overboard when they got in.

New York Yacht Club Commodore Bob McCullough came aboard to congratulate *Courageous*, and he went into the water. However, the commodore had anticipated this and had left his jacket behind. Vice Commodore Harry Anderson, who followed McCullough, had not taken that precaution. Harry managed to get to the foredeck of *Courageous* and it appeared that his rank and decorum would be accorded due respect. He seemed oblivious to the possibility that he, too, would get dunked. Suddenly, he was bobbing to the surface and reaching for his hat. The vice commodore did not

Bob McCullough (in white shirt), commodore of the New York Yacht Club . . .

Gets dunked by an animated Aussie . . .

Much to the delight of wet Alan Bond (center).

The commodore gets a helping hand from Vice Commodore Harry Anderson. For a while it appeared that Anderson, replete with his double-breasted yachting jacket, club tie, and straw hat, would avoid a dunking . . .

But such was not the case!

Having exchanged shirts and dunkings, Ted Turner gives Alan Bond a helping hand back aboard *Courageous*. (*Jack Walker photo*)

look pleased as he swam for the float, his NYYC straw hat jammed back on top of his head.

When the Aussies arrived they went into the water too, and then the crews exchanged shirts—an America's Cup tradition. The Race Committee arrived and received the same fate as the commodore and vice commodore. In addition, the Race Committee members were relieved of their neckties which became souvenirs of several Australian crew members.

Of course, the *Courageous* crew had champagne with which to celebrate on the way in from the race course. More appeared when they got to the dock, and the Swedes sent over some aquavit for Turner. Champagne, aquavit, beer, it all went down the same way— gurgled from an upended bottle or can. When everyone had been in the water, some several times, Turner got himself up on the dock and made a determined—if somewhat glassy-eyed—march to the

Ted Turner and an *Australia* crew member, having exchanged toasts, do a dance on *Courageous*'s foredeck.

With a dry shirt and a happy grin, Turner makes his way through the crowd on Bannister's Wharf to pay his respects to the America's Cup Committee aboard their yacht. Even *Independence*, suspended high above the water, and her hoisting rig get used as perches by photographers and spectators.

America's Cup Committee's boat, which was tied up at the end of Bannister's Wharf along with half a dozen others. Turner disappeared into the flying bridge, was seen to shake hands with several officials, and then he was back down on the dock.

From Bannister's Wharf Turner and his followers wove their way to the Armory through a sea of people. The press conference was jammed. Bill Ficker, Alan Bond, Noel Robins, and Ben Lexan were already there, and a noisy crowd awaited Turner. By now the champagne and the aquavit were beginning to take their toll. Turner made his way down America's Cup Avenue to Thames Street with a smiling Newport policeman on either arm. At one point Ted complained that he was being held too tightly, but when the officer let go and Turner's knees began to buckle Ted changed his mind. "You'd better hang on," he said.

They surged into the Armory accompanied by the roar of the crowd inside and followed by the mob outside that had paraded down the street behind Turner. Ted sat down behind the microphones and

As a final act of a watery celebration, firemen turn their hoses on the crowd and the 12-Meter crews.

plopped two bottles of aquavit in front of him. A photographer trying to get a picture removed the bottles—placing them on the platform in front of the speaker's table—and Turner disappeared under
the table to retrieve his bottles of pale gold liquid. All of this was
accompanied by laughter and applause.

I found myself seated next to Janie Turner. "My mother is not
going to like this," she shouted over the hub-bub. "She doesn't like
alcohol."

"That's all right," I said, "it looks like it's going to be a very
short night."

"About 15 minutes," Janie agreed. "You know he didn't even
recognize me when he came in—walked right by me."

In spite of his state, and who can blame him for that, Turner
managed to say nice things about his former opponents. "I never
raced against such good sportsmen as my friends from Australia," Turner managed to say in clear but measured words. "I love the Australians . . . I love everybody in the room."

"I love the Australians . . . I love
everybody in the room," Ted Turner
tells the press conference audience—an
empty bottle of aquavit in his hands—
while Gary Jobson (left), Bill Flicker
(*Intrepid*'s skipper in 1970), Alan
Bond, Noel Robins, and other crew
members (standing) look on.

Moments later, Turner's crew hoists him up on their shoulders and carries him out of the Armory—home to sleep it off!

It was not really so much a press conference as a celebration. Alan Bond managed to get in a few words, as did Noel Robins, but all attention was focused on the superstar from Atlanta. Turner looked like he was about to say something else, when his crew swept him up on their shoulders and carried him out of the Armory, out into oblivion.

Immediately following Turner's departure from the Armory, there was a prize award ceremony at the Ida Lewis Yacht Club. Turner, of course, did not make it, but Lee Loomis was there giving his speech about how Ted Hood was the real hero, much to Hood's obvious embarrassment.

It was a fine, relaxed social affair with which to wind up the summer. Toasts were raised, farewells were said, and while the merri-

Ted Turner being escorted (held upright) by two Newport policemen following his victory over *Australia* and his celebration thereof. (*UPI photo*)

ment continued on the Ida Lewis porch a figure could be seen headed for shore down the long dock from the island clubhouse. It was Noel Robins, all alone, swinging his crippled legs one in front of the other.

"Each of us deals with losing in his own way," said Gordon Ingate, still dealing with it himself, "I watched Noel walking down that dock alone and I tried to imagine what he must have been thinking."

The press listens to the answers to written questions submitted to the 12-Meter skippers before the press conference in the Rhode Island Armory, which served as press headquarters for the summer.

Courageous 1977, defender of the America's Cup. (Dan Nerney photo)

Chapter *XVI* THE FUTURE

Once again the Americans had proven that the America's Cup is almost impossible to win. But the challengers keep coming, and the defenders keep putting it on the line. Why?

It is relatively easy to understand the motivation of a challenger. The amount of money required is really not an issue. Either it is obtained or it is not. None of the people involved is likely to go broke because of a challenge. The dollars, francs, and kroner may be dear, but they come from expendable funds. The amount of money needed adds to the quest, making it more important to the challenger than, say, a Soling World Championship.

The challenger may be up against fearful odds—a 126-year winning streak is awesome—but the greater the odds, the sweeter the victory if it is achieved. Therefore, the challenger can rationalize the possibility of defeat because it is, after all, expected. Everyone who has tried to win the America's Cup before has been beaten. If he gets closer than anyone ever has, that is a victory in itself. If he should win, he becomes the first. He has been able to do what no one else has done in the entire history of the sport of sailing—the America's

Cup being almost as old as the sport itself. Can there be a bigger challenge anywhere?

The defender must have a completely different attitude. He must put forward almost superhuman effort. The slightest oversight can spell disaster. It is all on the line, and the challengers keep getting better and better. The chances of defeat keep increasing, but if he wins he has merely done what was expected of him. Lots of people before him have been able to do what he has done—most of them with a disdainful yawn while doing it. But, if he should lose . . . It would be the ultimate personal disaster.

Ted Turner certainly proved that he was capable of putting together a superb effort. His was near perfection. When it is considered that at the beginning he was given very little chance—considered by many to be a bit of a clown—he silenced his detractors decisively. Turner's effort was all the greater because he did not do it alone. It was the effort of a cohesive team. He picked his crew and he let each crew member do his job. As this is written, it is too close to the event to view Turner's effort in full perspective, but there are signs that when compared to previous America's Cup defense efforts, this one may have been the most thorough, the best executed.

Why, then, should Ted Turner be talking about doing it again even before his name is engraved on the trophy? What is there left to prove? Yet, Turner is determined to do it again, and is already planning a defense effort for 1980.

Alan Bond has said he will be back. His challenge was surely a worthy one. His yacht was exceptional—almost good enough—perhaps more than good enough had *Australia* not had the misfortune to meet Turner's *Courageous*.

Bond still has a few problems with the America's Cup, however. He apparently does not fully understand what it is, and until he does he is bound to have difficulty winning it. At the closing press conference Bond reiterated his position of 1974 when he complained that he could not obtain the excellence in sails that the defender displayed. Bond wants equal access to American sailcloth and sailmakers. But it must be understood that the America's Cup is not a class championship to determine who are the best sailors. It is, and has always been, a contest to see which country can put together the best combination of design, building, and sailing skills in the largest and most prestigious yachts. Already this principle has been compromised by allowing challengers to acquire sails, cloth, and hardware from countries other than their own. Indeed, all the challengers except *Gretel II* used Barient winches which were designed and manufactured in the U.S. The rationale was that these winches are available worldwide and should therefore be allowed aboard challengers. To bow to Bond's request would be to change the America's Cup, to cheapen it, to make it just like so many other competitions. As it is, it is unique, and it is the combination of skills required to win or to keep it which is its essential quality.

"But you Americans have so much, your country is so big, you are impossible to beat." These are the pleadings of Bond in the frustration of his two losses. But that is exactly what makes the challenge worthwhile.

What about the French? The baron has done more than anyone since Sir Thomas Lipton for the spirit of America's Cup racing. His is a single effort—not the product of syndicates. His challenger, and he has really had only *France I*, has not been good enough to get to the finals in three tries, but he remains undaunted. There is, probably, something in the French character that lacks the killer instincts necessary to win the America's Cup. This is not a derogation; perhaps this lack is a virtue, depending on one's own values. Even losing, the French and the baron himself seem to enjoy the challenge. They are great sportsmen.

Bruno Bich, the baron's son, is now a U.S. citizen and a member of the New York Yacht Club. Bruno says he will build his own 12-Meter to *defend* the Cup and race against his father. That event will be worth the price of admission!

The Swedes will be back, although they went home looking like they'd been hit by a freight train. For them the America's Cup was a sobering experience, but it was an experience from which they learned much. They have a good chance to win the Cup next time.

The day after *Gretel II* was eliminated from the semifinals their syndicate members and supporters sported buttons which read, "G III." They did not go home with their tails dragging, but all who could stayed until the America's Cup was over. They will return.

Gordon Ingate, who both skippered *Gretel II* and spearheaded the syndicate, has a curious philosophy about the America's Cup. The *Gretel II* effort in 1977 was aimed more at maintaining Australia's image than winning the Cup, and when Ingate entered *Gretel* it was to salvage two Australian challenges that had apparently collapsed. They came with a determination to do their best, and under slightly different circumstances they might have pulled it off. Yet it is difficult to imagine how Ingate could ever win the America's Cup.

"I think that probably the America's Cup should not be won. It should be competed for, but never won." Ingate's ideal would be to have it go seven races and have the defender win the last race by one second.

Newport and the America's Cup have an interwoven destiny. Even the foreign challengers feel this bond. Many of the Australians, French, and Swedes said that if they won the Cup they thought they would like to defend it in Newport. Surely such sentiments would evaporate in the harsh light of practical reality if they ever got the chance. It is difficult and expensive to mount a challenge far away from home particularly when the rules require that your boat and equipment come from there. However, the sentiment is unmistakably present. Newport and the America's Cup are inseparable.

Some day the Cup *will* be won by a challenger, and perhaps Gordon Ingate is right. When that happens it will be the end of a long era and the mystique will evaporate. Isn't it likely that the solons of the New York Yacht Club will breathe a collective sight of relief? Perhaps, instead of replacing the America's Cup with the head of the losing skipper—as Cup tradition demands—they will proclaim him a hero for releasing them from the ever-increasing burden of mounting a defense. However, as long as the Cup stays in the 44th Street clubhouse the New York Yacht Club is bound to defend it, and with each successful defense the determination to keep it intensifies. They will keep it forever if they can.

But if they can't? When an incredulous race committee watches in disbelief as the challenger crosses the finish line to win the last race. When the spectator fleet goes berserk in its congratulations of the winning challenger. When the commodore hands over the ugly urn with ceremonial dignity. When the center of the hexagonal room in which the America's Cup has stood is empty. Then the mystique will be gone. The quest which has fascinated and driven so many for so long will have disappeared like an elusive wisp. Then it will be realized that it is all over, and the "100 Guinea Cup" which has been prized and sought after for so long will join a multitude of old silver collecting dust on some yacht club's trophy shelf.

But it hasn't happened yet. The America's Cup remains firmly bolted to its oak table in a place of sacred honor at the New York Yacht Club.

And there it must remain.

Courageous and *Australia* (right) beating for the finish line.

APPENDICES

CONDITIONS GOVERNING THE SELECTION OF THE CHALLENGER

CONDITIONS

GOVERNING THE RACES FOR A MATCH TO SELECT

A CHALLENGING YACHT

FOR THE AMERICA'S CUP 1977

The Conditions which shall govern the races for the match between the Yacht Club d'Hyeres, the Royal Göteborg Yacht Club, the Sun City Yacht Club, and the Royal Sydney Yacht Squadron in the International Twelve Metre Class to select a challenger for the 1977 America's Cup, as agreed upon by the above yacht clubs, are as follows:

NOTE: Whenever time is referred to in these Conditions, it is Eastern Daylight Savings Time.

1. DATE AND NUMBER OF RACES

a. Round Robin

A Round Robin series between the four contestants will take place from August 4 to August 9, 1977.

Two races will be scheduled each day for each contestant of approximately one-half the length of the standard America's Cup course as described in Section 2 hereof.

Each yacht will race each of the other yachts three times for a total of nine races, one point being awarded for each race won. The original pairing will be decided by a draw and will then follow a rotation plan established by the race committee.

A yacht not participating in one or several or all races of the Round Robin will be awarded zero point for each race in which it did not participate, but will not be eliminated and may participate in the Semi-Finals. In the Round Robin, if only one yacht starts in a division it will not be necessary for that yacht to complete the course. There will be no lay days in the Round Robin.

b. SEMI-FINALS

The result of the Round Robin will decide the pairing of the Semi-Finals. The boat having won the greatest number of races during the Round Robin will meet the boat having won the least races in the Round Robin, while the boats having won the second and third most races will meet each other. In the event of a tie in the Round Robin, the placing shall be decided in favor of the boat having the most wins against the boat he is tied with. In the event of a direct tie between the boats involved, the result of the first race shall be disregarded. In the event that two boats were still tied, the placing shall be decided by the toss of a coin.

The first race of the Semi-Finals shall be sailed on August 11, 1977, and the races shall be sailed on every succeeding day; provided, however, that immediately at the conclusion of each race or upon a race being postponed for the day or abandoned the Race Committee shall inquire of each contestant whether he is willing to start the next day, and each contestant shall reply within one hour. Should either contestant reply in the negative, one day shall intervene before starting the next race.

However, each contestant shall only be entitled to request two lay days in the course of the Semi-Finals, except that a third day may be requested by each contestant after she has completed four races. *August 22, 1977 shall not be used as a lay day.*

The Semi-Finals shall be decided by the best four out of seven races of *each* pair. Should the Semi-Finals be incomplete by August 22, 1977 (on the conclusion of any race held that day), the Semi-Finals will be decided by the most races won. In the event of a *tie* the result of the first race in each pairing shall be disregarded in order to determine the two winners of the Semi-Finals.

c. FINALS

The first race of the Finals shall be sailed on August 25, 1977, unless the Semi-Finals are finished in advance of August 22, 1977. In this situation, the start of the Finals will be advanced by one day for each three days that the Semi-Finals are finished in advance of August 22, 1977.

The races shall be sailed on every succeeding day; provided however, that immediately at the conclusion of each race or upon a race being postponed for the day or abandoned the Race Committee shall inquire of each contestant whether he is willing to start the next day, and each contestant shall reply within one hour. Should either contestant reply in the negative, one day shall intervene before starting the next race.

However, each contestant shall only be entitled to request two lay days in the course of the Finals, except that a third day may be requested by each contestant after four races have been completed. *September 8, 1977 shall not be used as a lay day.*

The Finals shall be decided by the best four out of seven races. Should the Finals be incomplete by September 8, 1977 (on the conclusion of any race held that day), the Finals will be decided by the most races won. In the event of a tie the result of the first race shall be disregarded in order to determine the winner of the Finals.

2. COURSES

Races shall start at one of the Rendezvous Buoys which will become the Starting Mark, the locations and descriptions of which will be supplied in writing by the Race Committee to the competitors prior to August 4, 1977, and stipulated in the Sailing Instructions. Competitors are to be advised on the morning of each race day of the starting mark to be used that day.

Races shall be approximately 24 and 3/10 nautical miles in length (except four Round Robin series). Races shall consist of six legs. The first leg, to be approximately 4½ nautical miles in length, shall be from the Starting Mark to a mark to windward; the second leg shall be from the windward mark equidistant from the

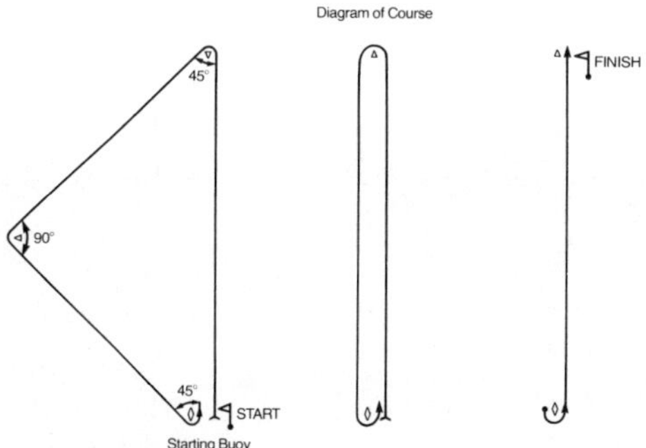

Starting Mark and the windward mark at a point on the circumference of a circle the diameter of which is the first leg; the third leg shall be from the gybe mark back to the Starting Mark; the fourth leg shall be from the Starting Mark to the windward mark; the fifth leg shall be from the windward mark to the Starting Mark; and the sixth leg shall be from the Starting Mark to the windward mark, at which the finish line shall be established.

Marks are to be left on the same hand as the Starting Mark.

The Magnetic course of the first leg shall be signaled, and the mark vessel shall be started not less than 10 minutes prior to the warning signal and will lay the *windward mark.*

The various rounds of the course will resemble the diagram on the preceding page.

There shall be included in the Sailing Instructions detailed arrangements for moving the *windward mark* after the first leg, in the event of a shift of wind, for either or both the fourth and sixth legs.

The course will not be shortened in the Semi-Finals and Finals.

3. **START**

The warning signal, unless the race is postponed by the Race Committee, shall be made as nearly as practicable at 1200 hours; and the starting signal, at 1210 hours. No race shall be started after 1410 hours.

In the Semi-Finals there shall be 10 minutes between the starts of the two pairings, and therefore the start of the first pairing shall be no later than 1355 hours.

In the Round Robin there shall be 10 minutes between starts and the first pairing will start as nearly as practicable at 1100 hours. No race shall start after 1540 hours.

4. **SIGNALS**

The warning signal shall be made ten minutes before the start. Five minutes after the warning signal the preparatory signal shall be made. Five minutes after the preparatory signal the starting signal shall be made. The time of the starting signal shall be taken as the time of the start of both yachts.

5. **POSTPONEMENTS OR ABANDONMENT**

The Race Committee in case of fog or heavy weather shall have the right to notify the contending yachts by 0900 hours on the morning of the race not to leave their moorings until notified later, either (1) to proceed to the designated Rendezvous Buoy or (2) that the race has been postponed for the day.

Except as above provided, the time of the warning signal shall not be postponed by the Race Committee except as follows:

a. In case of fog.

b. If, in its opinion, at the time appointed for the warning signal, the starting area is not sufficiently clear or the wind is too variable or too light or too strong or the sea is too rough reasonably to test the relative speed of the two yachts.

c. In case a yacht, after she has left her mooring for the start of a race and before the warning signal, is in a serious collision or accident, not the result of a defect in her hull or in her sails, rigging, gear, or the handling thereof; or in case the Race Committee is notified before the warning signal that a person on board has been seriously injured after the yacht left her mooring for the start.

The Sailing Instructions shall specify the signals to be displayed in connection with postponements for the day or until later in the day. A copy of these Sailing Instructions shall be given to each yacht prior to the start of the Round Robin.

The Race Committee may abandon a race as provided under Racing Rule 5.1 (b) because of foul weather endangering the yachts or for other reasons directly affecting safety.

6. **TIME LIMIT**

If in any race of the Semi-Finals or Finals neither yacht completes the first four legs in 4 hours, or if neither yacht completes the course in 5½ hours, such a race shall be resailed, provided the finishing date of the series is not exceeded. In the Round Robin, there will be no time limit, but the Race Committee may shorten course in order to complete a race or to sail two races per day or may abandon a race if the wind is calm.

7. **RACES RESULTING IN A TIE**

A race resulting in a tie shall be resailed *provided the finishing date of the series is not exceeded.*

8. RACING RULES OF THE INTERNATIONAL YACHT RACING UNION TO GOVERN

The 1977 Racing Rules of the International Yacht Racing Union as the same shall exist at the time of the Races shall govern the Races, except insofar as the same may be inconsistent with other provisions of this Agreement, and particularly the provisions of Article 10 hereof, except that; Yachts are deemed to be racing from the time of the warning signal.

9. COMMUNICATIONS

During a race, from the time of the warning signal for the start until the finishing line has been crossed, a yacht shall not receive any prearranged communications or make use of any prearranged indications, such sommunications or indications not being available from the same medium to both yachts, as advice or assistance in handling the yacht during the race. While racing, radio direction finders may be used but not Loran or Decca or similar navigational systems.

10. MEASUREMENT RULE OF THE INTERNATIONAL YACHT RACING UNION TO GOVERN

The Measurement Rule of the International Twelve Metre Class as established by the International Yacht Racing Union and effective March 1976, shall govern this Match. Only the Certificate of Classification issued by Lloyd's Register of Shipping shall be accepted in connection with Rule 26 of the Rating Rule.

Yachts shall comply in every respect with the requirements regarding construction and equipment contained in the Deed of Gift and the Interpreting Resolutions applying to national origin of design and construction.

Bilges shall be kept as reasonably dry as possible while racing. No devices shall be fitted or employed which would permit the tilting of the mast athwartship.

11. TIME ALLOWANCE

There shall be no time allowance.

12. RATING

Yachts shall not rate over twelve metres.

13. NAMING THE COMPETING YACHTS

At least 1 day before the first race of the Round Robin, the Yacht Club d'Hyeres shall be informed of the name of the yacht selected by each of the competing clubs.

14. ACCIDENTS

a. In case a serious accident occurs to either yacht prior to the warning signal, she shall have such time as the Committees representing the two Clubs involved shall determine to be reasonable to effect repairs before being required to start, or, if such accident occurs after the warning signal, before being required to start in the next race; but no such allowance of time to repair shall extend the Semi-Finals beyond August 22, 1977, or the Finals beyond September 8, 1977.

b. If either yacht, except as provided in Article 5, paragraph c, shall be disabled after leaving her mooring for the start of the race through a defect in her hull, or in her sails, rigging, gear or the handling thereof, in *the Semi-Finals and Finals* the other yacht shall start and continue the race within the time limit; and if finished within the time limit, that race shall be won by that yacht.

c. If through the fault of either yacht, the other be destroyed or so injured after the warning signal as to be incapable of repair in time to complete the Semi-Finals before August 22, 1977, or the Finals before September 8, 1977, and the yacht so destroyed or injured is free from fault, the division of Semi-Finals or Finals shall be awarded to her.

15. DISQUALIFICATION

If a yacht is disqualified in any race, such race shall be awarded to the other yacht, provided the race was completed within the time limit. The yacht *infringed against* shall be declared the winner if the Race Committee finds that disablement caused by the *infringement* prevented such completion.

16. REPRESENTATIVES

Each Club shall by its Committee name a representative who shall have the right to be present at all measurements and shall have, when practicable, not less than 24 hours notice thereof. A representative from each competing Club shall have the right to be on board the Race Committee boat during the races and may be consulted by the Race Committee in regard to the matters referred to in Article 5. The representative mentioned in this clause need not be the same person.

17. MEASUREMENTS

The Yacht Club d'Hyeres and the New York Yacht Club shall each select a Measurer. These two, together with a Measurer appointed by the International Yacht Racing Union, shall constitute a Measurement Committee; and the decision of that Committee on questions of measurement and on questions of interpretations of the Measurement Rule, shall be final. All measurements, except displacement, shall be taken or checked within two weeks prior to 1200 hours on August 3, 1977, by the Measurement Committee, and Measurement Certificates of all yachts shall be signed by at least two of the three Measurers composing the Measurement Committee, and shall be filed with the Race Committee no later than 1200 hours on August 1, 1977.

18. RE-MEASUREMENTS AND INSPECTIONS OF SIDE MARKS

If either yacht in any way changes her L.W.L. or sail plan as officially taken, she must obtain a re-measurement by special appointment before the next race and must report the alteration to the New York Yacht Club Measurer and to the representatives of the four Contestants' Clubs by 2100 hours of the day before the race following such alteration and must arrange with the Measurer for re-measurement and, if required, be in Brenton Cove by 0600 hours of the day of said race, and be at the disposition of the Measurer until 0700 hours if necessary for purposes of re-measurement.

If either yacht shall take on or remove ballast or dead weight, she must notify the Measurer of the New York Yacht Club and the representatives of the four Contestants' Clubs and be at the disposition of the Measurer for inspection of marks. The representatives of each Club shall have the right to be present at all re-measurements and inspections of marks and shall be given such notice thereof as time may permit; such notice shall be delivered to the Race Committee at Newport.

In the event that the Measurer is unable to obtain a measurement which he considers to be accurate before a race, a re-measurement shall be taken as soon as possible after the race; and a winning yacht so re-measured shall forfeit that race if she fails to rate Twelve Metres or less.

In the event that a yacht is out of the water and thereafter cannot be launched in time to engage in the next scheduled race, because of weather conditions or for other causes beyond its control, the representative of the Yacht Club d'Hyeres and other competing Yacht Clubs shall grant such yacht an additional day or days sufficient to allow such yacht to be launched and made ready for the next scheduled race, always provided the grant of such additional day or days does not extend the Semi-Finals beyond August 22, 1977, or the Finals beyond September 8, 1977.

Should either yacht desire to be hauled out, or should both yachts desire to be hauled out at the same time, either yacht or both yachts must have available to them Measurers and adequate facilities; and, if such facilities or Measurers are not available to either yacht or to both yachts, sufficient time must be granted by the aforesaid representatives so that either yacht or both yachts will have available adequate facilities to haul out, be measured and be launched, and time within which to complete such a maneuver.

19. DECISIONS OF THE RACE COMMITTEE

The decisions of the Race Committee taken in consultation with the representatives of the Challenging Clubs, as provided for in Article 16 and with respect to postponements and abandonments, shall be final and there shall be no appeal therefrom.

20. PROTESTS

In case of a protest between two yachts, a Protest Committee will be formed with members of the Race Committee. In case of a request for redress from the Race Committee in accordance with Racing Rule 68.5(a), a non-involved external Protest Committee will be convened.

July 23, 1977

YACHT CLUB D'HYERES

MARCEL L. BICH
Honorary Commodore

ROYAL GÖTEBORG YACHT CLUB

CHRISTER SALEN
Commodore

ROYAL SYDNEY YACHT SQUADRON

W. L. FESQ
Commodore

SUN CITY YACHT CLUB

J. B. FITZHARDINGE
Commodore

SAILING INSTRUCTIONS, AMERICA'S CUP OFFICIALS, AND SYNDICATE REPRESENTATIVES

AMERICA'S CUP 1977
SAILING INSTRUCTIONS
FOR THE
OBSERVATION TRIAL RACES, JULY 16–27
FINAL TRIALS, AUGUST 16–8 SEPTEMBER

These Races will be held under the observation of the America's Cup Committee of the New York Yacht Club.

Eligibility	Twelve Metre yachts competing for the selection as Defender of the America's Cup are elegible provided that a valid International Measurement Certificate is on file with the Race Committee.
Captains' Meeting	A Captains' Meeting for each Trial Race Series will be held on board the Race Committee's vessel BOBBARA at Goat Island in Newport at 1800 hours on 15 July and 15 August.
Rules	The 1977 IYRU Yacht Racing Rules will apply except as modified herein. Rule 32 shall not apply. Yachts will be racing from the time of their Warning Signal. Tenders must clear the starting area five minutes after course signals are displayed.
Race Rendezvous	Yachts will rendezvous at 1100 hours. A code flag (see Rendezvous Buoys) designating this location will be flown from the Ida Lewis Yacht Club by 0930 and the Race Committee will advise the yachts of this location. In addition, the Race Committee vessel will signal the designated location as it proceeds to the rendezvous by flying the appropriate code flag. Prior to 0930 the Race Committee may also advise the yachts of a postponement rendezvous time or cancellation of racing for the day.

Rendezvous Buoys | The following Code Flags will signal the intended rendezvous areas:

ALFA | Tracking System Bell Buoy "SE" 5.2 miles 185° from Brenton Reef Tower

BRAVO | Black & White Approach Buoy "NC" 2.2 miles 194.5° from Brenton Reef Tower

CHARLIE | W Or "DG-A" Fl 4 sec Buoy 5.1 miles 137° from Brenton Reef Tower

DELTA | W Or "DG-B" FL 4 sec Buoy 4.1 miles 140° from Brenton Reef Tower

ECHO | America's Cup Buoy 7.9 miles 150° from Brenton Reef Tower

FOXTROT | America's Cup Trial Buoy 8.1 miles 194.5° from Brenton Reef Tower

GOLF | R "2" Fl 4 sec Whistle, 1.2 miles 86.5° from Brenton Reef Tower

HOTEL | Special Mark—International Orange inflated buoy

Pairings | Yachts will race in pairs and will be notified by 2000 hours of the pairings for the following day.

Start and Finish Lines | The Start and Finish lines shall be between a yellow flag on the Committee vessel and the nearby government buoy or the special mark.

Course | The Course, with the exception of its length, shall be as described in Article 3, paragraph 2 of the Conditions Governing the Races for the America's Cup, Nineteen Seventy Seven. The length of the first leg shall be as specified in the signaled mark.

A code flag (see Marks) indicating the first mark will be flown from the forward hoist on the Race Committee vessel. The course of the first leg shall be signaled by three numeral pennants reading from top to bottom from an after hoist. When code flag WHISKEY is flown below the signal for the initial mark, the second (reaching) mark shall be eliminated and the course shall be windward-leeward with five legs.

Marks, with the exception of the starting mark, shall be international orange inflated buoys. The starting mark may be a government buoy or an international orange inflated buoy.

Marks | The following Code Flags will signal the initial mark of the course and will be flown from a forward hoist.

OSCAR | Mark—4.5 miles from the Starting Mark
PAPA | Mark—3.5 miles from the Starting Mark
TANGO | Mark—3.0 miles from the Starting Mark
UNIFORM | Mark—2.5 miles from the Starting Mark

Mark Shift | In the event of wind shifts after a race has started, the Race Committee may move the weather mark for the fourth leg and/or the sixth leg of the Course. The new magnetic bearing of the fourth mark and/or the finishing mark from the starting mark will be signaled by the Committee vessel or Auxiliary Committee vessel which will be moving on a course from the starting mark in a direction towards the yachts as they approach the starting mark. This vessel will be flying code flag "C" from a forward hoist and the new magnetic course from an after hoist and it will make a series of short sound signals as each yacht approaches. Each yacht shall visually acknowledge these signals to the Committee vessel.

The length of the new leg will be the same as the length of the first windward leg.

Should the new course displayed for the fourth mark and/or finishing mark be more than 45 degrees to port or 135 degrees to starboard of the course displayed for the previous windward mark, a special gate mark will be placed approximately 100 yards from the starting mark. This special gate mark will be an international orange inflated buoy with a black horizontal band. Yachts will cross between the special gate mark and the starting mark from the direction of the course from the previous mark before proceeding to the next mark.

Government Aids to Navigation

Government aids to navigation when not signaled as marks of the course may be passed on either hand, except: C "1" on River Ledge, R "4" gong off Brenton Pt., R "2A" Bell on Seal Ledge, Bell "1" on Cormorant Reef, must all be passed on their seaward side.

Starting Signals

The Warning Signal will be displayed 5 minutes after Course Signals. Each signal shall be lowered one minute before the next is hoisted.

	Warning Signal	Yellow Cylinder
5 min. later	Preparatory Signal	Blue Cylinder
5 min. later	Start Signal	Red Cylinder

Recall

Recall numbers shall be a yacht's sail number and will be displayed on large placards on the starting line side of the Committee vessel, accompanied by a sound signal. The placards will be removed from view as soon as the recalled yacht or yachts have wholly returned across the starting line or its extensions, as provided in Rule 8.2 (a).

General Recall

The next signal after a General Recall will be the Warning Signal. In the event of a General Recall, Rule 51.1 (c) shall not apply.

Communications and Navigation

During a race, from the time of the warning signal for the start until the finish line has been crossed, a yacht shall not receive any prearranged communications or make use of any prearranged indications, such communications or indications not being available from the same medium to both yachts, as advice or assistance in handling the yacht during the race. While racing radio direction finders may be used but not Loran or Decca or similar navigational systems.

Racing Rule Infringements

A yacht which infringes a racing rule should acknowledge blame by displaying her ensign, in which case the Race Committee may signal General Recall and re-start the race or Abandon a race underway.

Practice Starts

If a practice start is invoked, Code flag "Z" shall be flown from an after hoist, prior to the Warning Signal. Both yachts shall cease racing when the race is abandoned and shall return to the prestart side of the starting line to await new signals. Additional practice starts shall be indicated by the continued display of Code flag "Z".

Protests

For Rule 68.3 (a), International Code Flag "B" shall be used. Written protests shall be submitted to the America's Cup Committee aboard its Committee vessel, or its designee within one (1) hour after the protesting yacht returns to her berth. Hearings will be scheduled and conducted by the America's Cup Committee.

Additional Races

When the Committee Boat displays numeral Pennant 2 at the finish line, another race will follow.

Note

All times herein are Eastern Daylight Time and all bearings are magnetic. Yachts shall conform to applicable Coast Guard Regulations.

SAILING INSTRUCTIONS FOR
THE AMERICA'S CUP 1977

1. Conditions
The Race will be sailed under the "Conditions Governing the Races for the America's Cup Nineteen Seventy Seven", as amended March 17, May and June, all 1977.

2. Captains' Meeting
The Captains' Meeting will be held aboard the Race Committee Vessel BOBBARA at Dock C, Goat Island Marina, at 1430 hours, September 12, 1977.

3. Courses
Races shall start at the America's Cup Buoy anchored 7.9 nautical miles 150° magnetic from Brenton Reef Light and shall be approximately 24.3 nautical miles in length.

Races shall consist of six legs. The first, to be approximately 4.5 nautical miles in length, shall be from the starting buoy to a mark to windward; the second leg shall be from the first mark to a mark equidistant from the starting buoy and the first mark at a point on the circumference of a circle the diameter of which is the first leg; the third leg shall be from the second mark back to the starting buoy; the fourth leg shall be from the starting buoy to the first (weather) mark; the fifth leg shall be from the first (weather) mark to the starting buoy; and the sixth leg shall be from the starting buoy to the first (weather) mark, at which the finish line shall be established.

The various legs of the course will resemble the diagram on Page 5 of the Conditions.

Marks are to be left on the same hand as the starting mark (America's Cup Buoy) except as noted in "A" below.

The approximate magnetic course of the first leg shall be signalled not less than 10 minutes prior to the warning signal.

In the event of wind shifts after a race has started, the Race Committee may move the first (weather) mark for the fourth leg and/or the sixth leg of the course. The change will be signalled by a Race Committee vessel moving on a course from the America's Cup Buoy in a direction towards the yachts as they approach the America's Cup Buoy as follows:

A. Code Flag C will be flown from a forward hoist to indicate that the windward mark has been changed. In addition a green flag may be displayed below Code Flag C. When displayed this indicates that the America's Cup Buoy is to be left to starboard on the next rounding.

B. The approximate magnetic bearing of the new weather mark from the America's Cup Buoy will be displayed from an after hoist.

C. The Race Committee vessel will sound a series of short signals as each yacht approaches to call attention to the signals. Each yacht is requested to visually acknowledge these signals to the Committee vessel.

4. Marks
The marks, except the starting mark, will be inflated buoys, orange in color and cylindrical in shape. The starting mark is the America's Cup Buoy.

In the event that a mark is missing the Race Committee vessel which replaces it, in addition to displaying Code Flag M, will ring a bell during periods of low visibility.

5. Starting Line
The Starting Line will be between a yellow flag on the Committee Vessel and the America's Cup Buoy.

6. Finishing Line
The Finishing Line will be between a yellow flag on the Committee Vessel and the first (weather) mark. The Committee Vessel at the Finish may be a different vessel than at the Start.

When in position at the Finish Line, the Committee Vessel will display a Blue Cylinder until the time limit expires. In fog she will ring a bell rapidly, at intervals, for approximately five seconds. After sunset she will display the NYYC night signal (Green, Red, Green vertically) in place of the NYYC burgee.

7. Starting Procedures and Signals
   1150   Course Signals
   1200   Warning Signal .... Yellow Cylinder
   1205   Preparatory Signal .... Blue Cylinder
   1210   Starting Signal .... Red Cylinder
   Each cylinder shall be lowered one minute before the next is hoisted. Attention will be drawn to starting signals by a sound signal.
   Yachts will be racing from the time of the Warning Signal.

8. Recalls and General Recalls
   Rule 8.3(b) is modified to read: "Except as provided in Rule 31.2 (Disqualification), rule infringements before the warning signal for the new start shall be disregarded for the purpose of starting in the race to be restarted."
   The Committee Vessel will sound one blast on a horn for each yacht starting prematurely and will display a placard(s) on the starting line side of the Committee Vessel, indicating which yacht or yachts started prematurely. The placard(s) will be removed from view when the recalled yachts have wholly returned behind the starting line or its extensions.
   In the even of a general recall I.Y.R.U. Rule 51.1(c) shall not apply.

9. Signals
   Signals, unless otherwise specified in the Conditions or these Sailing Instructions, shall be in accordance with the I.Y.R.U. Rules.

10. Single Starter
   A yacht which appears alone at the starting line on a scheduled race day shall be accorded a start. If only one yacht ranks as a starter and she starts and finishes the race in accordance with the Conditions and Sailing Instructions she shall be declared the winner of that race.

11. Tenders and Support Boats
   Yachts shall release their tow and cast off from their support boats prior to the warning signal and in sufficient time to be at least 200 yards from them at the warning signal.
   While racing, competitors' support boats shall not approach closer to either of the competing yachts than approximately 200 yards, except as permitted by the Rules or except during periods of low visibility.

12. Willingness to Start on the Next Day
   After the leading contestant has finished or after the time limit has expired or after a race has been postponed until a later day or has been abandoned, the Race Committee will display Code Signal AQ inquiring the contestants' willingness to start the next day. Contestants must signal either Code Flag C (affirmative) or Code Flag N (negative) within one hour. Lack of response by a yacht will indicate "affirmative". The Committee will not lower their signal until both contestants have replied and their signals have been understood or the one hour has elapsed.

13. Protests
   The flag to signify a protest shall be International Code Flag B.
   Protests shall be made in accordance with the I.Y.R.U. Rules and delivered to the Race Committee Vessel BOBBARA at Dock C, Goat Island Marina, not later than four hours after the finish of the race concerned unless the Race Committee extends the time limit.
   Protests will be heard by the International Jury.

14. Note
   All times herein are Eastern Daylight Time and all bearings are magnetic.

AMERICA'S CUP OFFICIALS

America's Cup Committee

George R. Hinman, **Chairman**
Henry H. Anderson, Jr., **Secretary**
Robert N. Bavier, Jr.
Emil Mosbacher, Jr.
Robert W. McCullough
James Michael
Clayton Ewing
Briggs S. Cunningham

America's Cup Auxiliary Committee

Henry S. Morgan
Donald B. Kipp
Percy Chubb 2nd
Charles F. Adams

Race Committee

Frederick H. Scholtz, **Chairman**
C. Gaither Scott, **Secretary**
E. Wesley Oliver, Jr.
Robert B. Conner
Prescott W. N. Gustafson
Robert F. Walmsley, Jr.

Auxiliary Race Committee

Chauncey P. Dewey, Jr.
Charles F. Morgan
William H. Dyer Jones
Andrew A. Scholtz
Wesley W. Oliver
B. Devereux Barker III
Ronald L. Ward
Allan MacKenzie
Robert A. Bennett
John B. Sinclair
Charles C. Adams III

International Jury

Dr. Beppe Croce, **Chairman**
The Hon. Livius Sherwood
Robert Sloane

Measurers

A. E. Watts
Oskar Weber
Robert S. Blumenstock

International Race Committee

John Morgan, Chairman, Montreal
William Thomson, Darien, Ct.
Dr. A. R. G. Wallace, Newport, R.I.
Cdr. John Bonds, USN, Va. Beach, Va.
James Carroll, Bermuda
Wallace Ross, Darien, Ct.
Peter Geddes, Providence, R.I.
Noel M. Field, Jr., Providence, R.I.
Kim Collins, Pawcutuck, Ct.
Louis A. Burns, Newport, R.I.
Cdr. George Winslow, USN (Ret),
   Newport, R.I.
Bengt Julin, Sweden
Leeds Mitchell, Jr., Barrington, Mass.
Lawrence E. Metcalfe, Barrington, Mass.
Robert B. Puleston, Barrington, Mass.
Dr. J. E. Tappert, Gross Point, Mich.
Dr. Bernard Skinner, Montreal
T. B. Arneberg, Darien, Ct.
Dr. David H. Shonting, Newport, R.I.
Richard Stackpole, Newport, R.I.
R/Adm. Joseph C. Wylie, USN (Ret.)
John Quinn, Providence, R.I.
Cdr. Barry Byrne, USN, Newport, R.I.
Perry Lewis, Newport, R.I.

Victualers

Gene Sieck
Lucia Carpenter
Doreene Dewhurst
Linda Dwyer
Pel Fesq
Judy O'Neil
Muriel Wallace

SYNDICATE REPRESENTATIVES

Enterprise

Edward du Moulin
R/Adm. Sheldon H. Kinney
George F. Jewett, Jr.
Lowell North
Archibald Cox, Jr.
David R. Pedrick
Olin J. Stephens

Independence

Alfred Lee Loomis, Jr.
Frederick E. Hood
Ralph (Pete) Lawson
R/Adm. Arthur B. Engel
Capt. Victor Tyson

Sverige

H. M. Carl XVI Gustav
Christer Salén
Pehr G. Gyllenhammar
Pelle Petterson
Hans Blenner
Tore Daun

Gretel II

Commodore William L. Fesq
Sir William Northam
Sir William Pettingell
R. A. Dickson
John B. Reid
Norman B. Rydge
Peter Holmes a'Court
A. W. Byrne
Gordon Ingate
William Manning

France I and France II

Baron and Baronne Marcel Bich
Bruno Bich
Roger Laforest
Jean Paul Gateff
Gaston Burgaud
Comte de Rosbo
Pierre Goemans

Courageous

Alfred Lee Loomis, Jr.
R. E. Turner III

THE RACES—REPORTS OF THE RACE COMMITTEES

CHALLENGERS' ROUND ROBIN RACES

YACHT CLUB D'HYERES

ROUND ROBIN RACES

Date August 4, 1977		Race #1	Division I
Course America's Cup		Distance	13.5 miles
Direction to Weather Mark 250 °M		Distance	2.5 miles
Time of Official Start 11:15:00 hrs.			

Yacht Sverige		Yacht Australia		Delta
Start	11:15:46 hrs.	11:16:01	hrs.	:15 sec. S
1st Mark	hrs.		hrs.	:13 sec. A
2nd Mark	hrs.		hrs.	:14 sec. A
3rd Mark	hrs.		hrs.	:31 sec. A
4th Mark	hrs.		hrs.	1:42 sec. A
5th Mark	hrs.		hrs.	1:35 sec. A
Finish	13:38:35 hrs.	13:36:17	hrs.	2:18 sec. A

Wind at start 255 °M		8	knots
at Finish 250 °M		9	knots

YACHT CLUB D'HYERES

ROUND ROBIN RACES

Date August 4, 1977		Race #1	Division II
Course America's Cup		Distance	13.5 miles
Direction to Weather Mark 245 °M		Distance	2.5 miles
Time of Official Start 11:25:00 hrs.			

Yacht France		Yacht Gretel II		Delta
Start	11:25:31 hrs.	11:25:43	hrs.	:12 sec. F
1st Mark	hrs.		hrs.	:32 sec. F
2nd Mark	hrs.		hrs.	:35 sec. F
3rd Mark	hrs.		hrs.	:11 sec. F
4th Mark	hrs.		hrs.:	17 sec. F
5th Mark	hrs.		hrs.	1:31 sec. G
Finish	13:46:32 hrs.	13:44:04	hrs.	2:28 sec. G

Wind at start 245 °M		10	knots
at Finish 250 °M		9	knots

YACHT CLUB D'HYERES

ROUND ROBIN RACES

Date August 4, 1977 — Race #2 — Division I
Course America's Cup — Distance 13.5 miles
Direction to Weather Mark 240 °M — Distance 2.5 miles
Time of Official Start 14:40:00 hrs.

Yacht Sverige	Yacht Gretel II	Delta
Start 14:40:06 hrs.	14:40:06 hrs.	:00 sec.
1st Mark hrs.	hrs.	:25 sec. S
2nd Mark hrs.	hrs.	:18 sec. S
3rd Mark hrs.	hrs.	:13 sec. S
4th Mark hrs.	hrs.	:06 sec. G
5th Mark hrs.	hrs.	:07 sec. G
Finish 16:52:26 hrs.	16:52:05 hrs.	:21 sec. G

Wind at start 240 °M 10 knots
at Finish 250 °M 9 knots

YACHT CLUB D'HYERES

ROUND ROBIN RACES

Date August 4, 1977 — Race #2 — Division II
Course America's Cup — Distance 13.5 miles
Direction to Weather Mark 240 °M — Distance 2.5 miles
Time of Official Start 14:50:00 hrs.

Yacht Australia	Yacht France	Delta
Start 14:50:11 hrs.	14:50:16 hrs.	:05 sec. A
1st Mark hrs.	hrs.	:22 sec. A
2nd Mark hrs.	hrs.	:29 sec. A
3rd Mark hrs.	hrs.	:54 sec. A
4th Mark hrs.	hrs.	2:16 sec. A
5th Mark hrs.	hrs.	5:03 sec. A
Finish 17:01:05 hrs.	17:05:29 hrs.	4:24 sec. A

Wind at start 245 °M 13 knots
at Finish 235 °M 11 knots

YACHT CLUB D'HYERES

ROUND ROBIN RACES

Date August 5, 1977 — Race #3 — Division I
Course America's Cup — Distance 13.5 miles
Direction to Weather Mark 210 °M — Distance 2.5 miles
Time of Official Start 13:55:00 hrs.

Yacht Sverige	Yatch France	Delta
Start 13:55:12 hrs.	13:55:42 hrs.	:30 sec. S
1st Mark hrs.	hrs.	:11 sec. F
2nd Mark hrs.	hrs.	
3rd Mark hrs.	hrs.	:18 sec. F
4th Mark hrs.	hrs.	:15 sec. S
5th Mark hrs.	hrs.	:08 sec. F
Finish 15:54:22 hrs.	15:55:04 hrs.	:42 sec. S

Wind at start 210 °M 11 knots
at Finish 225 °M 11 knots

YACHT CLUB D'HYERES

ROUND ROBIN RACES

Date August 5, 1977 — Race #3 — Division II
Course America's Cup — Distance 13.5 miles
Direction to Weather Mark 210 °M — Distance 2.5 miles
Time of Official Start 14:05:00 hrs.

Yacht Australia	Yacht Gretel II	Delta
Start 14:05:01 hrs.	14:05:02 hrs.	:01 sec. A
1st Mark hrs.	hrs.	:30 sec. A
2nd Mark hrs.	hrs.	:36 sec. A
3rd Mark hrs.	hrs.	:35 sec. A
4th Mark hrs.	hrs.	:59 sec. A
5th Mark hrs.	hrs.	:48 sec. A
Finish 16:06:24 hrs.	10:07:00 hrs.	:36 sec. A

Wind at start 210 °M knots
at Finish 220 °M 11 knots

YACHT CLUB D'HYERES
ROUND ROBIN RACES

Date August 6, 1977   Race #4   Division I
Course America's Cup   Distance   13.5 miles
Direction to Weather Mark 235 °M   Distance   2.5 miles
Time of Official Start   11:10:00 hrs.

Yacht Gretel II		Yacht France		Delta
Start	11:10:22 hrs.	11:10:58 hrs.		:36 sec. G
1st Mark	hrs.	hrs.		1:02 sec. G
2nd Mark	hrs.	hrs.		
3rd Mark	hrs.	hrs.		1:37 sec. G
4th Mark	hrs.	hrs.		1:03 sec. G
5th Mark	hrs.	hrs.		2:03 sec. G
Finish	13:22:15 hrs.	13:23:58 hrs.		1:43 sec. G

Wind at start 240 °M   7.5   knots
at Finish 235 °M   10   knots

YACHT CLUB D'HYERES
ROUND ROBIN RACES

Date August 6, 1977   Race #4   Division II
Course America's Cup   Distance   13.5 miles
Direction to Weather Mark 235 °M   Distance   2.5 miles
Time of Official Start   11:20:00 hrs.

Yacht Australia		Yacht Sverige		Delta
Start	hrs.	hrs.		:11 sec. S
1st Mark	hrs.	hrs.		1:05 sec. A
2nd Mark	hrs.	hrs.		1:14 sec. A
3rd Mark	hrs.	hrs.		1:16 sec. A
4th Mark	hrs.	hrs.		1:16 sec. A
5th Mark	hrs.	hrs.		1:19 sec. A
Finish	13:33:30 hrs.	13:34:53 hrs.		1:23 sec. A

Wind at start 220 °M   8   knots
at Finish 235 °M   10   knots

YACHT CLUB D'HYERES
ROUND ROBIN RACES

Date August 6, 1977   Race #5   Division I
Course America's Cup   Distance   13.5 miles
Direction to Weather Mark 230 °M   Distance   2.5 miles
Time of Official Start   14:20:00 hrs.

Yacht Australia		Yacht France		Delta
Start	14:20:09 hrs.	14:20:07 hrs.		:02 sec. F
1st Mark	hrs.	hrs.		:23 sec. A
2nd Mark	hrs.	hrs.		:31 sec. A
3rd Mark	hrs.	hrs.		:46 sec. A
4th Mark	hrs.	hrs.		1:34 sec. A
5th Mark	hrs.	hrs.		1:38 sec. A
Finish	16:18:10 hrs.	16:19:55 hrs.		1:45 sec. A

Wind at start 250 °M   10   knots
at Finish 245 °M   12   knots

YACHT CLUB D'HYERES
ROUND ROBIN RACES

Date August 6, 1977   Race #5   Division II
Course America's Cup   Distance   13.5 miles
Direction to Weather Mark 230 °M   Distance   2.5 miles
Time of Official Start   14:30:00 hrs.

Yacht Gretel II		Yacht Sverige		Delta
Start	14:30:07 hrs.	14:30:17 hrs.		:10 sec. S
1st Mark	hrs.	hrs.		1:16 sec. S
2nd Mark	hrs.	hrs.		1:21 sec. S
3rd Mark	hrs.	hrs.		1:34 sec. S
4th Mark	hrs.	hrs.		1:51 sec. S
5th Mark	hrs.	hrs.		1:48 sec. S
Finish	16:30:37 hrs.	16:29:51 hrs.		:46 sec. S

Wind at start 245 °M   10   knots
at Finish 245 °M   12   knots

YACHT CLUB D'HYERES
ROUND ROBIN RACES

Date August 7, 1977   Race #6   Division I
Course America's Cup   Distance   13.5 miles
Direction to Weather Mark 230 °M   Distance   2.5 miles
Time of Official Start 12:05:00 hrs.

Yacht Australia	Yacht Gretel II	Delta
Start 12:05:52 hrs.	12:05:13 hrs.	0:39 sec. G
1st Mark ___ hrs.	___ hrs.	1:08 sec. G
2nd Mark ___ hrs.	___ hrs.	
3rd Mark ___ hrs.	___ hrs.	3:04 sec. G
4th Mark ___ hrs.	___ hrs.	2:51 sec. G
5th Mark ___ hrs.	___ hrs.	2:31 sec. G
Finish 14:50:24 hrs.	14:45:59 hrs.	4:25 sec. G

Wind at start 245 °M   6   knots
    at Finish 240 °M   6   knots

Remarks:
Windward leg changed to 265° for 4th leg
Windward leg changed to 230° for 6th leg

YACHT CLUB D'HYERES
ROUND ROBIN RACES

Date August 7, 1977   Race #6   Division II
Course America's Cup   Distance   13.5 miles
Direction to Weather Mark 230 °M   Distance   2.5 miles
Time of Official Start   12:15:00 hrs.

Yacht Sverige	Yacht France I	Delta
Start 12:15:20 hrs.	12:15:29 hrs.	0:09 sec. S
1st Mark ___ hrs.	___ hrs.	0:40 sec. S
2nd Mark ___ hrs.	___ hrs.	
3rd Mark ___ hrs.	___ hrs.	0:32 sec. S
4th Mark ___ hrs.	___ hrs.	0:50 sec. S
5th Mark ___ hrs.	___ hrs.	1:35 sec. S
Finish 15:00:22 hrs.	15:03:25 hrs.	3:03 sec. S

Wind at start 245 °M   6   knots
    at Finish 230 °M   7   knots

Remarks:
Windward leg changed to 265° for 4th leg
Windward leg changed to 230° for 6th leg

ELIMINATION RACES FOR THE CHALLENGERS
ROUND ROBIN RACES

RACE	DATE	DIVISION I	WINNER	TIME	DIVISION II	WINNER	TIME	A	F	G	S
1	Aug 4	S & A	A	1:48 sec.	F & G	G	2:28 sec.	1		1	
2	Aug 4	S & G	G	0:21 sec.	A & F	A	4:24 sec.	1		1	
3	Aug 5	S & F	S	0:42 sec.	A & G	A	0:36 sec.	1			1
4	Aug 6	G & F	G	1:43 sec.	A & S	A	1:23 sec.	1		1	
5	Aug 6	A & F	A	1:45 sec.	G & S	S	0:46 sec.	1			1
6	Aug 7	A & G	G	4:25 sec.	S & F	S	3:03 sec.			1	1
							Wins	5	0	4	3
							Losses	1	6	2	3

For scoring purposes, the result of the Round Robin Series is determined by the score at the conclusion of six races. Had a full series of nine races been sailed, *Sverige* would have scored one point for the race with *Gretel II*, since *Gretel II* had notified the Race Committee that she would not race. This was agreed to by representatives of all challenging yacht clubs.

YACHT CLUB D'HYERES

ROUND ROBIN RACES

Date __August 8, 1977__   Race #7   Division I
Course __America's Cup__   Distance __13.5 miles__
Direction to Weather Mark __260__ °M   Distance __2.5 miles__
Time of Official Start __10:55:00__ hrs.

	Yacht France I	Yacht France II	Delta
Start	10:55:48 hrs.	10:55:24 hrs.	:24 sec. F2
1st Mark	hrs.	hrs.	:37 sec. F1
2nd Mark	hrs.	hrs.	:47 sec. F1
3rd Mark	hrs.	hrs.	:57 sec. F1
4th Mark	hrs.	hrs.	1:37 sec. F1
5th Mark	hrs.	hrs.	1:51 sec. F1
Finish	12:51:25 hrs.	12:54:11 hrs.	2:46 sec. F1

Wind at start __255__ °M   13   knots

at Finish __255__ °M   10   knots

YACHT CLUB D'HYERES

ROUND ROBIN RACES

Date __August 8, 1977__   Race #7   Division II
Course __America's Cup__   Distance __13.5 miles__
Direction to Weather Mark __260__ °M   Distance __2.5 miles__
Time of Official Start __11:05:00__ hrs.

	Yacht Australia	Yacht Sverige	Delta
Start	11:06:04 hrs.	11:05:27 hrs.	:37 sec. S
1st Mark	hrs.	hrs.	:50 sec. S
2nd Mark	hrs.	hrs.	:30 sec. S
3rd Mark	hrs.	hrs.	:26 sec. S
4th Mark	hrs.	hrs.	:53 sec. S
5th Mark	hrs.	hrs.	1:24 sec. S
Finish	13:04:22 hrs.	13:02:31 hrs.	1:51 sec. S

Wind at start __255__ °M   11   knots

at Finish __255__ °M   10   knots

YACHT CLUB D'HYERES

ROUND ROBIN RACES

Date __August 8, 1977__   Race #8   Division I
Course __America's Cup__   Distance __13.5 miles__
Direction to Weather Mark __255__ °M   Distance __2.5 miles__
Time of Official Start __13:50:00__ hrs.

	Yacht Australia	Yacht France I	Delta
Start	13:50:10 hrs.	13:50:16 hrs.	:06 sec. A
1st Mark	hrs.	hrs.	:30 sec. A
2nd Mark	hrs.	hrs.	:27 sec. A
3rd Mark	hrs.	hrs.	:36 sec. A
4th Mark	hrs.	hrs.	1:05 sec. A
5th Mark	hrs.	hrs.	:59 sec. A
Finish	15:40:45 hrs.	15:41:53 hrs.	1:08 sec. A

Wind at start __255__ °M   15   knots
at Finish __240__ °M   15   knots

CHALLENGERS' SEMI-FINAL TRIALS

YACHT CLUB D'HYERES
SEMI-FINAL TRIALS

Date August 11, 1977   Race #1   Division I
Course America's Cup   Distance   24.3 miles
Direction to Weather Mark 235 °M   Distance   4.5 miles
Time of Official Start 12:30:00 hrs.

Yacht Gretel II		Yacht Sverige		Delta
Start	12:30:02 hrs.	12:30:05	hrs.	:03 sec. G
1st Mark	hrs.		hrs.	1:04 sec. S
2nd Mark	hrs.		hrs.	1:29 sec. S
3rd Mark	hrs.		hrs.	1:00 sec. S
4th Mark	hrs.		hrs.	1:13 sec. S
5th Mark	hrs.		hrs.	:30 sec. S
Finish	16:56:08 hrs.	16:54:01	hrs.	2:07 sec. S

Wind at start 235 °M   9   knots
at Finish 235 °M   9   knots

YACHT CLUB D'HYERES
SEMI-FINAL TRIALS

Date August 11, 1977   Race #1   Division II
Course America's Cup   Distance   24.3 miles
Direction to Weather Mark 235 °M   Distance   4.5 miles
Time of Official Start 12:40:00 hrs.

Yacht Australia		Yacht France I		Delta
Start	12:40:52 hrs.	12:40:04	hrs.	:46 sec. F
1st Mark	hrs.		hrs.	1:09 sec. A
2nd Mark	hrs.		hrs.	:36 sec. A
3rd Mark	hrs.		hrs.	1:14 sec. A
4th Mark	hrs.		hrs.	1:28 sec. A
5th Mark	hrs.		hrs.	4:35 sec. A
Finish	17:01:38 hrs.	17:07:31	hrs.	5:53 sec. A

Wind at start 245 °M   8   knots
at Finish 235 °M   8   knots

Remarks:
Australia started two seconds early and was recalled.

YACHT CLUB D'HYERES
SEMI-FINAL TRIALS

Date August 12, 1977   Race #2   Division I
Course America's Cup   Distance   24.3 miles
Direction to Weather Mark 230 °M   Distance   4.5 miles
Time of Official Start 12:10:00 hrs.

Yacht Australia		Yacht France I		Delta
Start	12:10:09 hrs.	12:10:12	hrs.	:03 sec. A
1st Mark	hrs.		hrs.	:57 sec. A
2nd Mark	hrs.		hrs.	1:03 sec. A
3rd Mark	hrs.		hrs.	1:28 sec. A
4th Mark	hrs.		hrs.	1:38 sec. A
5th Mark	hrs.		hrs.	3:37 sec. A
Finish	16:09:37 hrs.	16:09:56	hrs.	:19 sec. A

Wind at start 230 °M   7   knots
at Finish 260 °M   12   knots

Remarks:
Direction to weather mark changed to 220° at 4th mark.

YACHT CLUB D'HYERES
SEMI-FINAL TRIALS

Date August 12, 1977   Race #2   Division II
Course America's Cup   Distance   24.3 miles
Direction to Weather Mark 210 °M   Distance   4.5 miles
Time of Official Start 12:20:00 hrs.

Yacht Sverige		Yacht Gretel II		Delta
Start	12:20:04 hrs.	12:20:20	hrs.	:16 sec. S
1st Mark	hrs.		hrs.	
2nd Mark	hrs.		hrs.	2:43 sec. S
3rd Mark	hrs.		hrs.	2:36 sec. S
4th Mark	hrs.		hrs.	2:02 sec. S
5th Mark	hrs.		hrs.	:16 sec. G
Finish	16:14:08 hrs.	16:13:10	hrs.	:58 sec. G

Wind at start 210 °M   9   knots
at Finish 250 °M   12   knots

Remarks:
Wind direction change to 220° on 4th leg.
Direction to weather mark changed to 220°.

YACHT CLUB D'HYERES

SEMI-FINAL TRIALS

Date August 14, 1977　　　　Race #3　　Division I

Course America's Cup　　　　Distance　24.3 miles

Direction to Weather Mark 235 °M　　Distance　4.5 miles

Time of Official Start 12:10:00 hrs.

	Yacht Sverige	Yacht Gretel	Delta
Start	12:10:03 hrs.	12:10:06 hrs.	:03 sec. S
1st Mark	hrs.	hrs.	1:11 sec. S
2nd Mark	hrs.	hrs.	1:20 sec. S
3rd Mark	hrs.	hrs.	2:30 sec. S
4th Mark	hrs.	hrs.	
5th Mark	hrs.	hrs.	
Finish	hrs.	15:37:58 hrs.	

Wind at start 240 °M　　16　knots

at Finish 245 °M　　20　knots

Remarks:
Protest at Start by Gretel II.
Sverige dismasted at approximately 13:42 on second weather leg.
Under tow by Swedish tender with 41' Coast Guard escort.
No injuries.

YACHT CLUB D'HYERES

SEMI-FINAL TRIALS

Date August 14, 1977　　　　Race #3　　Division II

Course America's Cup　　　　Distance　24.3 miles

Direction to Weather Mark 235 °M　　Distance　4.5 miles

Time of Official Start 12:20:00 hrs

	Yacht Australia	Yacht France	Delta
Start	12:20:05 hrs.	12:20:10 hrs.	:05 sec. A
1st Mark	hrs.	hrs.	2:28 sec. A
2nd Mark	hrs.	hrs.	2:53 sec. A
3rd Mark	hrs.	hrs.	3:28 sec. A
4th Mark	hrs.	hrs.	5:15 sec. A
5th Mark	hrs.	hrs.	8:50 sec. A
Finish	15:31:15 hrs.	15:40:09 hrs.	8:54 sec. A

Wind at start 235 °M　　16　knots

at Finish 230 °M　　18　knots

Remarks:
Australia flying code flag Charlie at end of race.

United States Yacht Racing Union

STANDARD PROTEST FORM

PROTESTOR: Sail No......S 3...... Yacht's Name ....SVERIGE........ Class .....12 meter.....

Helmsman ....Pelle Pettersen........ Signature ....
print

PROTESTEE: Sail No. ......International Race Committee...... Class ....

Chairman, ...John D. Morgan....... Whom I have ...... have not ...... tried to inform
print

Sponsoring Club ....Yacht Club d'Hyeres........ Race date & number ..3,...Aug. 14, 1977..

Time and whereabouts of incident ....

Rule(s) applicable ......Sailing Instruction..

Direction & Strength: Wind .... Current ....

Time protest flag was shown ......As soon as possible..............................

Witnesses ....

....

Received by ....J. D. Morgan........ Time .... Date ....

Address: Protestor ......Hammersmith Farm, Newport, R.I.......................

Protestee ......America's Cup Office, Goat Island.......................

Description of the Incident

To the Race Committee for the America's Cup semi-finals; third race, August 14, 1977.

The Swedish boat SVERIGE hereby lodges a protest against the Race Committee for not having abandoned the race on the 14th of August as the wind raised up to 29-30 knots during the second windward leg. SVERIGE lost her mast in the heavy sea. According to the sailing instructions the race should have been abandoned at about 23 knots, as the wind vane from a southerly direction. SVERIGE claims that the race shall be abandoned. SVERIGE set her protest flag; as soon as she had taken care of the mast. SVERIGE means that the Race Committee has infringed the sailing instructions and the conditions governing the race of August 14, 1977.

Signed by: Pelle Petterson

Facts found

SVERIGE was dismasted on the 4th leg of her race against GRETEL II while beating to windward on August 14th. At the time of the dismasting the wind was blowing approximately 27 knots from 245° magnetic. Subsequent to the incident the wind did increase to a maximum of 30 knots in a brief squall. SVERIGE lodged a protest against the Race Committee claiming that the Sailing Instructions indicated that a race would be abandoned if the wind exceeded 23 knots.

Decision and grounds for decision including applicable rules

The Jury disallowed SVERIGE'S protest for the following reasons:

1. The official Sailing Instructions contain no wind limit.

2. A statement was made at the Skipper's meeting not to start a race in a southerly breeze exceeding 23 knots. At the start the wind velocity was substantially below this limit.

3. The Race Committee was within its authority in not abandoning the race.

Signed: John C. Quinn

F. Gregg Bemis

William W. Poole

August 15, 1977

YACHT CLUB D'HYERES

SEMI-FINAL SERIES

Date August 16, 1977   Race #4   Division I

Course America's Cup   Distance 24.3 miles

Direction to Weather Mark 205 °M   Distance 4.5 miles

Time of Official Start 12:05:00 hrs.

	Yacht Australia	Yacht France I	Delta
Start	12:05:15 hrs.	12:09:08 hrs.	3:53 sec. A
1st Mark	hrs.	hrs.	
2nd Mark	hrs.	hrs.	6:36 sec. A
3rd Mark	hrs.	hrs.	6:23 sec. A
4th Mark	hrs.	hrs	7:48 sec. A
5th Mark	hrs.	hrs.	9:14 sec. A
Finish	15:36:23 hrs.	15:46:39 hrs.	10:16 sec. A

Wind at start 205 °M   15 knots

at Finish 203 °M   10 knots

Remarks:
Collision at the start.
Australia flying protest flag.

YACHT CLUB D'HYERES

SEMI-FINAL SERIES

Date August 16, 1977   Race #4   Division II

Course America's Cup   Distance 24.3 miles

Direction to Weather Mark 205 °M   Distance 4.5 miles

Time of Official Start 12:15:00 hrs.

	Yacht Sverige	Yacht Gretel II	Delta
Start	12:15:58 hrs.	12:15:40 hrs.	:18 sec. G
1st Mark	hrs.	hrs.	
2nd Mark	hrs.	hrs.	:47 sec. S
3rd Mark	hrs.	hrs.	1:02 sec. S
4th Mark	hrs.	hrs.	1:35 sec. S
5th Mark	hrs.	hrs.	1:18 sec. S
Finish	15:53:17 hrs.	15:54:10 hrs.	:53 sec. S

Wind at start 205 °M   13 knots

at Finish 205 °M   12 knots

Remarks:
Gretel II Lay Day requested August 17

FACTS

In the fourth race between AUSTRALIA and FRANCE held on August 16th a collision occurred shortly before the start. Both yachts had been sailing on a close hauled port tack approximately 1 minute and 30 seconds prior to the start, with AUSTRALIA approximately 1 length to windward and slightly less than a boat length astern. FRANCE began to bear away; AUSTRALIA also bore away, swinging her bow across FRANCE'S stern. FRANCE continued to bear away through a jibe onto the starboard tack. Upon realizing FRANCE'S intention to continue bearing away through a jibe, AUSTRALIA, feeling she could not clear FRANCE'S stern by turning to windward, bore off as quickly as possible using both rudder and trim tab. After her jibe, FRANCE continued her turning arc towards a close hauled starboard course. During the maneuvering, hails were exchanged. Approximately ten seconds after the completion of FRANCE'S jibe, her bow struck AUSTRALIA approximately one meter forward of her port shrouds.

FRANCE protested AUSTRALIA for a violation of Rule 36, and AUSTRALIA protested FRANCE for violations of Rules 40 and 41.

DECISION

The Jury disallows FRANCE'S protest and allows the protest of AUSTRALIA. FRANCE is disqualified for the following reasons:

1. FRANCE violated Rule 41.2 in that she jibed on to starboard tack without allowing AUSTRALIA a sufficient opportunity to keep clear.

2. Rule 41.3 clearly places the onus of satisfying the Jury upon FRANCE, which she was unable to do.

Signed: John C. Quinn, Chm.

YACHT CLUB D'HYERES
SEMI-FINAL TRIALS

Date __August 18, 1977__   Race __#5__

Course __America's Cup__   Distance __24.3 miles__

Direction to Weather Mark __255__ °M   Distance __4.5 miles__

Time of Official Start __12:00:00__ hrs.

	Yacht Sverige		Yacht Gretel II		Delta
Start	12:00:06 hrs.		12:00:05 hrs.		:01 sec. G
1st Mark	hrs.		hrs.		:35 sec. S
2nd Mark	hrs.		hrs.		:35 sec. S
3rd Mark	hrs.		hrs.		:54 sec. S
4th Mark	hrs.		hrs.		:56 sec. S
5th Mark	hrs.		hrs.		1:10 sec. S
Finish	15:23:31 hrs.		15:25:42 hrs.		2:11 sec. S

Wind at start __260__ °M   __12__ knots

at Finish __260__ °M   __16.5__ knots

Remarks:
Lay Day August 19

YACHT CLUB D'HYERES
SEMI-FINAL TRIALS

Date __August 20, 1977__   Race __#6__

Course __America's Cup__   Distance __24.3 miles__

Direction to Weather Mark __255__ °M   Distance __4.5 miles__

Time of Official Start __12:45:00__ hrs.

	Yacht Sverige		Yacht Gretel II		Delta
Start	12:45:33 hrs.		12:45:01 hrs.		:32 sec. G
1st Mark	hrs.		hrs.		1:29 sec. G
2nd Mark	hrs.		hrs.		1:20 sec. G
3rd Mark	hrs.		hrs.		1:30 sec. G
4th Mark	hrs.		hrs.		:55 sec. G
5th Mark	hrs.		hrs.		:22 sec. G
Finish	16:18:38 hrs.		16:17:53 hrs.		:45 sec. G

Wind at start __255__ °M   __12__ knots

at Finish __245__ °M   __15__ knots

Remarks:
Sverige crossed starting line early; had to restart

YACHT CLUB D'HYERES
SEMI FINALS

Date __August 21, 1977__   Race __#7__

Course __America's Cup__   Distance __24.3 miles__

Direction to Weather Mark __215__ °M   Distance __4.5 miles__

Time of Official Start __13:45:00__ hrs.

	Yacht Gretel II		Yacht Sverige		Delta
Start	13:45:18 hrs.		13:45:11 hrs.		:07 sec.
1st Mark	hrs.		hrs.		1:23 sec.
2nd Mark	hrs.		hrs.		:38 sec.
3rd Mark	hrs.		hrs.		:45 sec.
4th Mark	hrs.		hrs.		:52 sec.
5th Mark	hrs.		hrs.		1:04 sec.
Finish	17:18:17 hrs.		17:16:19 hrs.		1:58 sec.

Wind at start __215__ °M   __10__ knots

at Finish __230__ °M   __13__ knots

Remarks:
Gretel II recalled at start, crossed line 4 sec. early.

CHALLENGERS' FINAL TRIALS

YACHT CLUB D'HYERES
FINAL TRIALS

Date   August 25, 1977   Race #1

Course   America's Cup   Distance   24.3 miles

Direction to Weather Mark 015 °M   Distance   4.5 miles

Time of Official Start   12:20:00 hrs.

Yacht Australia	Yacht Sverige	Delta
Start	12:20:15 hrs.	12:20:12 hrs.	:03 sec. S
1st Mark	hrs.	hrs.	3:12 sec. S
2nd Mark	hrs.	hrs.	3:54 sec. S
3rd Mark	hrs.	hrs.	1:47 sec. S
4th Mark	hrs.	hrs.	:13 sec. A
5th Mark	hrs.	hrs.	1:09 sec. A
Finish	16:36:56 hrs.	16:37:47 hrs.	:51 sec. A

Wind at start   015 °M   12   knots

at Finish   330 °M   12   knots

Remarks:
Course at 4th leg 315°
Course at 6th leg 345°
Lay Day August 26

YACHT CLUB D'HYERES
FINAL TRIALS

Date   August 27, 1977   Race #2

Course   America's Cup   Distance   24.3 miles

Direction to Weather Mark 230 °M   Distance   4.5 miles

Time of Official Start   12:00:00 hrs.

Yacht Australia	Yacht Sverige	Delta
Start	12:00:05 hrs.	12:00:09 hrs.	:04 sec. A
1st Mark	hrs.	hrs.	:41 sec. A
2nd Mark	hrs.	hrs.	:31 sec. A
3rd Mark	hrs.	hrs.	:23 sec. A
4th Mark	hrs.	hrs.	:37 sec. A
5th Mark	hrs.	hrs.	:27 sec. A
Finish	15:39:08 hrs.	15:39:33 hrs.	:25 sec. A

Wind at start   235 °M   15   knots

at Finish   225 °M   14   knots

YACHT CLUB D'HYERES
FINAL TRIALS

Date   August 29, 1977   Race #3

Course   America's Cup   Distance   24.3 miles

Direction to Weather Mark 245 °M   Distance   4.5 miles

Time of Official Start   12:00:00 hrs.

Yacht Australia	Yacht Sverige	Delta
Start	12:00:38 hrs.	12:00:08 hrs.	:30 sec. S
1st Mark	hrs.	hrs.	1:03 sec. A
2nd Mark	hrs.	hrs.	:57 sec. A
3rd Mark	hrs.	hrs.	:51 sec. A
4th Mark	hrs.	hrs.	1:07 sec. A
5th Mark	hrs.	hrs.	1:26 sec. A
Finish	15:20:21 hrs.	15:21:11 hrs.	:50 sec. A

Wind at start   242 °M   14   knots

at Finish   240 °M   20   knots

Remarks:
Start at the America's Cup Buoy

YACHT CLUB D'HYERES
FINAL TRIALS

Date   August 30, 1977   Race #4

Course   America's Cup   Distance   24.3 miles

Direction to Weather Mark 230 °M   Distance   4.5 miles

Time of Official Start   12:10:00 hrs.

Yacht Australia	Yacht Sverige	Delta
Start	12:10:06 hrs.	12:10:34 hrs.	:28 sec. A
1st Mark	hrs.	hrs.	2:48 sec. A
2nd Mark	hrs.	hrs.	4:35 sec. A
3rd Mark	hrs.	hrs.	6:45 sec. A
4th Mark	hrs.	hrs.	4:45 sec. A
5th Mark	hrs.	hrs.	5:53 sec. A
Finish	16:58:46 hrs.	17:12:05 hrs.	13:19 sec. A

Wind at start   240 °M   7   knots

at Finish   350 °M   12   knots

DEFENDER'S OBSERVATION TRIALS

WINNERS — OBSERVATION TRIALS

DATE	PAIRINGS	RACE #1	TIME	RACE #2	TIME	C.	E.	I.
7/16	C. & E.	Courageous	:27 sec.	(Disqualified) Courageous	:49 sec.	1	1	
7/17	C. & I.	Courageous	:46 sec.	Courageous	1:17 sec.	2		0
7/18	E. & I.	Enterprise	2:19 sec.	Independence	:49 sec.		1	1
7/19	E. & C.	(Enterprise) Abandoned						
7/20	E. & C.	Enterprise	2:46 sec.	Enterprise	1:24 sec.		2	
7/21	C. & I.	Courageous	:6 sec.	Courageous	:18 sec.	2		
7/22	E. & I.	Independence	:41 sec.	Independence	1:45 sec.			2
7/23	E. & C.	Enterprise	:7 sec.	Enterprise	1:36 sec.		2	
7/24	C. & I.	Independence	:28 sec.	Courageous	:57 sec.	1		1
7/25	I. & E.	No racing due to high winds and seas						
7/26	I. & E.	(Disqualified) Enterprise	1:03 sec.	Enterprise	1:59 sec.		1	1
7/27	C. & E.	Courageous	:43 sec.			1		

	C.	E.	I.
Observ.	7-6	7-6	5-7
Prelim.	7-1	4-6	2-6
	14-7	11-12	7-13

NEW YORK YACHT CLUB
37 WEST 44TH STREET
NEW YORK, N.Y. 10036

COURAGEOUS vs. ENTERPRISE #1
ENTERPRISE vs. COURAGEOUS #1
and
ENTERPRISE vs. COURAGEOUS #2

Second Race of the Observation Trials
16 July 1977

FACTS

Approaching the second downwind leeward mark, to be left to port, ENTERPRISE (L) to leeward was overlapped by COURAGEOUS (W) to windward; both were running on the port tack with spinnakers set. Approximately three to four boat lengths from the mark, L hailed that she was taking W to windward of the mark and then luffed. At between three and two boat lengths from the mark W hailed "Mast abeam" and both yachts bore away to the extent that W momentarily jibed on to starboard tack and that L was sailing by the lee.

At approximately one boat length from the mark there was contact between the yachts about amidships, followed shortly thereafterwards by a second contact as the two yachts passed to windward of the mark.

Subsequently both yachts came up to hard on the wind with L overlapped to leeward of W. W then tacked and in the process her stern made contact with L just aft of the shrouds.

DECISIONS

Respecting Protest #1, whether or not there was a proper basis for hailing "Mastline", L responded and both yachts bore away. W as windward yacht is still required to keep clear of L (see Appeal No. 15 and No. 130—now I.Y.R.U. Case No. 48). Furthermore, whether or not L had lost her right to luff above proper course, she had reached the point of no return at which she could no longer leave the mark to port and provide room for W to do likewise. Hence her proper course was to pass to windward of the mark along with W.

W, therefore, is disqualified for infringing rule 37.1.

Respecting Protest #2, W's reliance on rule 42 is misplaced. Both yachts had passed beyond the mark; both were then outside the two boat length circle; neither was in the act of rounding. Accordingly, rule 42 was not applicable. The collision in Protest #2 occurred when W, in tacking, did not keep clear of L. Accordingly, W is disqualified under rule 41.1.

July 17, 1977

The America's Cup Committee

George R. Hinman, Chairman
Henry H. Anderson, Jr.
Robert N. Bavier, Jr.
Emil Mosbacher, Jr.

Robert W. McCullough
James Michael
Clayton Ewing
Briggs S. Cunningham

DEFENDER'S FINAL TRIALS

NEW YORK YACHT CLUB
FINAL SELECTION TRIALS

Date August 16, 1977   Race #1

Course America's Cup (Delta)   Distance   24.3 miles

Direction to Weather Mark   °M   Distance   4.5 miles

Time of Official Start   hrs.

Yacht Courageous		Yacht Enterprise		Delta
Start	hrs.	hrs.	:12 sec. C
1st Mark	hrs.	hrs.	:52 sec. C
2nd Mark	hrs.	hrs.	:47 sec. C
3rd Mark	hrs.	hrs.	:48 sec. C
4th Mark	hrs.	hrs.	:43 sec. C
5th Mark	hrs.	hrs.	:56 sec. C
Finish	hrs.	hrs.	:56 sec. C

Wind at start   °M   knots
at Finish   °M   knots

NEW YORK YACHT CLUB
FINAL SELECTION TRIALS

Date August 16, 1977   Race #2

Course Windward/Leeward/Windward   Distance

Direction to Weather Mark   °M   Distance

Time of Official Start   hrs.

| Yacht Courageous | | Yacht Enterprise | | Delta |
Port tack		starboard tack		
Start	hrs.	hrs.	SAME
1st Mark	hrs.	hrs.	:48 sec. C
2nd Mark	hrs.	hrs.	:26 sec. C
Finish	hrs.	hrs.	:33 sec. C

Wind at start   °M   knots
at Finish   °M   knots

NEW YORK YACHT CLUB
FINAL SELECTION TRIALS

Date August 17, 1977   Race #1

Course America's Cup   Distance   24.3 miles

Direction to Weather Mark 230 °M   Distance   4.5 miles

Time of Official Start 12:25:00 hrs.

Yacht Courageous		Yacht Independence		Delta
Start	12:25:12 hrs.	12:25:08 hrs.	:04 sec. I
1st Mark	hrs.	hrs.	1:19 sec. C
2nd Mark	hrs.	hrs.	:58 sec. C
Finish	13:48:48 hrs.	13:49:38 hrs.	:50 sec. C

Wind at Start 230 °M   15   knots
at Finish 230 °M   15   knots

Remarks:
Race Start at Dumping Ground "B" Bouy
Race shortened because of severe weather warnings.
Finish at Dumping Ground "B" Bouy. 10.8 miles

NEW YORK YACHT CLUB
FINAL SELECTION TRIALS

Date August 18, 1977   Race #1

Course America's Cup   Distance

Direction to Weather Mark   °M   Distance

Time of Official Start   hrs.

Yacht Enterprise		Yacht Independence		Delta
Start	hrs.	hrs.	:27 sec. E
1st Mark	hrs.	hrs.	:44 sec. E
2nd Mark	hrs.	hrs.	:51 sec. E
3rd Mark	hrs.	hrs.	:42 sec. E
4th Mark	hrs.	hrs.	1:14 sec. E
Finish	hrs.	hrs.	1:02 sec. E

Wind at Start   °M   knots
at Finish   °M   knots

NEW YORK YACHT CLUB
FINAL SELECTION TRIALS

Date August 18, 1977   Race #2

Course Windward/Leeward/Windward   Distance

Direction to Weather Mark 260 °M   Distance   3.5 miles

Time of Official Start _____ hrs.

Yacht Independence	Yacht Enterprise		Delta
Start _____ hrs.	_____ hrs.	:02 sec. I
1st Mark _____ hrs.	_____ hrs.	:20 sec. I
2nd Mark _____ hrs.	_____ hrs.	:21 sec. I
3rd Mark _____ hrs.	_____ hrs.	1:07 sec. I
Finish _____ hrs.	_____ hrs.	:58 sec. I

Wind at Start _____ °M   18   knots
    at Finish _____ °M   knots

NEW YORK YACHT CLUB
FINAL SELECTION TRIALS

Date August 19, 1977   Race #1

Course   America's Cup   Distance   19 miles

Direction to Weather Mark 110 °M   Distance   3.5 miles

Time of Official Start   11:35:00 hrs.

Yacht Enterprise	Yacht Courageous		Delta
Start 11:35:11 hrs.	11:35:04 hrs.	:07 sec. C
1st Mark _____ hrs.	_____ hrs.	:23 sec. C
2nd Mark _____ hrs.	_____ hrs.	:25 sec. C
3rd Mark _____ hrs.	_____ hrs.	:32 sec. E
Finish _____ hrs.	_____ hrs.	8:21 sec. C

Wind at Start   110 °M   6   knots
    at Finish   195 °M   less than 5   knots

Remarks:
Protest on second leg, Enterprise against Courageous

PROTEST
ENTERPRISE vs. COURAGEOUS
Final Trials—August 19, 1977

FACTS

After rounding the reaching mark in light airs COURAGEOUS (W) was passed by ENTERPRISE (L) to windward. COURAGEOUS then crossed ENTERPRISE'S stern and proceeded to overtake her to windward—both yachts flying spinnakers.

As W gradually overtook L passing a boat length (LOA or LWL in distance) to windward W hailed "mastline" and L retorted in the negative. A second hail followed in approximately 10 seconds and a third after another interval. L claims that the first hail was premature and that W did not achieve mastline until the third hail. Both yachts had been sailing approximately parallel courses subject to alterations from time to time of up to 10 degrees to maintain boatspeed.

FINDINGS & DECISION

Although L displayed a protest flag timely after the incident, the flag for a considerable period of time later in the race lay, still attached to the shroud, on the deck so that on approaching the finish line it appeared as though she had withdrawn the protest. Shortly before finishing, however, she reset the flag in a conspicuous position.

When the reason for failure to fly the protest flag, as required by rule 68.3 (a), is the result of negligence by the Protestor, it would not normally merit exonerating her for the omission. Notwithstanding, and despite the fact that the protest was defective in lacking a diagram, thereby making it difficult to develop the facts, the Protest Committee have elected to hear it and render a decision in the interest of clarifying certain procedures under rule 38.

The hailing of "mastline" must be done with extreme precision since even though in the instant case it had been clearly established by the time of the third hail, as agreed upon by both parties, it results in a dramatic change in the rights and obligations of the two yachts. An incorrect call of "mastline" could affect the outcome of a race.

Likewise, any hail of "mastline" must under the rule come from the helmsman of the windward yacht. Conversely, although there is no requirement under the rules, responding hails should come from the helmsman of the Leeward yacht rather than randomly from crew members. This makes for an orderly ship and obviates the type of confusion to which random hails contributed in the well known collision in the 1970 America's Cup Match.

While there was a conflict in the evidence relating to the timing of the first hail of "mastline", it was found not to have been premature. The protest is therefore disallowed.

August 21, 1977

America's Cup Protest Committee:

George R. Hinman, Chairman
Henry H. Anderson, Jr.
Robert N. Bavier
Emil Mosbacher
Clayton Ewing
James Michael
Briggs S. Cunningham

NEW YORK YACHT CLUB
FINAL SELECTION TRIALS

Date August 20, 1977   Race #1

Course America's Cup   Distance 15.5 miles

Direction to Weather Mark 240 °M   Distance 3.5 miles

Time of Official Start 11:20:00 hrs.

Yacht Courageous		Yacht Independence		Delta
Start	11:20:06 hrs.	11:20:26	hrs.	:20 sec. C
1st Mark	hrs.		hrs.	:52 sec. C
2nd Mark	hrs.		hrs.	:58 sec. C
3rd Mark	hrs.		hrs.	1:00 sec. C
4th Mark	hrs.		hrs.	:44 sec. C
Finish	13:31:40 hrs.	13:32:34	hrs.	:54 sec. C

Wind at start 240 °M   11   knots

 at Finish 245 °M   15   knots

Remarks:
Course shortened at 5th mark.

NEW YORK YACHT CLUB
FINAL SELECTION TRIALS

Date August 20, 1977   Race #2

Course WLW   Distance 17.5 miles

Direction to Weather Mark 240 °M   Distance 3.5 miles

Time of Official Start 14:40:00 hrs.

Yacht Courageous		Yacht Independence		Delta
Start	14:40:20 hrs.	14:40:06	hrs.	:14 sec. I
1st Mark	hrs.		hrs.	:34 sec. I
2nd Mark	hrs.		hrs.	:23 sec. I
3rd Mark	hrs.		hrs.	:40 sec. I
Finish	16:34:52 hrs.	16:34:09	hrs.	:43 sec. I

Wind at start 235 °M   16   knots

 at Finish 255 °M   15   knots

Remarks:
Course shortened and finished at 4th mark
Length 14.0 miles
Practice Start 14:25:00
Courageous 14:25:06   Independence 14:25:05

NEW YORK YACHT CLUB
FINAL SELECTION TRIALS

Date   August 25, 1977   Race #1

Course   America's Cup   Distance   24.3 miles

Direction to Weather Mark   345 °M   Distance   4.5 miles

Time of Official Start   11:40:00 hrs.

	Yacht Courageous		Yacht Enterprise		Delta
Start	11:40:00 hrs.		11:40:09 hrs.		:09 sec. C
1st Mark	hrs.		hrs.		:12 sec. E
2nd Mark	hrs.		hrs.		less than :10 sec. E
3rd Mark	hrs.		hrs.		1:04 sec. E
4th Mark	hrs.		hrs.		:44 sec. C
5th Mark	hrs.		hrs.		:49 sec. C
Finish	15:44:07 hrs.		15:44:55 hrs.		:48 sec. C

Wind at start   345 °M   12 knots

at Finish   335 °M   13 knots

Remarks:
Both yachts displayed protest flags at start.

NEW YORK YACHT CLUB
FINAL SELECTION TRIALS

Date   August 25, 1977   Race #2

Course   Distance   12.5 miles

Direction to Weather Mark   335 °M   Distance   4.5 miles

Time of Official Start   16:30:00 hrs.

	Yacht Courageous		Yacht Enterprise		Delta
			premature start		
Start	16:30:04 hrs.		16:30:32 hrs.		:28 sec. C
1st Mark	hrs.		hrs.		:39 sec. C
2nd Mark	hrs.		hrs.		:40 sec. C
Finish	17:50:17 hrs.		17:51:28 hrs.		1:11 sec. C

Wind at start   335 °M   12 knots

at Finish   340 °M   9 knots

Remarks:
Start at Dumping Ground "B"
Course shortened at third mark to 7.5 miles

NEW YORK YACHT CLUB
FINAL SELECTION TRIALS

Date   August 26, 1977   Race #1

Course   America's Cup   Distance   24.3 miles

Direction to Weather Mark   210 °M   Distance   4.5 miles

Time of Official Start   12:35:00 hrs.

	Yacht Courageous		Yacht Independence		Delta
Start	12:35:19 hrs.		12:35:08 hrs.		:11 sec. I
1st Mark	hrs.		hrs.		1:25 sec. C
2nd Mark	hrs.		hrs.		1:09 sec. C
3rd Mark	hrs.		hrs.		:43 sec. C
4th Mark	hrs.		hrs.		1:35 sec. C
5th Mark	hrs.		hrs.		:40 sec. C
Finish	17:12:34 hrs.		17:13:22 hrs.		:48 sec. C

Wind at start   205 °M   6 knots

at Finish   200 °M   5 knots

Remarks:
Rendezvous ALFA — Tracking System Bell Bouy "SE"

NEW YORK YACHT CLUB
FINAL SELECTION TRIALS

Date   August 27, 1977   Race #1

Course   America's Cup   Distance   19.0 miles

Direction to Weather Mark   225 °M   Distance   3.5 miles

Time of Official Start   11:20:00 hrs.

	Yacht Enterprise		Yacht Independence		Delta
Start	11:20:09 hrs.		11:20:08 hrs.		:01 sec. I
1st Mark	hrs.		hrs.		:14 sec. I
2nd Mark	hrs.		hrs.		:17 sec. E
3rd Mark	hrs.		hrs.		:29 sec. E
4th Mark	hrs.		hrs.		:42 sec. E
5th Mark	hrs.		hrs.		:36 sec. E
Finish	14:10:59 hrs.		14:11:08 hrs.		:09 sec. E

Wind at start   225 °M   13 knots

at Finish   220 °M   11 knots

Remarks:
Start at "SE" Buoy

NEW YORK YACHT CLUB
FINAL SELECTION TRIALS

Date August 27, 1977   Race #2

Course America's Cup   Distance 19.0 miles

Direction to Weather Mark 225 °M   Distance 3.5 miles

Time of Official Start 15:05:00 hrs.

Yacht Independence			Yacht Enterprise		Delta
Start	15:05:08	hrs.	15:05:08	hrs.	:00 sec.
1st Mark		hrs.		hrs.	:32 sec. E
2nd Mark		hrs.		hrs.	:24 sec. E
3rd Mark		hrs.		hrs.	:18 sec. E
4th Mark		hrs.		hrs.	overlap E
5th Mark		hrs.		hrs.	:15 sec. E
Finish	17:15:30	hrs.	17:15:15	hrs.	:15 sec. E

Wind at start 225 °M   10   knots

at Finish 225 °M   15   knots

Remarks:
Start at SE buoy, race shortened, finished at 5th mark.
Independence showing protest mark at finish.

NEW YORK YACHT CLUB
FINAL SELECTION TRIALS

Date August 29, 1977   Race #1

Course America's Cup   Distance 19 miles

Direction to Weather Mark 245 °M   Distance 3.5 miles

Time of Official Start 11:15:00 hrs.

Yacht Courageous		Yacht Independence		Delta
Start	hrs.		hrs.	:09 sec. I
1st Mark	hrs.		hrs.	:09 sec. C
2nd Mark	hrs.		hrs.	:10 sec. C
3rd Mark	hrs.		hrs.	:19 sec. C
4th Mark	hrs.		hrs.	:56 sec. C
5th Mark	hrs.		hrs.	1:08 sec. C
Finish	13:53:45	hrs.	13:55:08	hrs.	1:23 sec. C

Wind at start 243 °M   18   knots

at Finish 245 °M   16   knots

Remarks:
Start at Dumping Ground B Buoy

NEW YORK YACHT CLUB
FINAL SELECTION TRIALS

Date August 30, 1977   Race #1

Course America's Cup   Distance 19 miles

Direction to Weather Mark 255 °M   Distance 3.5 miles

Time of Official Start 11:15:00 hrs.

Yacht Courageous			Yacht Enterprise		Delta
Start	11:15:03	hrs.	11:48:18	hrs.	:01 sec. C
1st Mark		hrs.		hrs.	1:14 sec. C
2nd Mark		hrs.		hrs.	1:32 sec. C
3rd Mark		hrs.		hrs.	1:15 sec. C
4th Mark		hrs.		hrs.	2:17 sec. C
5th Mark		hrs.		hrs.	2:08 sec. C
Finish	14:46:52	hrs.	14:48:18	hrs.	1:26 sec. C

Wind at start 255 °M   10   knots

at Finish 225 °M   8   knots

Remarks:
Start at Dumping Ground B Buoy
Change of course at third mark

AMERICA'S CUP 1977

NEW YORK YACHT CLUB
AMERICA'S CUP 1977

Date   September 13, 1977   Race #1

Course   America's Cup   Distance   24.3 miles

Direction to Weather Mark 225 °M   Distance   4.5 miles

Time of Official Start   12:10:00 hrs.

Yacht Courageous	Yacht Australia		Delta
Start	12:10:24 hrs.	12:10:10 hrs.	:12 sec. A
1st Mark	hrs.	hrs.	1:08 sec. C
2nd Mark	hrs.	hrs.	1:16 sec. C
3rd Mark	hrs.	hrs.	1:23 sec. C
4th Mark	hrs.	hrs.	1:12 sec. C
5th Mark	hrs.	hrs.	1:18 sec. C
Finish	15:37:59 hrs.	15:39:47 hrs.	1:48 sec. C

Wind at start   225 °M   12.5   knots

at Finish   205 °M   17   knots

Remarks:
Weather mark shifted for 6th leg
After race Courageous indicated willingness to race tomorrow.
At 16:25 Australia requested lay day tomorrow. Acknowledged.

NEW YORK YACHT CLUB
AMERICA'S CUP 1977

Date   September 15, 1977   Race #2

Course   America's Cup   Distance   24.3 miles

Direction to Weather Mark 050 °M   Distance   4.5 miles

Time of Official Start   12:10:00 hrs.

Yacht Courageous	Yacht Australia		Delta
Start	12:10:07 hrs.	12:10:06 hrs.	:01 sec. A
1st Mark	12:56:58 hrs.	12:57:46 hrs.	:48 sec. C
2nd Mark	13:29:57 hrs.	13:30:17 hrs.	:20 sec. C
3rd Mark	13:54:48 hrs.	13:55:32 hrs.	:44 sec. C
4th Mark	15:03:06 hrs.	15:13:51 hrs.	10:45 sec. C
5th Mark	16:16:40 hrs.	16:22:17 hrs.	5:37 sec. C
Finish	Time limit expired at 17:40:00		

Wind at start   050 °M   10   knots

at Finish   125 °M   3   knots

Remarks:
For 2nd weather leg, course changed to 110°
Wind at 5th mark — 6 knots
Time limit expired 17:40:00
Courageous approximately 570 yards from finish
Australia approximately 1.14 miles from finish

NEW YORK YACHT CLUB
AMERICA'S CUP 1977

Date   September 17, 1977   Race #3

Course   America's Cup   Distance   24.3 miles

Direction to Weather Mark 240 °M   Distance   4.5 miles

Time of Official Start   12:10:00 hrs.

Yacht Courageous	Yacht Australia		Delta
Start	12:10:15 hrs.	12:10:27 hrs.	:12 sec. C
1st Mark	13:00:54 hrs.	13:02:44 hrs.	1:50 sec. C
2nd Mark	13:40:02 hrs.	13:42:33 hrs.	2:31 sec. C
3rd Mark	14:05:37 hrs.	14:08:41 hrs.	3:04 sec. C
4th Mark	14:55:45 hrs.	14:59:12 hrs.	3:27 sec. C
5th Mark	15:40:36 hrs.	15:42:33 hrs.	1:57 sec. C
Finish	16:33:23 hrs.	16:35:55 hrs.	2:32 sec. C

Wind at start   238 °M   8   knots

at Finish   310 °M   8   knots

Remarks:
Course signalled at 11:50:00 hours
Second weather leg course changed to 275°. Wind 9-10 knots.
AQ hoisted 16:35:55
Code flag "C" observed on Courageous 16:43:00
Code flag "C" observed on Australia 17:05:30

NEW YORK YACHT CLUB
AMERICA'S CUP 1977

Date   September 18, 1977   Race #4

Course   America's Cup   Distance   24.3 miles

Direction to Weather Mark 265 °M   Distance   4.5 miles

Time of Official Start   12:10:00 hrs.

Yacht Courageous	Yacht Australia		Delta
Start	12:10:09 hrs.	12:10:09 hrs.	:00 sec.
1st Mark	12:53:32 hrs.	12:54:16 hrs.	:44 sec. C
2nd Mark	13:13:46 hrs.	13:14:34 hrs.	:48 sec. C
3rd Mark	13:33:58 hrs.	13:34:54 hrs.	:56 sec. C
4th Mark	14:17:01 hrs.	14:19:12 hrs.	2:11 sec. C
5th Mark	14:58:42 hrs.	15:01:17 hrs.	2:35 sec. C
Finish	15:42:31 hrs.	15:44:56 hrs.	2:25 sec. C

Wind at start   265 °M   14   knots

at Finish   260 °M   9   knots

Appendix D
THE MEASUREMENT RULE

The Measurement Rule of the International 12-Metre Class established by the International Yacht Racing Union and effective March 1976.

Yachts shall comply in every respect with the requirements regarding construction and equipment contained in the Deed of Gift and the Interpreting Resolutions applying to national origin of design and construction.

Bilges shall be kept as reasonably dry as possible while racing. No devices shall be fitted or employed which would permit the tilting of the mast athwartship.

The Twelve-Metre Class of racing sailboats is based on a quotient of the following formula that equals 12 metres, or 39.37 feet.

$$R = \frac{L + 2d + \sqrt{SA} - F}{2.37}$$

R = Rating (12 metres in this class).

L = Length of the hull measured approximately 7 inches above the load waterline. Corrections for girth are applied to this measurement.

d = The skin girth is measured on the surface of the hull from sheet to keel about midships. The chain girth measured at the same place is the length of line stretched taut from the sheer to the keel and is deducted from the skin girth to give the d component.

SA = Sail area includes the mainsail and the fore triangle bounded by the mast, forestay, and deck.

F = Freeboard, or height of hull above waterline.

2.37 = The mathematical constant.

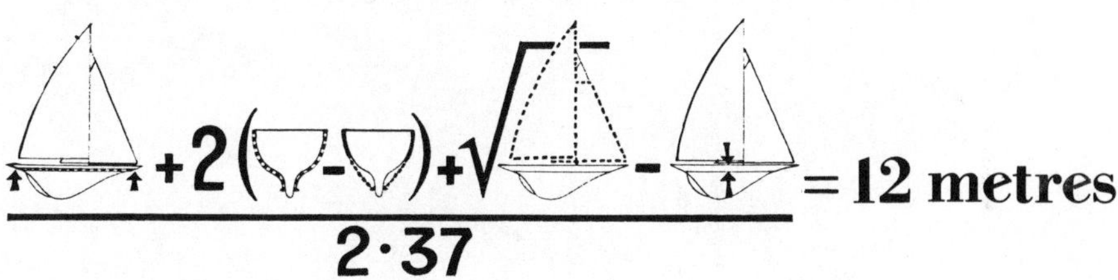

Each of the competing 12-Meters was measured before racing to be sure that it complied with the class rules. Here, New York Yacht Club measurer Bob Blumenstock (one of a committee of three) sights through a transit to read the tape held by Swiss measurer Oskar Weber.

Blumenstock stretches to reach tape held by Weber as they check the after waterline of *Gretel*.

Each yacht was weighed to conform to a new ruling which resulted when it was discovered that *Courageous* had been overweight in 1974. Here, *Gretel* is hoisted by *Sverige*'s crane at Fort Wetherill while a technician checks the electronic weight-measuring device.

Blumenstock and Weber, measuring *Sverige*'s spar, found that it was an inch and a half too long.

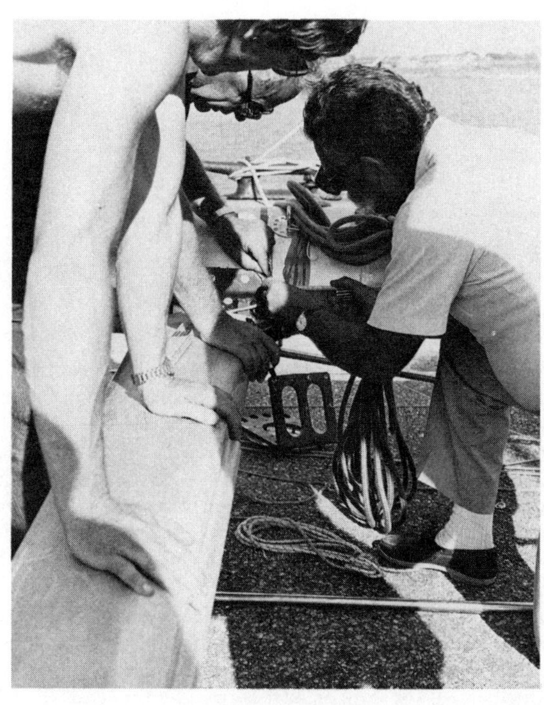

The measurers check to locate the new position for the main boom gooseneck to conform to the shortened mast length.

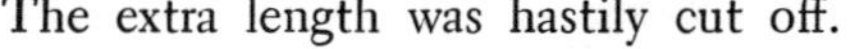

The extra length was hastily cut off.

SELECTING THE DEFENDER OF THE AMERICA'S CUP

In selecting the Defender of the America's Cup, the sole duty of the America's Cup Committee is to decide which yacht is most likely to be successful in the races against the foreign Challenger.

Unlike other sporting events, such as the pennant races before the World Series, the decision is intended to select, not the contender with the best record throughout the past season, but rather the yacht which has reached the highest peak just prior to the International Series. Once this basic objective of the trials is recognized, it becomes apparent why the selection cannot be made on a score card basis. Two examples serve to illustrate this point.

1. First of all take the weather. The relative performance of twelve metre yachts may vary widely in different weather conditions. One may be clearly superior in heavy winds and seas, and only marginally weaker in light airs. There is no way of predicting what weather will be experienced in the International Races and we must be prepared for all contingencies. As against this, the weather during the trials may be lopsided. In the case just cited, a score card method of selection, coupled with a spell of predominantly light weather during the trials, would mandate the elimination of the best overall yacht.

2. Again take the question of a boat's tuning. Some if not all of the potential defenders are new and are late to reach their peak. Others reach maturity earlier in the trials. In 1964 American Eagle peaked early and on a point basis might well have been chosen, yet by the conclusion of the final races it was clear that Constellation was the better boat.

What then are the criteria which guide the America's Cup Committee in making their selection? First of all, preponderant weight is given to performance in the final August trials. The purpose of the Observation and Preliminary trials in June and in

July is to permit each yacht to discover its weaknesses and correct them. Second, the Committee looks for as nearly as possible an all around vessel—one that will make a creditable showing in both light weather and heavy. Beyond that, they look at the composite of many elements:

3. tactics, sail handling, and starting skills, all of which reflect the human element;
4. hull performance upwind and down, absence of pitching or hobbyhorsing in adverse conditions, quality of the sail inventory, and soundness of gear as indicated by failures or lack of failures under racing conditions.

All of these judgements of necessity have a subjective element and they cannot be balanced by any mathematical formula, but experience shows that after watching all of these points, race after race under varying weather conditions, the Committee usually finds that one of the contenders is clearly outstanding. The biggest problem may be the weather. In the 1974 series the final trials provided after day of moderate to light airs, and it was clear that under these conditions there were two evenly matched yachts of outstanding quality. Finally, on the very last day, there was an 18 to 20 knot wind, sufficient to test both performance and gear, and when the race was over the defender had selected herself.

The job of the America's Cup Committee would be much simpler if a mathematical formula of selection were followed, and the Committee would be spared the deeply unhappy task of telling unsuccessful contenders that they had been eliminated. However, given the basic objective of *selecting the yacht best qualified to defend the America's Cup against foreign challenge* the method followed is probably the most effective that could be devised. To date its mission has been accomplished.

America's Cup Committee—1977
New York Yacht Club

Appendix F
CREW LISTS

COURAGEOUS

Richard Boyd
Robbie Doyle
John Edgecomb
Conn Finley
Bunky Helfrich
Gary Jobson
Bill Jorch
Marty O'Meara
Stretch Ryder
Dick Sadler
R. E. Turner III
Paul Fuchs

AUSTRALIA

Ross Annear
Rob Antill
Jack Baxter
David Forbes
Richard Goldsmith
Norman Hyett
Ken Judge
John Longley
Scott McAllister
Wayne McCurry
Noel Robins
Andy Rose
Mike Summerton
John Rosser
Lee Killingworth

ENTERPRISE

Lowell North
Malin Burnham
Richard du Moulin
John Marshall
Emrys Black
James Caldwell
Roderick Davis
Donald Kohlmann
Roger Le Blanc
Andrew MacGowan
Ken McKenzie

INDEPENDENCE

Robert Campbell
Eugene Hack
Frederick E. Hood
Frederick G. Hood
Richard B. Hood
Dubose R. Joslin
Pete Lawson
Steve Lirakis
Jeffrey G. Neuberth
Thomas O'Brien
Scott Perry
Reg Pierce
Arthur Santry

SVERIGE

Pelle Petterson
Bernt Ekström
Thomas Haraldsson
Gösta Holmin
Mats Karlsson
Börje Larsson
Figge Montan
Lennart Nilsson
Magnus Olsson
Lennart Roslund
Tommy Sandberg
Göran Tell
Svante Tengbom
Jan-Olof Andersson
Göran Rutgersson

GRETEL II

Gordon Ingate
Graham Newland
Gordon Marshall
Mark Ross
Peter Cole
Dick Lawson
Bob Ogilvie
John Freedman
Graeme Brown
Graeme Ewing
Bruce Gould
Jack Christoffersen
Joe Cooper
Peter Nicholson
Leon Cremer
Bill Dewar
David Kellett
Jack Gale
Geoff Gale

FRANCE I and FRANCE II

Pierre Delfour
Bruno Trouble
Michel Frotiee
Daniel Saulnier
Yann Labre
Dominique Surcouf
Philippe Herard
Patrice Quesnel
Laurent Esquier
Marc Bonduelle
Michel Maeder
Frederic Laffitte
Sebastian Ferrari
François Mascle
François Giraud
Roberto Succarini
Alain Caudrelier-Benac
Eric Mallet
Jean Gastenet
Jean Didier Marial
Dominique Jamard
Raymond Strauseisen
Frank Girard
Maurice Jarousseau
Jean Yves Grezillier
Jean Luc Esquier
Robin Fuger

Appendix G
RHODE ISLAND STATE YACHTING COMMITTEE

Dr. & Mrs. Fred R. Alofsin
Mr. & Mrs. Leonard J. Panaggio
Mr. & Mrs. Leeds Mitchell, Jr.
Dr. Robin Wallace
Commodore & Mrs. Robert B. Conner
  Ida Lewis Yacht Club
Commodore & Mrs. Robert Bestoso
  Newport Yacht Club
Commodore & Mrs. Bertram Lippincott, Jr.
  Conanicut Yacht Club

Mr. & Mrs. Ralph Lawson III
Mr. & Mrs. Prescott W. N. Gustafson
Dr. & Mrs. Charles P. Shoemaker
Mr. Gary Lash
Mr. & Mrs. Louis Burns
Mr. & Mrs. William A. Shore
Commodore & Mrs. John Nicholas Brown
Mr. & Mrs. Murray Davis
Mr. & Mrs. William Benisch
Mr. & Mrs. James O. Roberson

THE DEED OF GIFT
AND RESOLUTIONS

THE DEED OF GIFT OF THE AMERICA'S CUP

This Deed of Gift, made the twenty-fourth day of October, one thousand eight hundred and eighty-seven, between George L. Schuyler as sole surviving owner of the Cup won by the yacht AMERICA at Cowes, England, on the twenty-second day of August, one thousand eight hundred and fifty-one, of the first part, and the New York Yacht Club, of the second part, as amended by an order of the Supreme Court of the State of New York dated December 17, 1956.

WITNESSETH—

That the said party of the first part, for and in consideration of the premises and of the performance of the conditions and agreements hereinafter set forth by the party of the second part, has granted, bargained, sold, assigned, transferred, and set over, and by these present does grant, bargain, sell, assign, transfer, and set over, unto said party of the second part, its successors and assigns, the Cup won by the schooner yacht AMERICA, at Cowes, England, upon the twenty-second day of August, 1851. To have and to hold the same to the said party of the second part, its successors and assigns, IN TRUST, NEVERTHELESS, for the following uses and purposes:

This Cup is donated upon the condition that it shall be preserved as a perpetual Challenge Cup for friendly competition between foreign countries.

Any organized Yacht Club of a foreign country, incorporated, patented, or licensed by the legislature, admiralty, or other executive department, having for its annual regatta an ocean water course on the sea, or on an arm of the sea, or one which combines both, shall always be entitled to the right of sailing a match for this Cup, with a yacht or vessel propelled by sails only and constructed in the country to which the Challenging Club belongs, against any one yacht or vessel constructed in the country of the Club holding the Cup.

The competing yachts or vessels, if of one mast, shall be not less than forty-four feet nor more than ninety feet on the load water-line; if of more than one mast they shall be not less than eighty feet nor more than one hundred and fifteen feet on the load water-line.

The Challenging Club shall give ten months' notice, in writing, naming the days for the proposed races; but no race shall be sailed in the days intervening between November 1st and May 1st. Accompanying the ten months' notice of challenge there must be sent the name of the owner and a certificate of the name, rig, and following dimensions of the challenging vessel, namely, length on load water-line; beam at load water-line and extreme beam; and draught of water; which dimensions shall not be exceeded; and a custom-house registry of the vessel must also be sent as soon as possible. Center-board or sliding keel vessels shall always be allowed to compete in any race for this Cup, and no restriction nor limitation whatever shall be placed upon the use of such center-board or sliding keel, nor shall the center-board or sliding keel be considered a part of the vessel for any purposes of measurement.

The Club challenging for the Cup and the Club holding the same may, by mutual consent, make any arrangement satisfactory to both as to the dates, courses, number of trials, rules and sailing regulations, and any and all other conditions of the match, in which case also the ten months' notice may be waived.

In case the parties cannot mutually agree upon the terms of a match, then three races shall be sailed, and the winner of two of such races shall be entitled to the Cup. All such races shall be on ocean courses, free from headlands, as follows: The first race, twenty nautical miles to windward and return; the second race an equilateral triangular race of thirty-nine nautical miles, the first side of which shall be a beat to windward; the third race (if necessary) twenty nautical miles to windward and return; and one week day shall intervene between the conclusion of one race and the starting of the next race. These ocean courses shall be practicable in all parts for vessels of twenty-two feet draught of water, and shall be selected by the Club holding the Cup; and these races shall be sailed subject to its rules and sailing regulations so far as the same do not conflict with the provisions of this deed of gift, but without any time allowances whatever. The challenged Club shall not be required to name its representative vessel until at a time agreed upon for the start, but the vessel when named must compete in all the races, and each of such races must be completed within seven hours.

Should the Club holding the Cup be for any cause dissolved, the Cup shall be transferred to some Club of the same nationality, eligible to challenge under this deed of gift, in trust and subject to its provisions. In the event of the failure of such transfer within three months after such dissolution, said Cup shall revert to the preceding Club holding the same, and under the terms of this deed of gift. It is distinctly understood that the Cup is to be the property of the Club subject to the provisions of this deed, and not the property of the owner or owners of any vessel winning a match.

No vessel which has been defeated in a match for this Cup can be again selected by any Club as its representative until after a contest for it by some other vessel has intervened, or until after the expiration of two years from the time of such defeat. And when a challenge from a Club fulfilling all the conditions required by this instrument has been received, no other challenge can be considered until the pending event has been decided.

AND the said party of the second part hereby accepts the said Cup subject to the said trust, terms, and conditions, and hereby covenants and agrees to and with said party of the first part that it will faithfully and fully see that the foregoing conditions are fully observed and complied with by any contestant for the said Cup during the holding thereof by it; and that it will assign, transfer, and deliver the said Cup to the foreign Yacht Club whose representative yacht shall have won the same in accordance with the foregoing terms and conditions, provided the said foreign Club shall, by instrument in writing lawfully executed, enter with said party of the second part into the like covenants as are herein entered into by it, such instrument to contain a like provision for the successive assignees to enter into the same covenants with their respective assignors, and to be executed in duplicate, one to be retained by each Club, and a copy thereof to be forwarded to the said party of the second part.

IN WITNESS WHEREOF, the said party of the first part has hereunto set his hand and seal, and the said party of the second part has caused its corporate seal to be affixed to these presents and the same to be signed by its Commodore and attested by its Secretary, the day and year first above written.

In the presence of	GEORGE L. SCHUYLER, (L.S.)
H. D. Hamilton.	THE NEW YORK YACHT CLUB
(Seal of the New York Yacht Club)	by Elbridge T. Gerry, Commodore
	John H. Bird, Secretary

RESOLUTION ADOPTED BY THE BOARD OF TRUSTEES ON MARCH 27, 1958

WHEREAS, a question has been raised on behalf of certain individuals, citizens of a foreign country, interested in a possible challenge for the America's Cup, as to whether a challenge would be accepted by the New York Yacht Club if the challenger were designed in the United States but the hull built in the country of the challenging Club; and

WHEREAS, by the original Deed of Gift of the America's Cup dated July 8, 1857, it was expressly provided that the Cup should be "perpetually a Challenge Cup for friendly competition between foreign countries;" and

WHEREAS, by the second Deed of Gift dated January 4, 1882, it was provided that the yacht challenging for the Cup and the yacht defending it must be "constructed" in the country to which challenging and defending Clubs respectively belong; and the above recited provision that the Cup should be "perpetually a Challenge Cup for friendly competition between foreign countries" was again set forth; and

WHEREAS, by the third and present Deed of Gift dated October 24, 1887, it was again provided that the Cup should be "a perpetual Challenge Cup for friendly competition between foreign countries," and the second paragraph thereof contained the provision above referred to that the challenging and defending yachts shall be constructed in the countries they respectively represent;

NOW, THEREFORE, in view of the expressed intent of the donors of the America's Cup that it should be "perpetually a Challenge Cup for friendly competition between foreign countries" and the fact that in accordance with that intent and commencing with the first race for the Cup in 1870 down to the present time every challenger has been both designed and constructed in the country of the challenging Club and every defender has been both designed and constructed in the country of the defending Club so that every challenger and every defender has been in all respects truly representative of the countries of the challenging and the defending clubs and the Cup has become by tradition the symbol of the yachting supremacy of the country of the Club winning the challenge match;

RESOLVED that the word "constructed" wherever it appears in the Deed of Gift of the America's Cup shall always be construed as "designed and built."

W. MAHLON DICKERSON,
Secretary

RESOLUTION ADOPTED BY THE BOARD OF TRUSTEES
ON DECEMBER 7, 1962

WHEREAS, certain citizens or subjects of foreign countries, members of yacht clubs which qualify under the Deed of Gift of the America's Cup, and which yacht clubs are considering challenging for the America's Cup, have raised the question as to whether the obtaining of components (other than raw materials), fitting and sails, or the use of design facilities such as a towing tank, outside the country of the challenging club would be construed as falling outside of the Board's Resolution of March 27, 1958, construing the word "constructed" in the Deed of Gift as "designed and built"; and

WHEREAS, by Resolution dated March 27, 1958, the Board construed the word "constructed" wherever it appears in the Deed of Gift of the America's Cup as meaning "designed and built"; it is

RESOLVED, that the word "designed" includes the use of a design facility such as a towing tank, and that the word "built" includes components, fittings and sails; and

WHEREAS, the Board recognizes that components, fittings and sails and the availability of design facilities such as towing tanks may not be obtainable in the country of the challenging club; it is

RESOLVED, that recognizing that such design facilities may not be available and components, fittings and sails may not be obtainable in the country of the challenging club, the New York Yacht Club, at the instance of a challenging club, will consider a request for permission to obtain certain of the aforesaid components, fittings and sails and to use the aforesaid design facilities in any country other than that of the defending club;

RESOLVED, that whenever the Deed of Gift of the America's Cup is printed, this Resolution with preamble adopted December 7, 1962 and the Resolution with preamble adopted by the Board of Trustees on March 27, 1958, interpreting the word "constructed" to mean "designed and built," be printed with the Deed of Gift.

W. MAHLON DICKERSON
Secretary

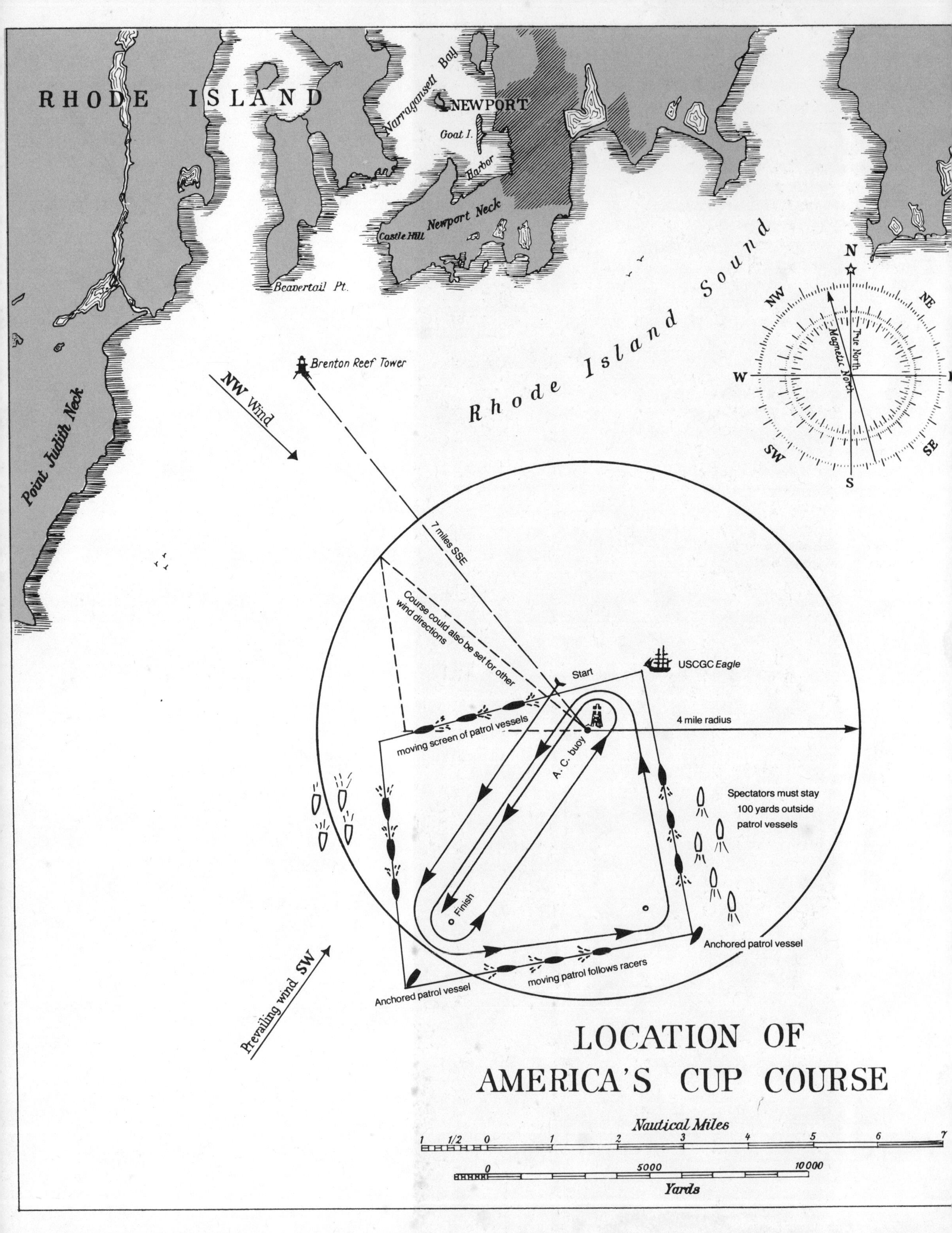

LOCATION OF AMERICA'S CUP COURSE